To Lyn Purnell

With my very best wishes to the winner of the prize – hope you enjoy it.

Henry Sandon

16th July 1990.

BRITISH POTTERY AND PORCELAIN

for pleasure and investment

BRITISH POTTERY AND PORCELAIN

for pleasure and investment

Revised Edition

By HENRY SANDON

JOHN GIFFORD
LONDON

ISBN 07071 0628 1

First published in Great Britain by
John Gifford., 125 Charing Cross Road, London WC2
1st Edition 1969
2nd Edition 1980

Photoset in Great Britain by
Photobooks (Bristol) Ltd.,
28/30 Midland Road, St. Philips, Bristol
and printed by
Clarke Doble & Brendon Ltd.,
Plymouth

CONTENTS

List of Colour Plates

List of Black and White Photographs

Preface to the New Edition

In the ten years since this book was first published there have been a number of movements in the field of collecting British pottery and porcelain. Although no British ceramics have yet been sold at auction at the enormous prices realised for some very early Chinese or Meissen pieces, many prices have gone up, very considerably.

Particularly noteworthy increases have been seen in the field of what might be called the more primitive pottery types, especially early slipwares and delftwares. Fine slipware dishes by Toft and Talor have now broken through the £10,000 barrier, which has already been broken by a saltglazed pew group. Fine delftware has escalated, rare shapes, blue dash chargers and dated pieces particularly increasing in price. Many salt-glazed items, such as early Fulham bellarmines have increased enormously in value, although white saltglaze has not yet taken off.

Eighteenth century porcelain has generally shown a steady increase in price. Some items have gone up fast, especially good blue and white (once the poor relation), early Worcester silver shapes, Caughley and Lowestoft. Chelsea prices, except for some extremely rare figures and decorations, have not increased greatly and may represent a great chance of future increase.

Early nineteenth century ceramics tend to be a fraction of the value of equivalent earlier pieces and there must be great bargains to be had in the wares of this period. Especially underpriced are tea and dinner services, which can often be bought at prices which are lower than the equivalent modern service bought new from a shop and this surely is rather strange. Wares of the Victorian period have seen some dramatic increases. Parian figures have made a reasonable increase—pieces that fetched £10–15 now fetch £60–70—but the finest items must still have a long way to go, as their qualities can be very great. In the field of painted vases and plaques the greatest increase has been in the works of Solon at Minton and the Stinton family and Harry Davis at Worcester. A vase painted with Highland cattle subjects by John Stinton that was happily sold by a Worcester antique dealer for £28 just ten years ago was just as happily bought for £900 this year. Enormous increases have been seen in most Martinware, Doulton vases and figures, de Morgan dishes and vases. Even in the twentieth century such items as the earliest wares by the great craftsman potter Bernard Leach and his Japanese assistant Shoji Hamada at the St. Ives Pottery have increased a hundred fold in value and the very finest of the limited editions of our present day have produced similar results.

At the risk of blowing my own trumpet, I must say that I prophesied most of these things as being due for greater appreciation because of their inherent qualities in the first edition of this book and there must still be many more things that are due for an upsurge.

However, it is wrong to go into the buying of ceramics purely as an investment—far better buy stocks and shares if you want to invest. I firmly believe that you should buy a piece only because you love and desire it. If it turns out to be a good investment this is just a bit of gilt on the gingerbread. But as the investment angle is quite an important one still, I have attempted to give a guide to likely wares which ought to increase in value in this new edition of the book. Happy collecting—

Acknowledgements

My thanks are due to all who have assisted in the preparation of this book, especially to my fellow Curators, the staff of the numerous factories whose work is represented in the book, and dealers, collectors and potters who have kindly provided photographs or allowed their pieces to be photographed. It should not be assumed that pieces credited to dealers are still in their collections as they may have been disposed of.

Especial thanks are due to the following factories: - The Belleek Pottery Ltd., and Mr. T. Campbell; Bristol Pottery and Mr. A. Newsam; Coalport China Ltd. and Mr. F. E. Ridgway; Doulton & Co. Ltd. and Mr. D. Eyles; Mason's Ironstone China Ltd. and Mrs. E. E. Jenkins; Mintons Ltd. and Mr J. E. Johnson; Spode (W. T. Copeland & Sons Ltd.) and Mr. H. Holdway; Josiah Wedgwood & Sons Ltd. and Mr. W. A. Billington; Worcester Royal Porcelain Co. Ltd. and Professor R. W. Baker; to the Museums and their Curators whose pieces are illustrated in the book; Mr. & Mrs. Thornton Taylor, Mr. J. Twitchett, Mr. R. Williams of Messrs. Winifred Williams; private collectors, Mr. P. D. Newbrook, Mr. K. A. Raybould and Dr. B. Watney; to Mr. N. French for drawing the marks in Appendix III and my wife for typing the manuscript; the London auction houses of Bonhams, Christies, Phillips and Sothebys and my son John Sandon for much help in connection with the revised edition.

Introduction

This book is intended to be a general introduction to British pottery and porcelain.

Really, the subject is such a vast one that to hope to cover it in one volume is attempting the impossible and this book can only hope to show the possibilities open to a collector. Within these covers both the experienced and the novice collector will find the history of the most collectable and important factories and styles briefly dealt with and a number of suggestions as to what to collect for pleasure and investment.

The realisation that ceramics—the general term which includes all wares made of clay or fusible stone—can provide both pleasure and investment is not a new one. Discerning collectors have, for many years, found that money soundly invested in fine pieces can make a good profit, as well as giving the owner the pleasure of having the piece to enjoy. It is not unusual to hear of ceramic items bought ten years or so ago fetching five or ten times as much as their purchase prices on resale.

There is no reason to believe that this process will not continue in the future. In fact it shows every sign of acceleration, as inflation has caused a move away from many ordinary forms of fixed rate interest investments into works of art. Inevitably the supply of the very finest objects of the past has tended to dry up and the tendency has been recently for lesser pieces to be more sought after and avenues of collecting to open that have not previously been considered. The most recent movement has been in the field of limited editions and this book gives the present day collectable items and tips on possible future trends.

THE DEVELOPMENT OF CERAMICS IN BRITAIN

Few things in life have a deeper meaning for us than ceramics. The Old Testament tells us that man was created from dust of the earth and this suggests the importance that articles made of clay had for primitive man.

Nowadays we are surrounded by ceramics: even though some more mass manufactured materials, such as plastics and concrete, have made inroads into our previous dependence upon clay, it is extraordinary what a number of ceramic items are still a part of our lives. From the houses we live in built of bricks and roofed with tiles, to the pottery, china or porcelain vessels in which we cook or wash and from which we eat and drink, from the beautiful pottery and porcelain of the past and the finest productions of the present which we may be lucky enough to own in our homes or enjoy looking at in museum collections to its most modern application to scientific purposes and computer components it is easy to appreciate the hold that ceramics have upon people.

Many cultures in the past have looked upon pots as objects of special significance. Vessels have often been buried in graves to help the dead in their after-life; great artistic cultures have done this, such as the ancient Chinese, Egyptians, Greeks and Romans and the more primitive cultures of America. These pots are often the most important source of information on the life of the people of those times; for instance the painting on Greek red and black figures vases and the pots from Peru with moulded scenes representing human activities and even depicting the actual people.

By the thirteenth century in Britain, the time from which the ceramics dealt with in this book begin, pottery making had gone through many phases, most of them reflecting movements into and invasions of this country from Europe. The earliest pottery that is found, from the prehistoric periods of the New Stone Age and Bronze Age show not only the influence of such migrants as the Beaker people but a gradually improving quality. The earliest pots were so poor that they could not stand on the fire and water had to be heated by having hot boiling stones (known as pot boilers) dropped into them to heat up the water.

All this early pottery was hand made by various methods of shaping, such as coiling, and it was not until the Iron Age, a century or so before the Roman invasion, that the potter's wheel was introduced. Late Iron Age pottery can be very beautiful but examples are so seldom sold at auction that the chances of acquiring any are very remote.

The Roman legions brought their own style of pottery to this country, a style based very much on wheel thrown shapes of a very refined form, all the throwing marks—the horizontal marks formed by the pulling up of the sides of the vessel by the potter's fingers—being erased by special turning tools to leave a cleared smooth surface. Ornamentation was very frequent, either put on in the form of slip decoration (slip is the technical name for liquid clay) or incised into the clay with a pointed stick.

The finest quality Roman pottery was imported into this country from Gaul and Germany, the best known type being called 'terra sigilata', a red gloss ware either of plain shape or with moulded decoration on the outside of the vessels, ranging from simple vine leaves to very elaborate scenes depicting such subjects as the triumphs of Hercules. Copies of these wares were made by the Romano-British potters at Colchester and other wares of note were made in this country at Castor in Northamptonshire and the New Forest, the best of this having a smooth hard black surface with white slip decoration. Examples of these wares are to be seen in many Museums.

The two centuries that followed the return of the Roman Legions to Rome are referred to as the Dark Ages. Ceramics, like all the arts, fell to a very low ebb, crude hand made vessels were often the people's only possessions and although the standard of the arts began to improve in the seventh century with the establishment of order under the Saxon Kings, especially in the field of metal work, pottery was very slow to recover.

It is not until the Norman Conquest that a great improvement in British ceramics is seen. Pottery began to be a more important part of life; although the wealthy used vessels made of metal and the poor used vessels of wood, jugs, pitchers and cooking pots were used in great quantities, especially in the kitchens of castles and tiles were made for the use of churches and abbeys. These vessels were frequently decorated with applied strips of clay and covered, or partly covered, with lead based glazes which, with various additions, produced colours ranging from brown and yellow to green.

In the Tudor period pots became smaller, although of greater range and included such objects as candlesticks and chamber pots, the typical glaze being of a bright green colour, nowadays called Tudor Green. At the end of the fifteenth and in the first half of the sixteenth centuries a fine, hard, red body, almost a stoneware, began to be made, covered with a lead based manganese glaze and now generally called Cistercian ware, as examples are frequently found in the ruins of Cistercian abbeys. But this ware was in quite common use domestically in the form of jugs and mugs and curious drinking vessels often with more than one handle, known as tygs.

In the second half of the sixteenth century the finest wares in use in this country were stonewares from Germany and the rare and very expensive fine porcelain imported from China. In competition with these the

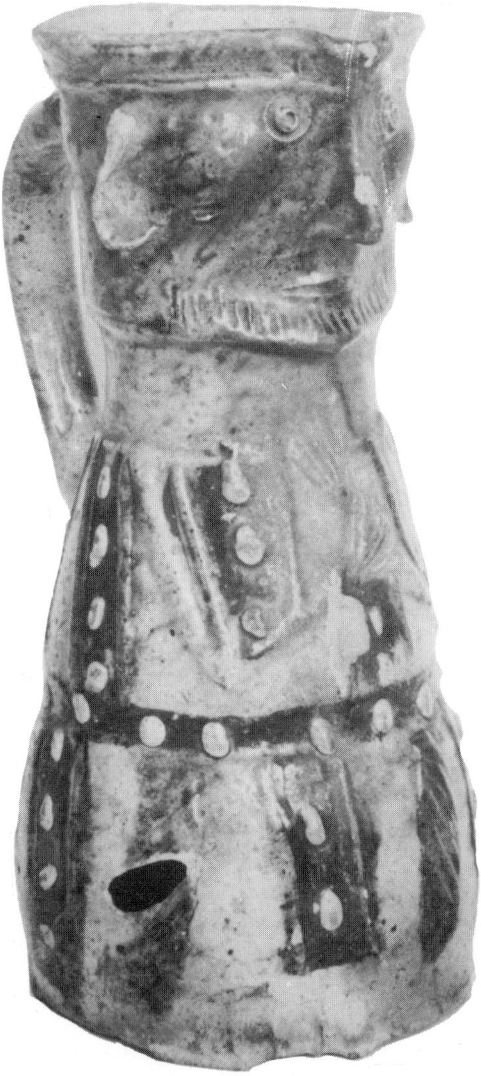

Plate 1. Jug in the shape of a man, with applied details partly coloured green and dark brown, with a yellow glaze, 14th or 15th century from Leadenhall Street, London.
Guildhall Museum

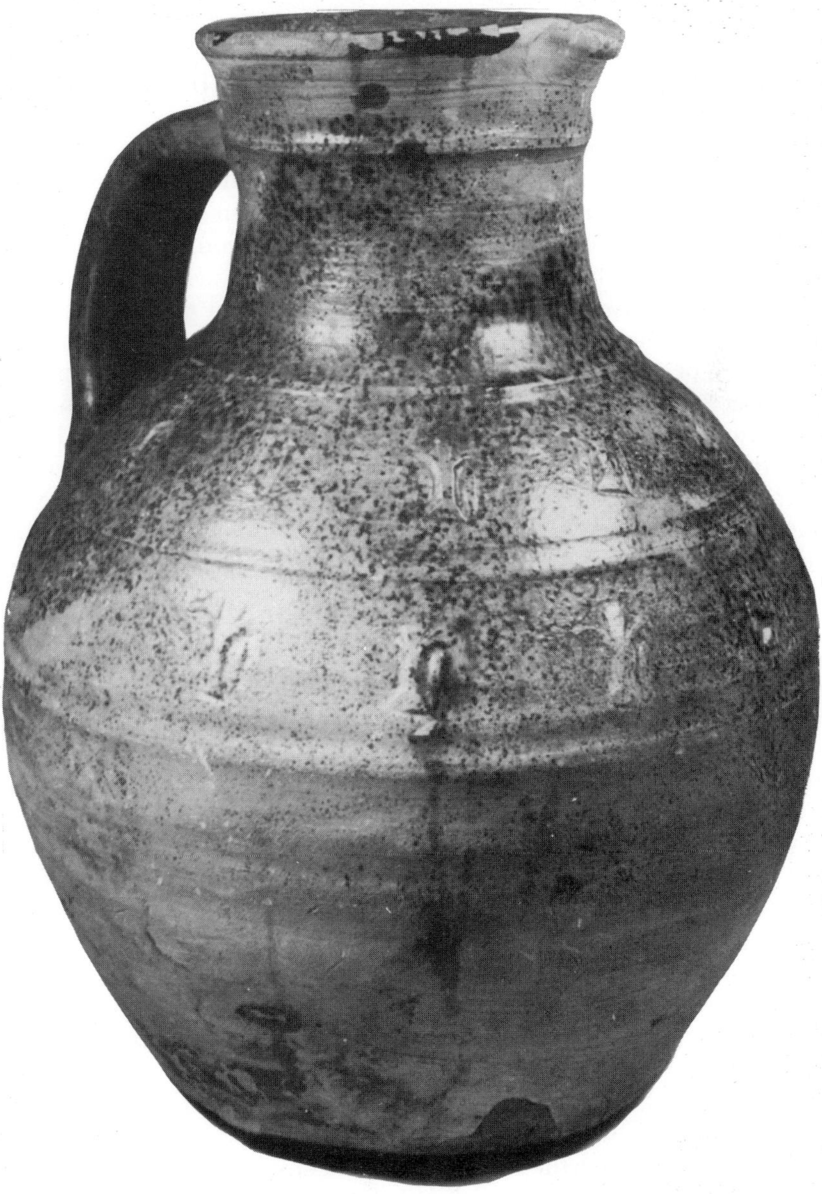

Plate 2. Medieval green glazed jug with applied fleur-de-lys ornament of the 14th or 15th century, found in St. Mary Axe in the City of London.

Guildhall Museum

production of delft (that is, earthenware covered with a tin glaze) began, firstly the pieces known as 'Malling' ware because of the finding of some examples at West Malling in Kent, one of which is mounted in silver and hall-marked 1581–82, which are covered with a rich blue glaze and were probably made in London.

At about this time other potters making delft began setting up in London and later in Bristol, Liverpool and several other centres. Delft ware was a great success and could be regarded as the poor man's Chinese porcelain, being an attempt to copy the whiteness and decoration of the fine Oriental pieces, the cost of which were very great.

England was also making stoneware by the end of the seventeenth century, at first in imitation of German wares. Stoneware is made of a special form of clay, mixed with sand and fired to such a high temperature that it becomes partly vitrified, being able to hold liquids without the necessity of a glaze. The first stoneware maker was John Dwight at Fulham in London. The Elers brothers made fine red stonewares in the area now known as the Potteries in Staffordshire and drab brown stonewares were being made in Nottingham by the year 1700. Stoneware could be glazed by the throwing of salt into the kiln at the highest point of the firing; this led to the typical 'orange peel' appearance of the surface.

A much more traditional English form of decoration, known as 'slip ware' continued to be made in an almost unbroken tradition from medieval times right up to the present day: vessels decorated with trailed on or painted slip. The greatest exponents of this difficult but traditional English form of decoration were in Wrotham, Kent and Staffordshire.

In the first half of the eighteenth century, North Staffordshire really began to come into its own as the centre of pottery making it still remains. Great individual potters founded their small factories in the area, attracted by its abundant sources of clay and fuel. Potters such as Astbury and Whieldon followed by the Woods and Josiah Wedgwood, experimented with all forms of earthenware from figure groups decorated with coloured glazes and vessels formed of different coloured blended clays of the early years of the century to the later jasper wares. This half century probably produced the finest and most strikingly original earthenwares made in this country.

But the death knell of vigorous, strong, rough English earthenwares was rung in the 1740's when England finally discovered the secret of making porcelain; although earthenware was an unconscionable time a dying and is not dead yet, its rough qualities changed in an attempt to imitate porcelain. The great tradition of English pottery, however, has frequently reared its strong head at various times, as for instance in the vigorous figures of Walton and Sherratt, the Victorian chimney ornaments, the wares of the Martin brothers and of the artist potters of the present day.

English porcelain, although at first made as copies of Chinese and European porcelain, was of a soft paste or artificial body. Each of the many factories that sprang up in the years following Chelsea and Bow had their own secret recipes, of frit, bone or soapstone body, factories such as Longton Hall, Lowestoft, Lund's Bristol, Worcester, Caughley and the various Liverpool factories all making soft paste porcelain and Plymouth, Champion's Bristol and New Hall all making hard paste.

The differences between say a Worcester teabowl and a Staffordshire earthenware cup of the 1750's—the one a fine, thin, white, translucent, beautifully potted body, the other crude, thick, heavy and opaque—must have caused the potters of Staffordshire to despair and the invention of transfer printing onto porcelain was an additional thorn in their flesh. But they fought back with Wedgwood's Queen's ware, a fine, cream coloured earthenware and similar wares which because of their cheaper price and also because of the great quantities of cheap imported wares pouring in from China caused a number of English porcelain factories to go out of business and some of the others to cheapen their productions and to increase the use of blue transfer printing.

The speedy development of bone china, the invention of which was claimed by Spode, gave a much needed jolt in the arm for fine, translucent ware, although porcelain of various forms was still continued by some of the finest factories of the early nineteenth century, Swansea, Nantgarw, Derby and the various Worcester factories.

Bone china was the predominant material of the nineteenth century, although it had its rivals in parian ware and coloured transfer prints and wares from many fine earthenware factories. The development of the craftsman potter's movement, artists working often on their own or with a few others in small potteries, typified by the Martin brothers of the late nineteenth century and Bernard Leach of our own century, has been of great importance in opening our eyes to the pure forms of pottery and the realisation that pots do not have to be decorated to be aesthetically pleasing.

Although the cheaper ceramics made nowadays are mass produced in modern factories, the general standards are high and in the case of some factories, as high as those of the past. Some of the most important items made are in the form of limited editions, in which a strictly limited number of each figure or vase is made and these will undoubtedly be the great collector's pieces of the future.

COLLECTING CERAMICS

What to collect! The field is virtually limitless. A lot of people start a collection by having had something left or given to them that they like and which takes their fancy, causing them to look for more of the particular form. This is a rather haphazard way of forming a collection, although it can result in a unified whole and it is as well to remember that some of the world's finest collections are closely defined in scope.

Other collections can be very wide ranging, such as examples from every English porcelain factory of the eighteenth century, or a large collection of teapots of different periods and styles. This sort of collection can be very exciting, although of a jackdaw form and it is necessary to gain an early appreciation of quality unless one is to end up ready to buy anything that comes within the scope of the collection, be it of good or bad quality.

Here the question of the cost of making a collection comes up and this must be clearly faced before making a start.

While the rarest and finest quality British ceramics of an established collectable form will undoubtedly cost a lot of money, very interesting collections can still be built up for a reasonable amount, in the following ways.

If a collector does not mind a little bit of damage to a piece, the cost can often be surprisingly low and the item can give just as much aesthetic pleasure, if it is not so damaged as to be objectionable. Unless a piece is a very rare one, such as a Worcester Dr. Wall period coloured ground vessel, a Thomas Toft dish or a rare eighteenth century figure in which a little damage does not greatly reduce its value, damaged wares should cost very much less than perfect ones. These can not only give as much pleasure as perfect ones, but can teach us a very great deal, as it is possible to see and understand the material so much more if a vessel has a small chip, for instance, exposing the body.

Here a general word of warning must be given. Although damaged wares should be bought at a reasonably low price from dealers and at sales, they are not so easy to sell again if you ever need to do so. Often does one hear of a purchaser having been persuaded to buy a damaged piece by the dealer saying, 'well, the piece is so old that you must expect a bit of damage, and you are getting it at a much lower price than it would be if it were perfect'. This is no doubt true, but if the purchaser comes to try to sell it at a later time, even to the same dealer, he usually receives a reply to the effect that, 'Oh, we do not buy damaged wares; collector's do not want them'.

So, apart from a certain range of wares, such as delft, where a little bit of damage is regarded as acceptable because of the fragile and crumbly nature of the material, you should eschew damaged pieces if your sole object is to buy for selling again later at a profit. However in the last few years it is becoming clear that the values of damaged fine quality pieces can go up quite substantially. This seemingly strange fact can be explained by the realisation that, in general, art of the finest quality is getting rarer, as the supply is tending to dry up. Great scope therefore exists in seeking such pieces, although, of course, it is vital to ensure that ones' appreciation is keen enough to appreciate the often subtle differences between a fine and ordinary piece. I hope that the photographs in this book may help, as they have all been carefully chosen for the inherent qualities of the pieces shown.

Therefore do not shun a bit of damage in a fine piece, especially as nowadays it is possible to have excellent repairs done.

The second way of building up a collection at reasonable price is to uncover some field that is not, as yet, appreciated or sought. In recent years we have seen some extraordinary sudden surges of interest and consequent increase in values, in certain periods and styles. A good example of this is Art Nouveau which a few years ago was suddenly sought and the price of which jumped rapidly. The same applies to Staffordshire figures and fairings. In the last few months we have seen some startling rises in the values of eighteenth century blue and white porcelain, especially underglaze blue prints, for many years the poor relation of onglaze decorated porcelain.

The only difficult thing is to find the gold mine before others do. This may sound an impossible thing to do, especially when one looks around at what is left and despairs of finding anything of quality so far undiscovered. Everything seems so cheap and tawdry.

And yet this is not so!

Very great quantities of fine ceramics, not as yet on the beaten track of collectors for one reason or another, lie around at relatively low price. Attention is drawn to all of these in the body of the book and it will suffice to mention just Royal Worcester of the 'Stained Ivory' and 'Japanesque' periods, Hadley ware, Doulton stonewares and the better quality parian figures. It is still possible to get such pieces for very little, if one is fortunate, sometimes even for a few pounds.

There are two essential weapons in the armoury of anyone who wishes to enter the ofttimes dangerous waters of collecting antique ceramics and these are to develop a good eye for quality and to learn as much as possible about the different materials which are likely to be encountered.

Both of these essentials, if not already present, can be obtained by hard work. A good eye can be developed by frequent visits to good museum collections, to look at the pieces with open eye and mind in an attempt to see what particular qualities are in the piece that make it worthy of a place on the shelf. Do not be afraid to ask for criticism from knowledgable people of pieces you have bought, for often it is only by buying a few ghastly mistakes that progress is made.

It should go without saying that it is necessary to know as much as possible about the different materials, to be able to recognise, for example, soft paste and hard paste porcelain, salt glazed stoneware, parian ware and bone china. Basic knowledge of these basic bodies will not only add greatly to ones enjoyment of the items but will help to avoid the great disappointment that can come when modern hard paste forgeries of English eighteenth century soft paste porcelains are bought by mistake.

Knowledge such as this can quite quickly be gained if a representative collection of, say, small damaged pieces of as many different materials, styles and factories is built up and handled and studied as often as possible. Here a friendly disposed antique dealer is the best ally and is the more likely to help in the early stages in the hope of building up a useful client for the future.

Great help can come from attending the view days of sales, especially those sales of the highest standard where catalogues are detailed. At these view days you have the opportunity of handling the pieces and of putting your knowledge against the experts.

With a growing knowledge and confidence given by experience in looking and handling, the next vital step is to rely on one's own eye and judgement and not on the opinion of others, which might well be wrong, nor the reliance on marks under the piece, which may not be there, or faked if they are. A very great quantity of early ceramics are unmarked and forgeries will usually carry forged marks.

The aim should be the recognition of quality above all, ignoring marks, and the buying of a piece for its inherent beauty of shape and decoration, even if you do not know which factory made the piece. Such fine pieces can be found everywhere, especially in the many junk shops that seem to be springing up, if patience, tenacity and skill is shown.

Although marks are not the most important feature to look at they can still be very helpful and interesting, although they must be treated with caution. Therefore, I have given drawings of the marks most likely to be met in Appendix III.

It is important, when dealing with marks, to realise that the word 'England' on ceramics indicates generally that the piece was made in or after the year 1891, the word being added to comply with the American McKinley Tariff Act, and Made in England generally indicates a twentieth century date. These facts firmly kept in the mind will help to avoid a lot of confusion over dating. Also keep clearly in mind that numbers written or printed on a piece are usually pattern or shape numbers and not dates. Realise that a lot of people have a mistaken idea that their pieces are older than they actually are. 'They belonged to Grandma' and must be 200 years old at least but they lose sight of the fact that Grandma might have acquired them when she was 70 and they may be as recent as 50 years. Anyway, age in itself does not make a thing collectable or valuable, only fine qualities can do this.

In general I have not put an indication of current prices of pieces. This is a difficult thing to venture to indicate as prices can vary so much not only from day to day but from one sale to another.

The glossary which ends the book is important in that it gives details of manufacturing techniques and processes, materials and technical terms met with in the body of the book.

A lot of guidance can be obtained from the many art and antique collectors clubs that are now such a feature of the life of most town and country areas. Some organisations offer courses, seminars and study meetings and at these both the novice and experienced collector can learn from experts and from each other. The best of these are The Morley College Ceramic Circle, Morley College, 61 Westminster Bridge Road, London, S.E.1. (write to the Secretary); Keele University Course, Stoke-on-Trent (write to T. A. Lockett, 6 Tideswell Road, Hazel Grove, Stockport, SK7 6JG); The Antique Collectors Club, Clopton, Woodbridge, Suffolk; Geoffrey Godden, 17–19 Crescent Road, Worthing, Sussex. Geoffrey Godden has issued a series of tape recorded talks accompanied by illustrated brochures covering the history and wares of some individual factories and these will be found most helpful.

1 Medieval & Post Medieval

Medieval English pottery is very seldom to be met with, except in museums, so there is not a great deal of point in dwelling overlong on the subject in such a book as this. Medieval pottery was made purely for practical use, broken and thrown away, none were buried in graves with dead, as was the case with the Romans, and so we have the apparent anomaly that there are much greater quantities of Roman pots available than of the Medieval period.

The Medieval pots that have come down to us are generally of very high artistic quality, being mainly jugs, or pitchers, and cooking pots; the wares are often extremely casually made but show great freedom and life and are very vigorous. Throwing rings made by the fingers are nearly always left, often being treated as part of the form and pattern of the vessel. Decoration is usually a relatively simple form of applied strips of clay added on, or slip painting by brush in bold lines and spirals, or sometimes with just a small amount of green or yellowy-brown galena and lead glaze as the only decoration, often just splashed or dabbed on the rim and spout of the vessel like a bib. Handles are very powerful in form often of strap shape with stabbings into the clay which not only help the grip but provide decoration.

The finest period in the manufacture of these wares is usually given both by ceramic historians and archaeologists as 1275–1325 and while this is a bit cramping as a theory there seems no doubt that the general standard

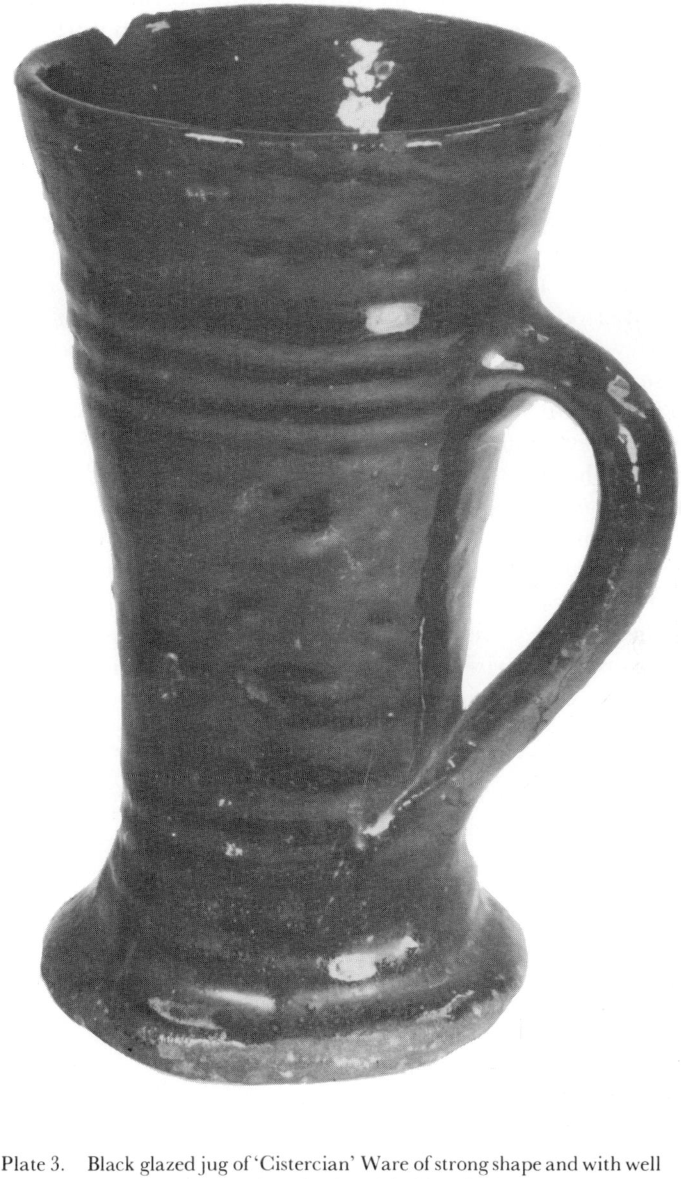

Plate 3. Black glazed jug of 'Cistercian' Ware of strong shape and with well proportioned and positioned handle, found in Moorfields, London. Height $5\frac{1}{2}$ in.

Guildhall Museum

tends to decline in the later fourteenth century. As well as pots, large quantities of wall and floor tiles were made, bearing stamped designs in slip which could often fit together to form elaborate overall patterns. Roof tiles were also made, the more elaborate having figures set on top to stand over a doorway, in the style of the Chinese. The rarest items were aquamaniles—water vessels in the shape of an animal standing on four feet, which were much more common in metal and have their modern counterpart as cow-creamers. In general, pottery was for common use or for the kitchens, the wealthier using metal objects on their tables.

In the Tudor period a characteristic light green lead glaze was used on the whiter, thinner pottery and this is often referred to as 'Tudor Green'. A mottled version of this, varying to olive green, was a later variant. In the late Tudor period and into the early seventeenth century, a fine, harder, red bodied ware was made, covered with lead glaze producing a dark manganese effect, sometimes reaching a blacky-brown. This ware is often termed 'Cistercian' ware as a quantity has been found in ruins of Cistercian Abbeys, but it was very widespread and made in many parts of the country. The most characteristic shape is a narrow drinking vessel of trumpet shape which could have one or more handles, and is called a tyg.

If seen, any of these wares should be grabbed, but it should be realised that pieces in good condition will undoubtedly be very expensive. A number of fine large pitchers of medieval shape, made in a pale buff body with a yellow glaze, were produced in the village of Verwood in the New Forest up until the early years of this century and you should beware of these as they can easily be mistaken for Medieval pieces.

FURTHER READING

Medieval English Pottery by B. Rackham

2 Delftware

Delft is the term applied in England to tin glazed earthenware made either in this country or in Holland, where so much of this ware was made in the town of Delft that the name has become associated with the material.

Ware of a similar kind was also made in Italy (this is called maiolica) and France and Germany (called faience) and the method of manufacture was brought to England by Flemish potters who produced the so-called 'Malling' jugs in the reign of Edward VI. These jugs were probably made in London but are called Malling as several were found in the village of Malling in Kent. They are variations of Rheinish stoneware shapes, decorated with tin glaze stained blue or turquoise, and are very rare, not usually being met with outside museums.

In the reign of Queen Mary these foreign potters were banished, but returned during the reign of Elizabeth, two potters named Jasper Andries and Jacob Jansen petitioning to settle in London in 1571. London quickly became established as the early centre of delft making, which could be regarded as the poor man's Chinese porcelain.

Delft is an interesting material, made of a clay that would fire a pale whitish colour in the biscuit kiln, covered with a glaze made of a lead base to which has been added tin oxide. The decoration, either in the form of cobalt to provide blue or such materials as manganese, iron oxide and antimony to produce purple, red and yellow respectively, was painted directly onto this raw glaze. This is a technically difficult thing to do as it is impossible to make any correction of mistakes. This led to the generally

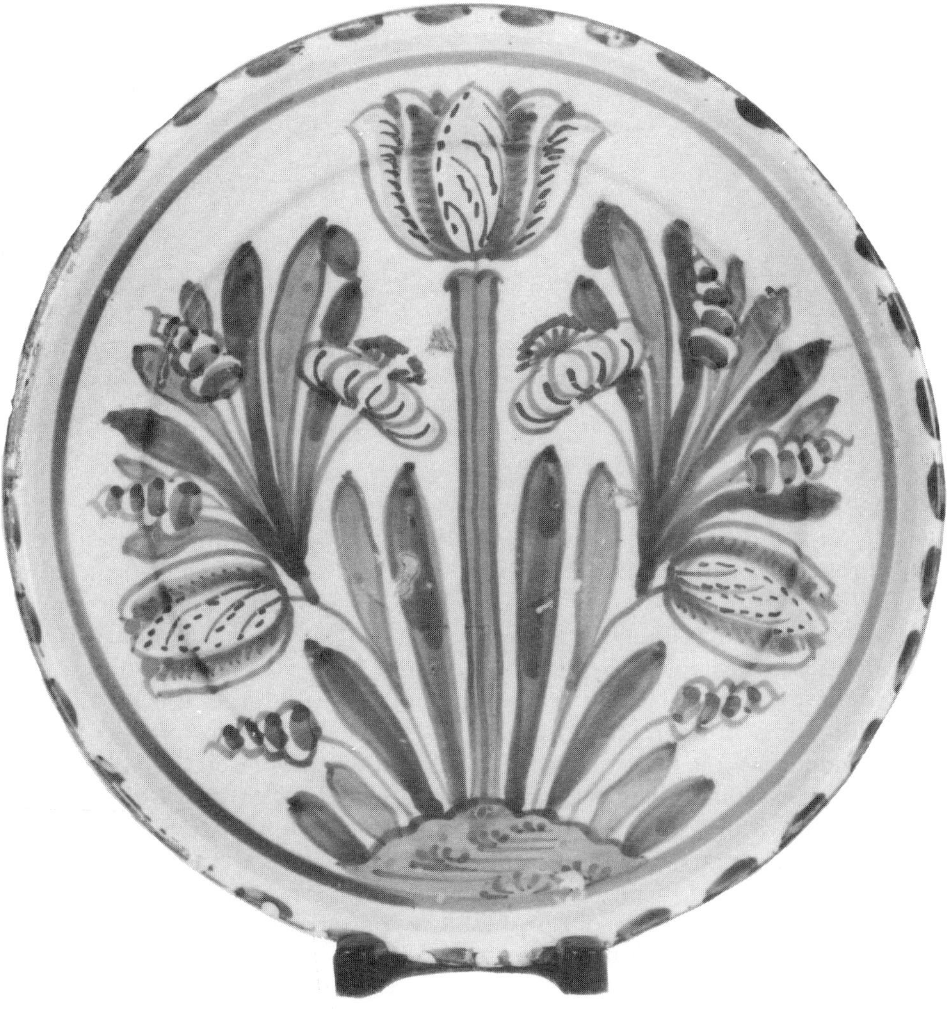

Plate 4. A Delft 'blue-dash' charger boldly painted in red, blue, yellow and green, with stylized tulips, the border with dashes in blue, 13½ in.

Phillips

rather crude effect of the basic decoration and a greatly simplified form of pattern as, although the great aim was to make the piece look as Chinese as possible, the technical difficulties weighed heavily against this. However a lot of delft wares, especially from the finest of the early English factories, are fine works of art, the verve and character of the paintings raising the resulting decoration to great heights.

Delft is a very soft material and the rims of plates and vases tend to chip and the glaze to flake off easily. It is very rare to find old delft without some form of damage, and this is not regarded as such a bad feature from the collector's point of view as similar damage on porcelain and the harder forms of earthenware. Once a piece of delft has been handled with understanding, the feel of the material will be with you for life—a soft and sensuous body that generally shows a yellowish white if a chip or break is visible. The tin glaze sits on top of the body and is rather shiny, although English delft usually does not have as hard and shiny a look as its Dutch counterparts. The natural white colour of the glaze generally has an additional colour tone caused either by additions to the glaze or by firing conditions; these colours vary from pink and green to blue. This is not particularly helpful in deciding the factory of origin, except that Lambeth wares of about 1740–1780 often have a greenish tone especially under the foot of pieces.

Colours used in decoration on delft were greatly restricted by the necessity to fire them at high temperatures. Blue, deriving from cobalt, was the most common and many pieces exist as just cobalt blue decoration on white. The other colours are green, which was produced from copper, yellow from antimony, orange from iron-rust, purple from manganese and red from iron-oxide. Red generally can be felt on the surface, as it did not easily sink into the glaze.

Some special methods of decoration on delft deserve special mention.

Powder Grounds were used on the 'Malling' jugs, probably by splashing or flicking the colour onto the body. In the eighteenth century, powdered manganese grounds were produced particularly at Wincanton and cobalt blue grounds elsewhere, these being obtained by blowing powdered colour onto the surface of the vessel through a tube which is covered at one end by gauze. Shaped 'reserves' could be left white by masking them with shaped pieces of paper, which when removed left a panel ready for decoration with other colours.

Bianco-sopra-bianco can be described as white upon white and refers to white colour upon a faintly tinted ground. This is a technique which was used by the Chinese and the beautifully subtle effects were eagerly copied by the English factories. The process does not seem to have been done at Wincanton nor in Ireland.

Wares of all sorts were produced and all of them are most collectable. The most common are the flatware pieces, ranging from small plates up to large dishes generally around 13 to 14 inches in diameter. Some of the early large dishes are called 'chargers', especially those which depict royal portraits, Adam and Eve and tulip studies. Some of these have blue dashes painted around the rim and these are termed 'blue-dash chargers'. It is possible that these may have been made for purely decorative purposes on the walls of houses and not for use and they certainly make a marvellous effect hanging suspended from holes in the footring on a wall, or standing on an oak dresser. Generally speaking the earliest plates have no footring, the more elaborate the footring becomes the later in date is the piece.

Great quantities of items were made for druggists' purposes; slabs on which pills were rolled, jars for the storage of wet and dry drugs (the former having spouts), and small pots, straight sided with flattened rim and small foot in which drugs were sold.

Bottles exist in fairly large numbers, having round bodies, long necks and flattened rims and large bowls were made, probably for punch. Little teaware was made in delft, although teapots, teabowls and saucers and tea caddies can sometimes be found.

A number of unusual pieces were made, such as 'flower bricks'—a rectangular hollow brick with round holes in the top—bleeding bowls, mugs, porringers, posset pots, and curious shoes.

An interesting field of delft collecting is tiles. A huge number of tiles were made in Holland and imported into this country to be used as wall tiles, especially for placing around the fire places in groups which make up into patterns of fours and larger groupings. The early Dutch tiles were very beautiful and decorative, but the quality of painting tended to decline through the eighteenth century. English tiles of this period, however, are generally of finer quality, the smaller corner patterns being especially well painted. Blue and white and polychrome tiles were made principally at Bristol and Liverpool and the latter made the beautiful tiles transfer printed in onglaze black by Sadler and Green. It is well worth looking for all of these tiles.

THE DELFT FACTORIES

It is very difficult indeed to ascribe delft wares to the correct factories. The material and techniques of manufacture were so similar that differences are slight and variable. Some pieces are, of course, documentary ones, referring to local events in the town in which they were made, such as parliamentary elections, plates and bowls with the names of boats known to be from a particular port, and these help in the ascription of other pieces.

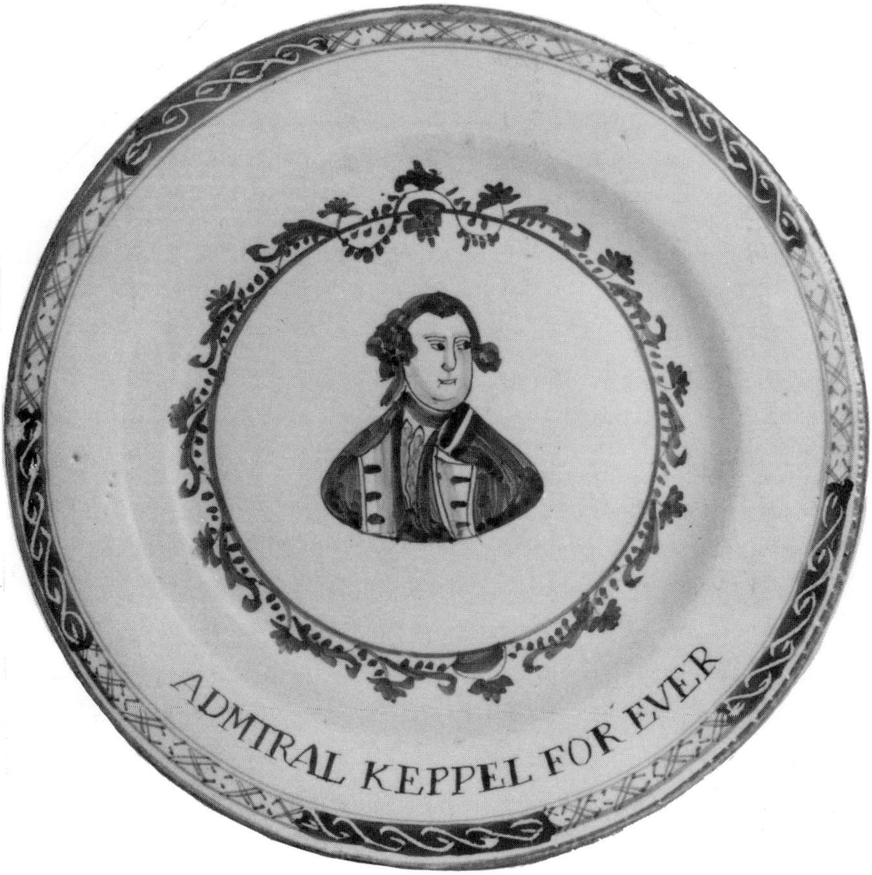

Plate 5. London Delft plate painted with a potrait of Admiral Keppel, the lettering in manganese, $10\frac{1}{2}$ in.

Phillips

LONDON

Aldgate. The pottery in Aldgate was founded by Joseph Johnson, who died in 1597 and it continued for a few years after his death probably making dry drug jars and the like. There was also a later factory near Hermitage Dock, which was called the Hermitage Pot-House when it was advertised for letting in 1724.

Lambeth. For a long time Lambeth was thought to have produced virtually all the delftware from London but both Aldgate and Southwark were in production before Lambeth started, probably in the mid seventeenth century. There were several delft potteries in the Borough, one at Howard House, Church Street which continued into the eighteenth century and another in Fore Street. On the site of the latter factory were found huge quantities of wasters by Dr. Garner which have helped in the ascription of a number of wares. There were also a number of other factories in Lambeth making different forms of earthenware and stoneware.

Southwark. Christian Wilhelm is described as making 'gallyware', the old term for tin-glazed earthenware, in 1618, and in 1628 he described himself as 'Gallipot-maker to the King' in a petition which granted him the position of 'Sole manufacturer of gallyware in England for 14 years'. He made wares in imitation of Chinese blue and white porcelain. Several other delft potteries were established in Southwark, lasting until the eighteenth century.

BRISTOL

Brislington. Bristol was a great ceramic centre from the Middle Ages, but delft was first made at Brislington, some two miles from Bristol. The Collins family set up a pottery there at first making earthenware, but gallipot makers are referred to early in the seventeenth century.

Temple Back Pottery. This was the earliest delft pottery in Bristol itself and was later called the Temple Pottery. Started by Edward Ward of Brislington in 1683. In the late eighteenth century Richard Frank and Joseph Ring made earthenware and creamware there after the popularity of delftware had declined. Temple Pottery has continued to this day, although no longer on the same site, under the title of the Bristol Pottery.

Limekiln Lane Pottery. Another centre of delft making from the late seventeenth century. One of the most famous apprentices here was John Bowen, to whom is attributed most of the plates with 'sponged' trees, although there is considerable doubt about this.

Avon Street. A delftware pottery run by Paul Townsend is believed to have been here between about 1735 and 1755.

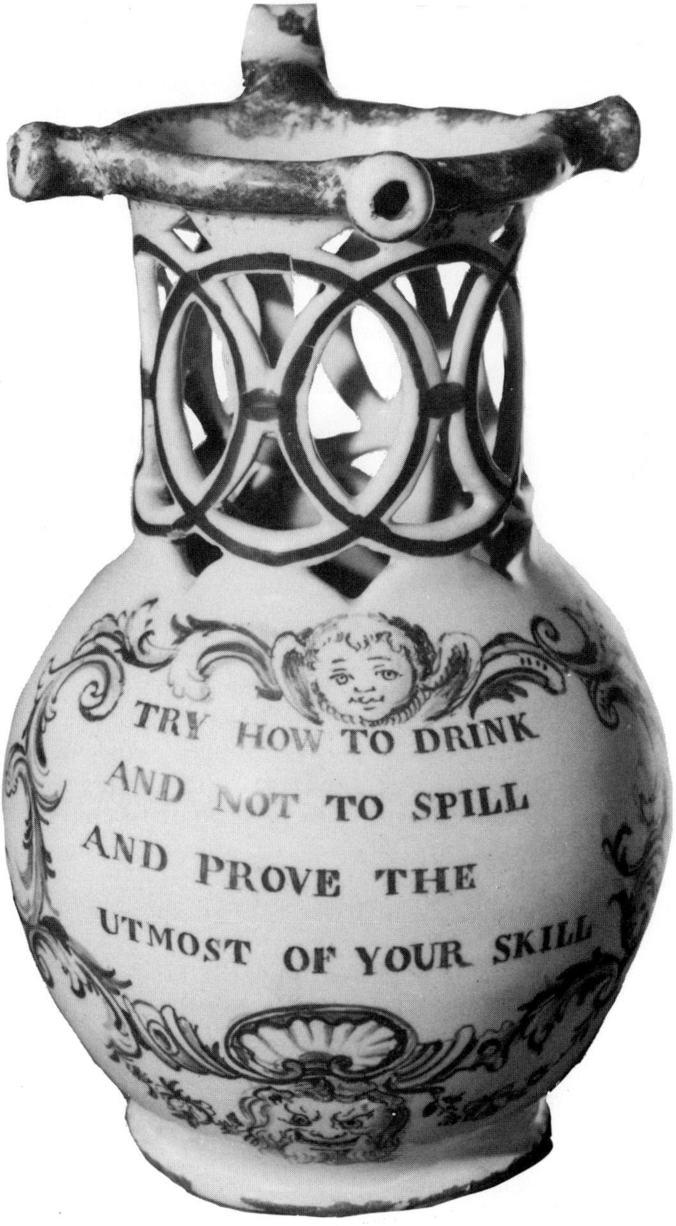

Plate 6. A Delftware puzzle jug, probably Bristol, mid 18th century. The point behind the inscription on the jug is well made that unless the drinker knew the way of closing the holes he would spill most of the drink over himself, 9 in.

Victoria & Albert Museum

Redcliff Backs. One of the most famous areas of ceramic making in Bristol, the delftware factory was run by Thomas Frank, who left Brislington in 1706. Thomas Frank continued the pottery after his father's death in 1757 and apprentices included the Taylor brothers, later to go to Brislington, and Joseph Flower. It used to be thought that Flower had a pottery of his own but it is now believed that he had merely a shop for decorating and sale of ceramics and glass. A number of pieces are known which have initials corresponding to those of Flower on their bases.

Other famous Bristol decorators include John Niglett, apprenticed at Brislington in 1714, to whom used to be attributed paintings in a Chinoiserie style on the strength of a dish in the Bristol Museum with the initials J N E on the back, and Michael Edkins who was credited with most of the other Chinoiserie style pieces on similar evidence.

LIVERPOOL

There were a number of factories producing delft in Liverpool, and, like those in Bristol, most of them were involved in the making of other forms of ceramics as well, especially after the popularity of delft began to fade. The principal factories were

Richard Holt in Lord Street. Probably the first to be established when Holt brought potters from Southwark in 1710.

Samuel Gilbody on Shaw's Brow. Probably started about 1714. Gilbody's son Samuel took over in 1752 and the factory made porcelain for a while. Shaw's Brow, now the site of the Liverpool Museums and Library, was a great ceramic centre.

Alderman Shaw off Dale Street. From about 1724.

Richard Chaffers on Shaw's Brow. From about 1747; he also made porcelain later.

Philip Christian on Shaw's Brow. From the 1750's. Another who was involved with porcelain, he apparently took over Richard Chaffer's factory in 1765.

Other delft makers included Samuel Poole of Trueman Street, George Drinkwater of Duke Street, John Dunbavan of St. Patrick's Hill, James Gibson on Cross Hill and Zachariah Barnes of the Old Haymarket. One of the finest journeyman decorators was Seth Pennington, especially famous for large punch bowls.

There are three features peculiar to Liverpool delft; tin-glazed stoneware, enamelled wares and transfer printing. The stoneware was a much harder and more durable body, resistant to hot liquids. These wares are rarely found now. Even rarer are the enamelled wares, which have enamel decoration put on after the glaze has been fired. Although frequently found

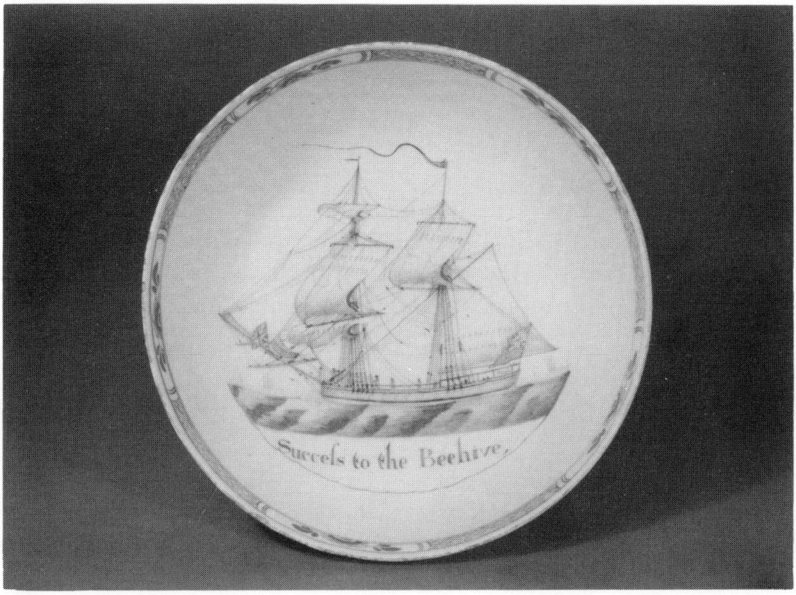

Plate 7. A fine Liverpool Delft ship's punchbowl painted in blue and iron red with a twin-masted ship, the *Beehive* diameter 10½in. The *Beehive* sloop was built at Bideford and sailed in 1776.

Phillips

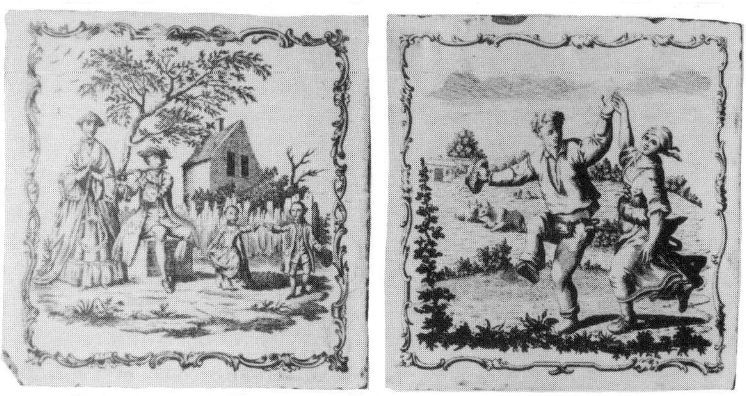

Plate 8. Two Liverpool Delft tiles, onglaze transfer printed by Sadler and Green, *c.*1760–65, 5 in. square.

City of Liverpool Museum

on Continental tin-glazed wares, in this country it appears unique to Liverpool.

Transfer printed wares can be found more frequently, the most commonly met with decoration being the 'Sailor's Farewell'; also to be found are the prints of 'Admiral Boscawen', the 'Sportsman's Arms' and the 'King of Prussia'.

Huge quantities of wall tiles were also made in Liverpool and these are generally of very fine quality. They can either be painted in a great variety of designs or onglaze printed by the firm of Sadler and Green. Beautiful scenes, generally of an amorous or humorous character, were frequently set in *rococo* scrolls, sometimes having the names of Sadler and Green at the botom.

WINCANTON

It is believed that this Somerset factory was started in the 1730's by Nathaniel Ireson and lasted for about twenty years. Although the factory did not produce the great quantity of ware that London, Bristol and Liverpool did, Wincanton wares are well documented by five known pieces with the name 'Wincanton' on them and by a large number of sherds which have been found on the site. These named pieces include a plate with powdered manganese border with a mimosa pattern in reserve panels and this is felt to be a typical Wincanton type.

IRELAND

Dublin. Was the most important centre. John Chambers started his 'Pot-House on the Strand' in about 1730, and this was possibly taken over by John Crisp who is known to have made delftware from Carrickfergus clay at 'The World's End on the Strand'. This was in turn taken over by David Davis. In 1752 Captain Henry Delamain took over the factory and it was in this period that the finest Irish wares were produced, a great quantity of blue and manganese painting of fine quality being produced. Delamain claimed to be the first to fire delft kilns with coal and not wood as was usual. The factory probably finished by 1771, put out of business by the increasing production of creamware.

Belfast. Little is known about this factory, which probably started in the late seventeenth century. A delft shoe is known marked H M R Belfast 1724.

Rostrevor, Co. Down. This factory is mentioned in the *Dublin Journal* in 1742; it used Carrickfergus clay and made armorial ware, punch bowls, teacups and saucers, basins of all sizes and chamber pots.

Limerick. Two armorial plates are known inscribed 'Made by John Strich Limerick, 4th June 1761', the glaze being stained pale blue.

SCOTLAND

The only factory was in Glasgow, called by Robert Dinwoodie, its founder, 'Delftfield' in April, 1748. After failures with the local clay, Carrickfergus clay was used and the factory exported huge quantities of ware to the New World, as much as 80,000 pieces in 1791. This, of course, was a very late date for the continuation of delft and the factory did not close until 1810, although it also made creamware. Very few pieces have been identified with certainty as Delftfield.

Summing up delft; although it is very difficult to be certain from which factory a piece may come it is a very collectable and displayable material. It is also one of the few forms of ceramics in which a bit of damage is not of great consequence, especially if it is merely chippings around the rim. A considerable quantity of delft is available at low prices for less important pieces of the mid to late eighteenth century to many hundreds of pounds for early blue-dash chargers.

FURTHER READING

English Delftware Pottery by Anthony Ray
English Delftware Tiles by Anthony Ray
English Delftware by F.H. Garner and M. Archer
Encylopaedia of English Tin-glazed Pottery by Louis Lipski (ed.) (forthcoming)

3 Slipware

Slipware is a very traditional English form of ceramics, but slip decoration —that is decoration on the surface of a vessel in the form of liquid clay on a different coloured or the natural body, has been practised for several thousand years.

Primitive countries like Peru produced fine slip decoration, painting cream coloured slip on to a red slipped body; China practised feathering, combing and marbling about a thousand years ago; fine Cypriot and Minoan pots with spiral and geometric decoration led the way to the finest imaginable slip painting on the Greek 'black figure' and 'red figure' wares of the sixth and fifth centuries B.C.

In Britain the earliest slip decoration was done during the Roman period, but it is not until the Middle Ages that a more national style of decoration began. Fine jugs were decorated with free brush strokes and spirals, but it is the wares dating from the seventeenth century with which we are concerned in this chapter—principally dishes, mugs and small pots.

The methods of slip decoration are varied, although they all have the same aim, of contrasting coloured slips with a different coloured body. The usual colour of the body was red, the wares generally being made from red clay. Slip may be painted on by brush, poured onto or into the vessel or trailed on from a slip trailer (the latter process being a little like the piping of decoration onto a cake), or blown on through a tube. White and brown slips were obtained by mixing natural clay with water and other colours

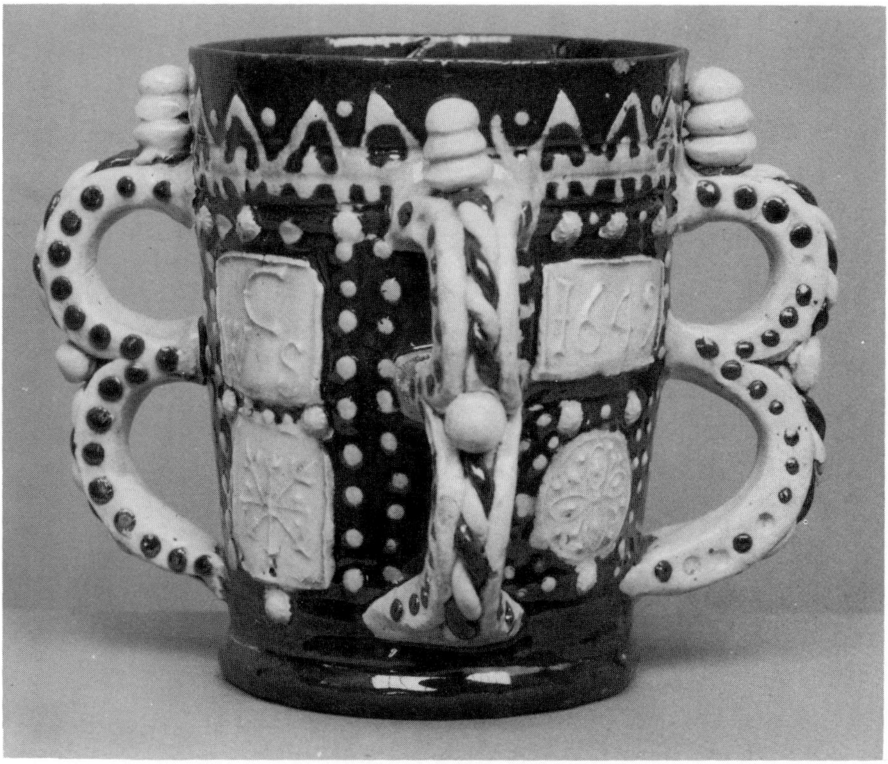

Plate 9. A slipware tyg of the type made at Wrotham in the 17th century, this example dated 1649.
Victoria & Albert Museum

could be obtained by the addition of metalic oxides. Slips of one colour could be put onto a bat of clay and different coloured slip trailed across the surface; the two colours could be merged by drawing across the lines a fine pointed stick when the lines would 'feather' in delightful effect; or the different coloured slips could be 'joggled' together, producing extraordinary, haphazard blends of colour and pattern, rather like modern art; more careful and difficult dotting and trellising of thicker slip could produce some splendid effects, such as the Wrotham pots and the dishes produced by the Toft & Malkin Schools; or sgraffito decoration could be practiced, the design cut through the layer of slip to show the natural colour of the body. When the bat of clay has partly dried to a 'cheese-hard' state, it is pressed over a mould of plaster to form the dish, the rim cut round with a knife and when dry can be lifted off fully formed and decorated.

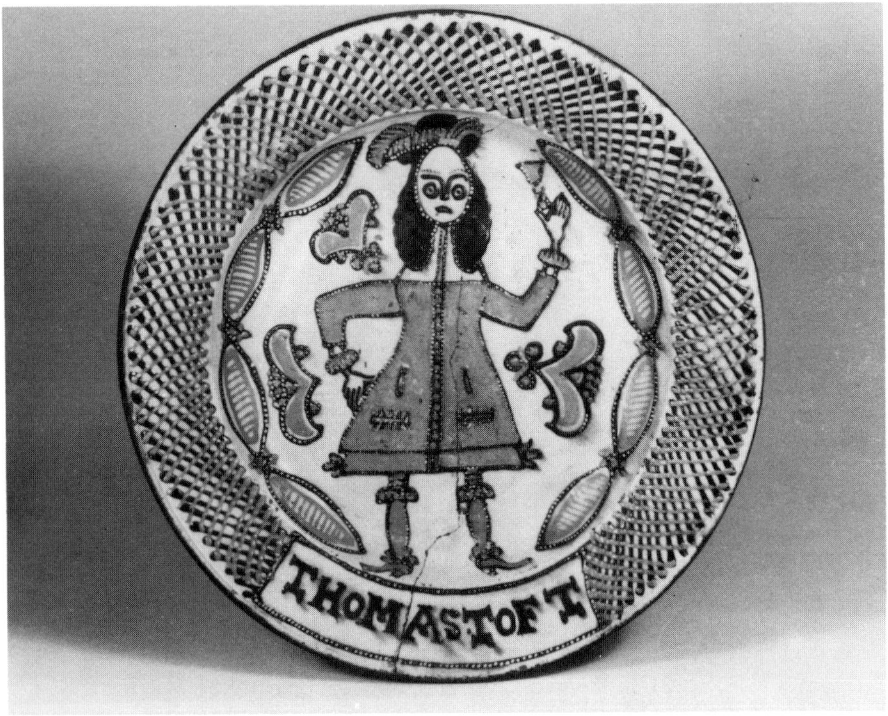

Plate 10. Large slipware dish decorated by Thomas Toft with a figure of a Cavalier holding a wine glass and an elaborate trellis border, *c.*1675, diameter 16½ in.

Stoke-on-Trent City Museum

Although the finest slipwares are now in museums or in a few private collections and it is rare for a dish by Thomas Toft, say, to get anywhere near the open market, not all the wares of this form would be regarded as great collectors' pieces now. In fact the greater majority of pieces produced were simple, homely pieces, such as puzzle jugs, miniature cradles, baking dishes with one or more compartments, money-boxes and jugs. Great quantities of these were made in many country centres right up to the early years of this century and pieces like Devon Harvest pitchers with typical sgraffito decoration, Sussex pots with painted slip decoration or baking dishes with trailed on slip can still be bought amazingly cheaply and represent some of the finest local peasant pottery imaginable.

Whole fields are open to the enquiring collector, such as the wares of Sussex, the West Country, Buckley in North Wales, each of these centres

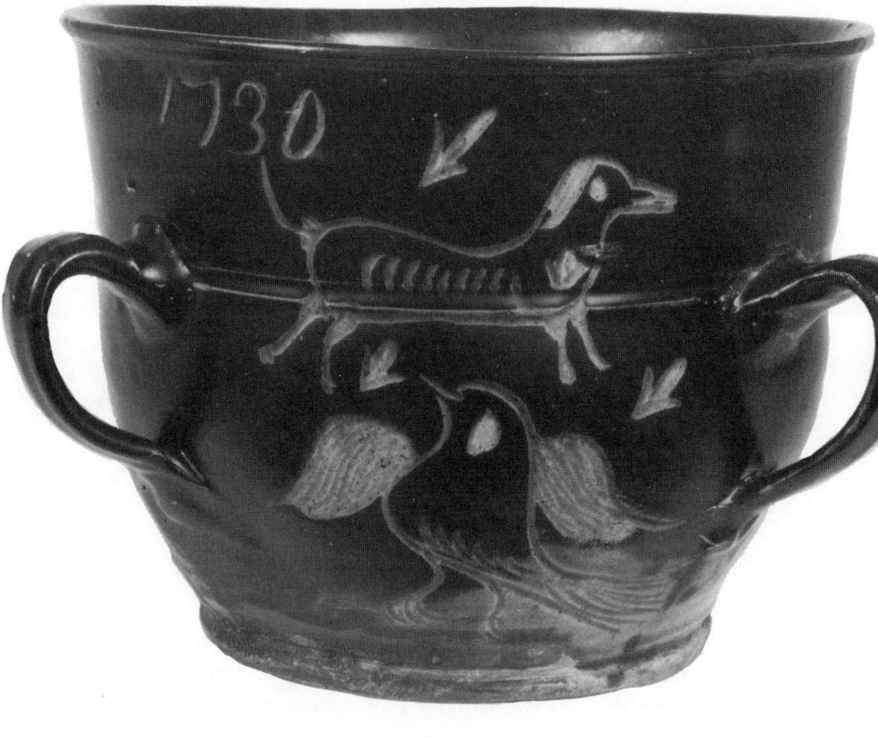

Plate 11. Large slipware handled bowl, decorated with sgrafitto birds and animals in yellow on deep brown and dated 1730, 10 in. diameter.
Rous Lench Collection (*Photograph: Phillips*)

having made enough wares to fill a dozen museums and there were many more areas as prolific as these. So although it is almost impossible to aspire to the purchase of Wrotham ware or Toft dishes and these can only be seen in museums the collector desirous of obtaining slip wares has plenty of scope.

One warning must be given. From 1865–1905 a curious pottery existed at Castle Hedingham in Essex, run by Edward Bingham, who frequently made pots decorated with slip in the Wrotham style and their crudity should not be confused with the genuine article.

FURTHER READING
English Slipware Dishes by R. G. Cooper

4 Stonewares and Saltglaze

Stoneware is a very high fired earthenware made of a special plastic clay and sand, which becomes partly vitrified and does not require glaze to enable it to retain liquids. Saltglazed stoneware was effected by throwing shovelfuls of common salt into the kiln at its highest temperature, the salt volatilized and formed the characteristic glaze on the exposed parts of the vessels, a glaze that is rather like orange peel with a pitted skin.

The ware first came into this country from the Rhineland in Germany, where it had been made from the Middle Ages. The first to be made in this country was by John Dwight in 1672 at Fulham potteries in London. The ware was referred to as 'Cologne' ware and was very largely copied from the German, one of the typical shapes being 'bellarmine' jugs, which have a curious bearded face on the front which is said to be a caricature of a Cardinal Bellarmine. Mugs and other vessels and also portrait busts and figures were produced in a putty colour or in coloured clays. Dwight also introduced red coloured teapots in imitation of Chinese wares, but he had his imitators.

A number of potters caused Dwight to attempt to enforce his patent in 1693, such potters as Wedgwood of Burslem and the Elers Brothers in Bradwell, Staffordshire and James Morley in Nottingham. These were great rivals to Dwight, whose family carried on the pottery after his death in 1703. The Elers found an abundance of fine red clay in Staffordshire and did a lot to build up the standards of potting in the area that was in due

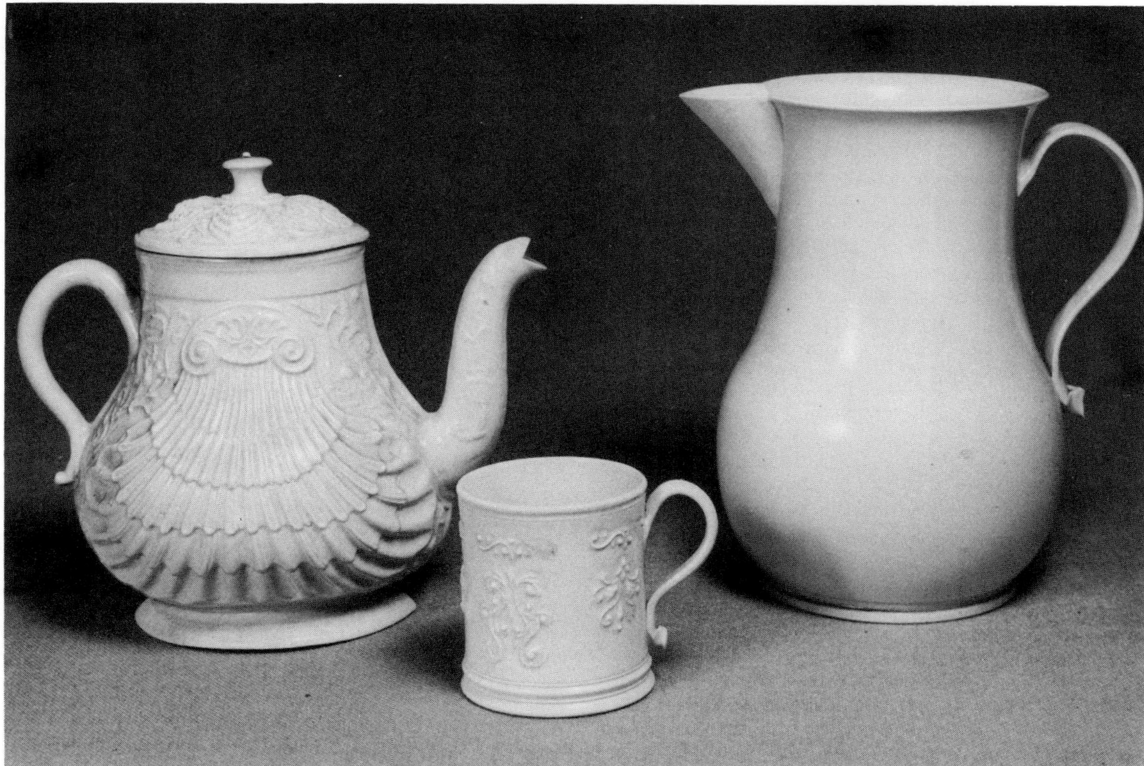

Plate 12. Three pieces of Staffordshire white saltglaze, the jug of plain, thrown shape, the other pieces with moulded decoration, the jug, 6½ in. *c.*1750.

Stoke-on-Trent City Museum

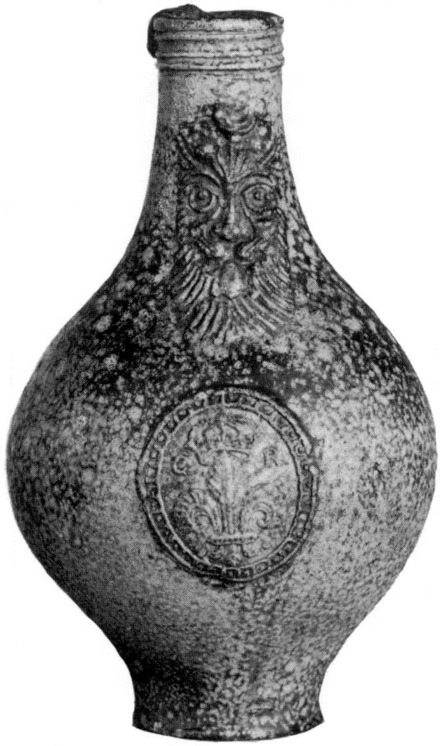

Plate 13. Saltglazed Stoneware Bellarmine Jug of typical form bearing monogram CR, second half of 17th century.

Victoria & Albert Museum

course to become The Potteries. Their ware was of superb quality, not only in form and potting but in material, a hard red stoneware of fine surface smoothness and compact body. Wares were generally thrown on a wheel and turned on a lathe, the only decoration being incised lines or applied clay decorations. Their wares are usually unglazed although it is possible that they introduced salt glazing into Staffordshire. They also made a black ware similar to the later black basalts made famous by Josiah Wedgwood. Although they guarded their secrets well, being said to employ only half wits who would not be able to pass on information, two potters—John Astbury and Josiah Twyford, who are said to have pretended to be idiots in order to gain knowledge, worked for them. They were later to make fine earthenware of their own.

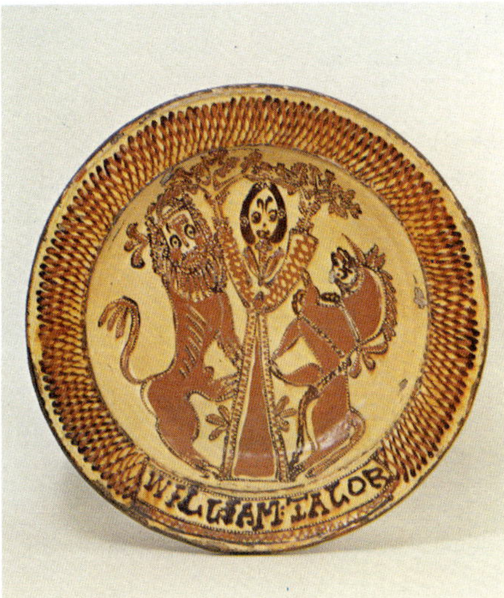

Plate I A Fine slipware charger by William Talor, trailed in brown and red slip with the head of Charles II in a stylized oak tree with Royal Supporters, 17½ in., late 17th century. Sold at Sothebys in 1978 for £15,400.

Sothebys

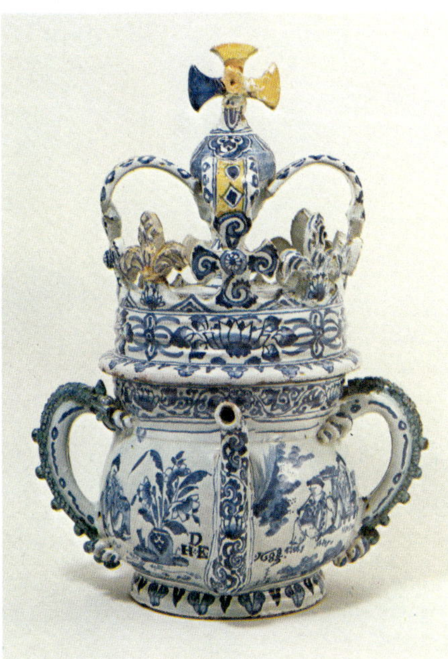

Plate II An impressive dated Delft posset pot and cover made in 1689, painted in blue with oriental type figures, the handle and crown picked out in green and yellow, inscribed HDE 168$\frac{8}{9}$

Sothebys

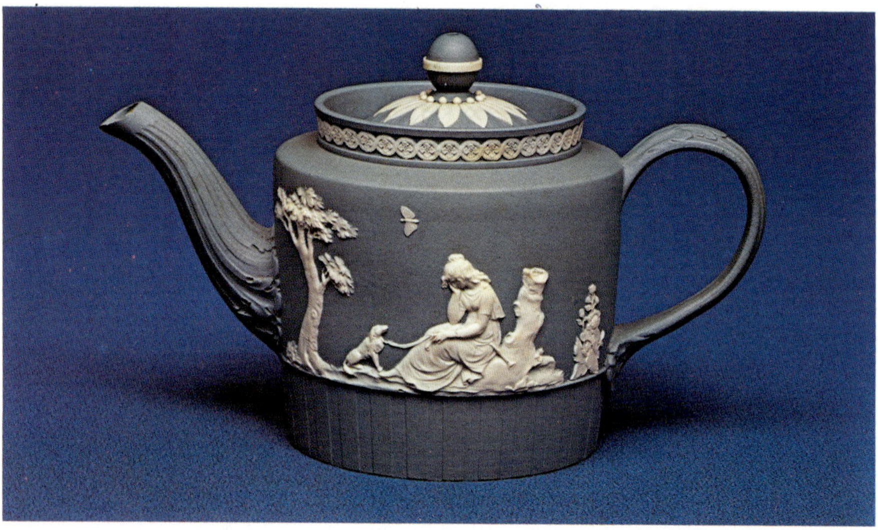

Plate III A Wedgwood blue jasperware teapot applied in white with a subject from the 'Domestic Employment' series designed by Lady Templeton, circa 1785, impressed 'Wedgwood' mark.

Josiah Wedgwood and Sons Ltd

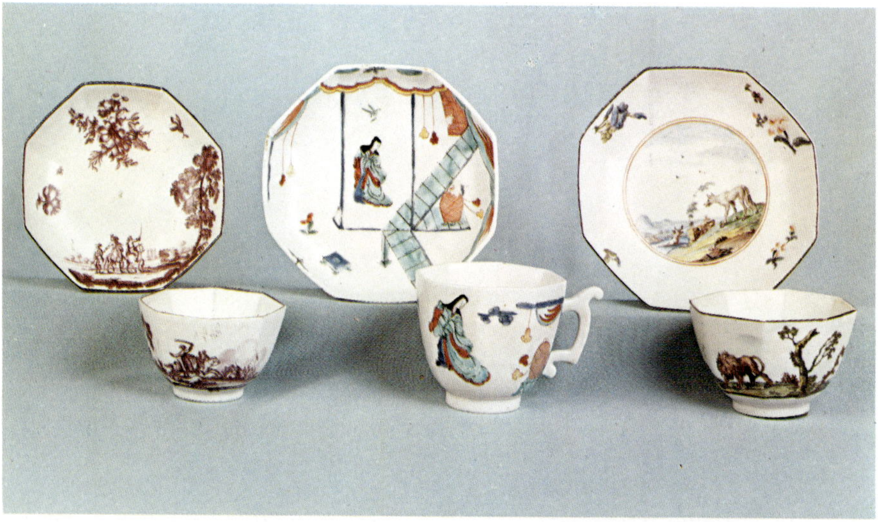

Plate IV A group of Chelsea octagonal teawares painted in the style of Meissen; the central cup after a Japanese design, the outside pieces with landscape and fable subjects by J. H. O'Neale, all Red Anchor period.

Christies

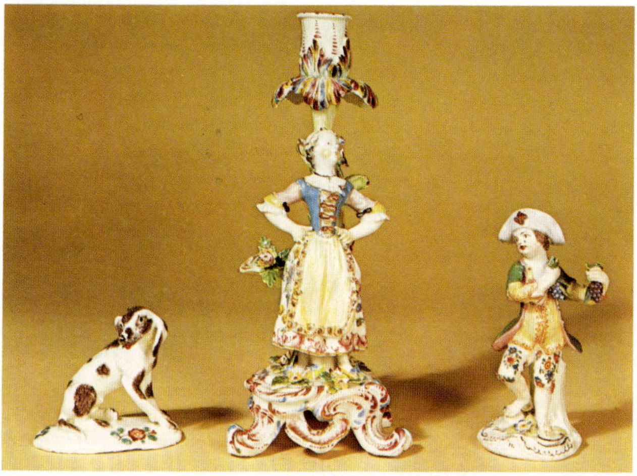

Plate V Three models from the Bow factory with contrasting decoration; The early figure of 'Autumn' is plain in design with high quality painting, as opposed to the later candlestick figure of a Dutch dancer bright enamels and on a Rococo base, the 'Dismal Hound' is charmingly simple and superbly potted, 3¼ in. high.

Phillips

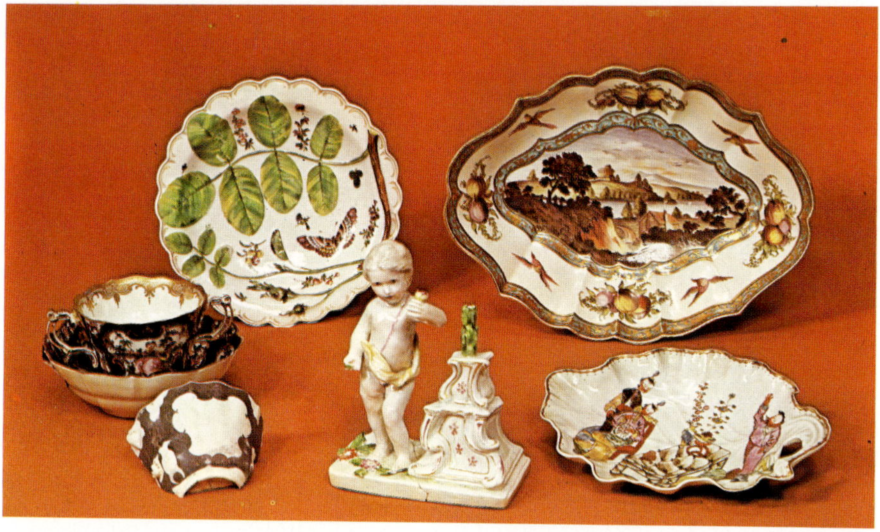

Plate VI Group of Worcester porcelain of the Dr. Wall period: Left: Chocolate cup and stand with scale-blue ground and figure panels, square mark; Plate of the 'Blind Earl' pattern embossed with rose leaves; Dish of Lord Henry Thynne type with fine quality landscape; Leaf dish in Canton style with Chinese figures; Figure of Cupid at Vulcan's Forge; all date from the late 1760's and 1770's. Shown with the cup is a 'waster' from the factory site with the blue ground before glazing.

Dysons Perrins Museum, Worcester

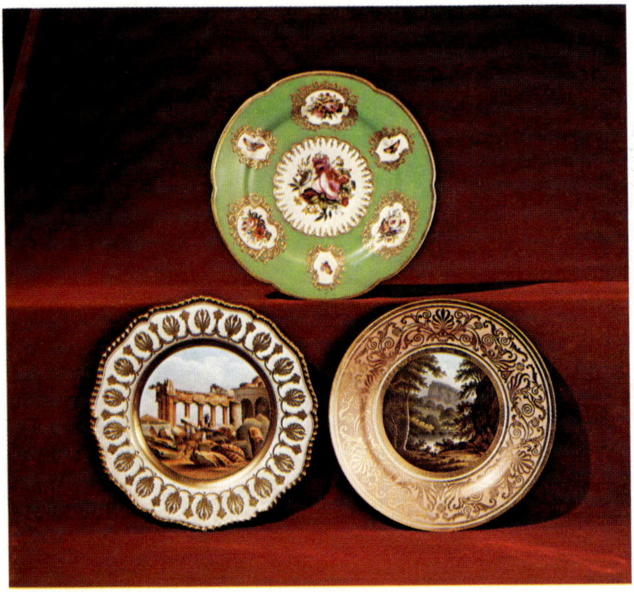

Plate VII Three Worcester plates from the Flight and Barr periods, typical of the fine quality services produced in the early 19th century to special orders.

Dyson Perrins Museum, Worcester

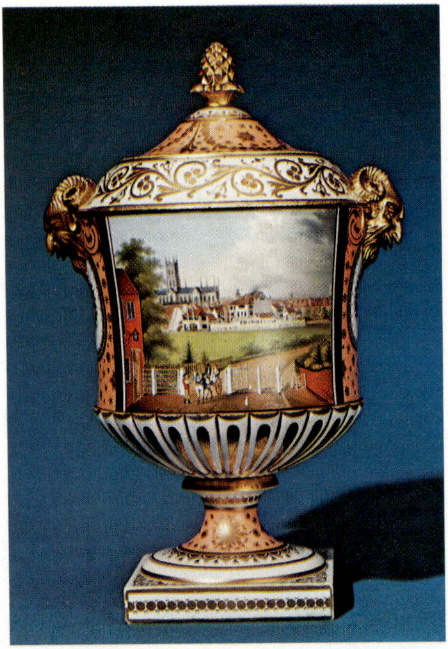

Plate VIII A Chamberlain's Worcester vase painted with a view of the city, Chamberlain's own factory shown prominently in the centre of the panel; note the high quality of gilding always found on such pieces.

Dyson Perrins Museum, Worcester

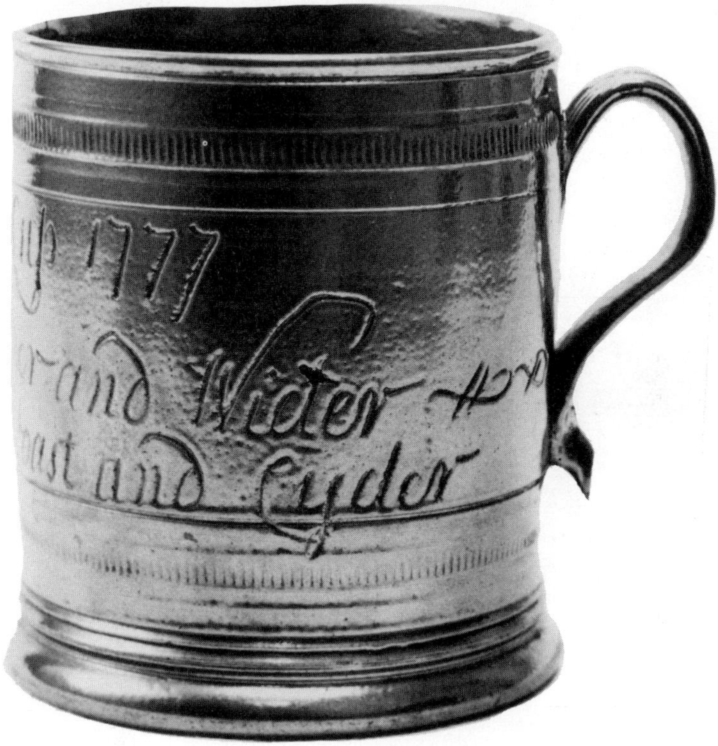

Plate 14. A Nottingham saltglazed tankard inscribed 'William Smith, his cup 1777 and if it had been higher and wider it would have held more Toast and Cyder'.
Author's Collection

The other great centre for stoneware was Nottingham, the earliest dated piece known being 1700. Most of the wares from this centre are saltglazed and covered with a shiny, irridescent brown surface. Mugs, cups, jugs and punch bowls were common, many having incised and rouletted decoration. The most curious pieces are vessels, probably tobacco jars, in the form of a bear with removable head, the representation of rough fur being given by the sprinkling of clay shavings into the wet body.

In Staffordshire in the first years of the eighteenth century great attempts were made to find a ware which could compete in quality with Chinese porcelain. Their answer to this problem was thin, light coloured saltglazed stoneware.

Astbury was one of the successes in this field, making a hard strong white

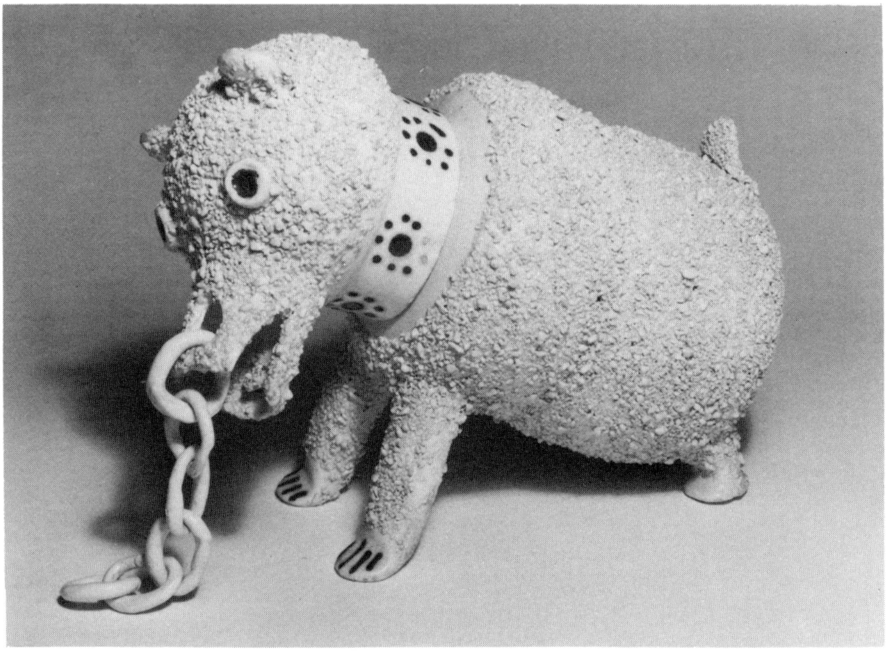

Plate 15. A Staffordshire saltglazed bear jar, the head forming the cover, applied with clay crumbs to simulate fur, 10 in., mid 18th century.

Phillips

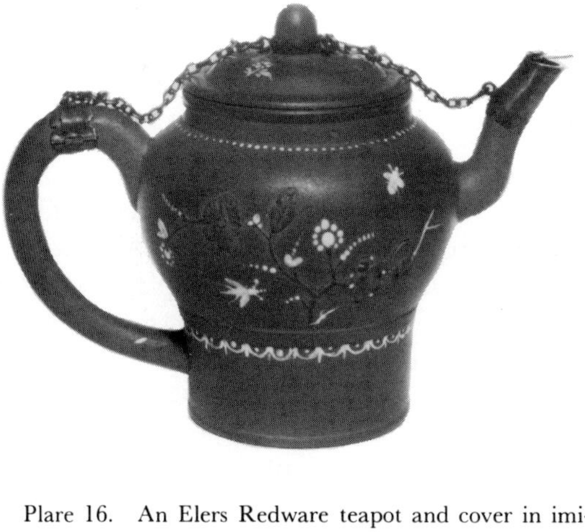

Plare 16. An Elers Redware teapot and cover in imitation of Chinese Yi Hsing ware, the side 'sprigged' with prunus sprigs picked out in white enamel, $4\frac{1}{4}$ in.

Sothebys

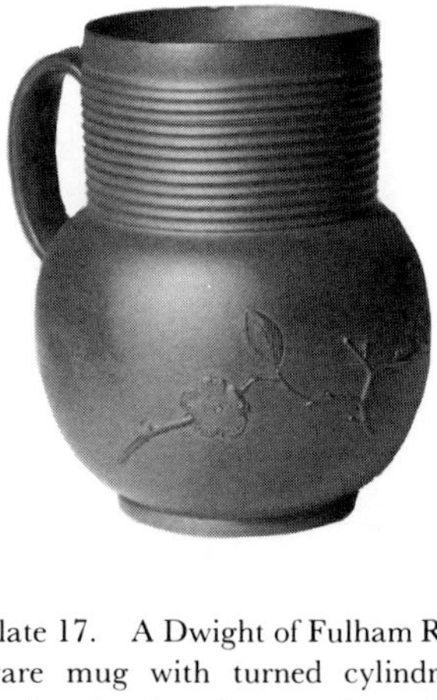

Plate 17. A Dwight of Fulham Redware mug with turned cylindrical neck and sprigged prunus decoration, 4 in. *c.*1685.

Phillips

body obtained by adding calcined flint to the local white clay. Numbers of potters followed his lead and many fine pieces were made, often of such thinness and quality that it is difficult to realise that they are opaque earthenware. So many potteries were making the ware that the smoke polution caused by the noxious gasses produced by the kilns not only caused serious illness but great clouds of smoke to hang over the area.

Dr Thomas Wedgwood produced a drab coloured ware decorated with applied work in white pipe clay. Aaron Wood is believed to have produced intricate moulded and pierced borders on wares and also elaborate figure model groups such as pew groups, depicting two figures seated on a pew. Other figures were made, often of a very primitive sort, frequently with details picked out in dark brown clay. Salt glazed agate ware was also made, the different coloured clays being blended and occasionally having splashes of blue. Enamel colours and scratch blue decoration was also used.

The manufacture of salt glaze had virtually ceased by the 1770's, having been overtaken by cream coloured earthenware. Stonewares have had a great revival in this present century, being one of the principal materials used by the craftsmen potters' movement.

FURTHER READING

Staffordshire Saltglaze Stoneware by Arnold Mountford

5 Astbury, Whieldon and Wedgwood

The names Astbury and Whieldon are used now to describe generic types of wares, although the two great potters themselves produced many fine pieces, which if proved to be by one of them can command high prices at auction.

Astbury we have met in the previous chapter, he it was who introduced pipe clay decoration and the use of calcined flint in Staffordshire. His glazed red stonewares frequently employ decoration produced by 'sprigging', that is by making ornamental bits in a separate mould and applying them onto the vessel. The rarest Astbury pieces are the small figures of musicians coloured in browns and greens under the glaze and these can fetch very great prices. Also made were agate and marbled wares.

Many of these items were also made by Thomas Whieldon. His wares are typified by different coloured glazes blended together to give some extraordinary effects, such as 'tortoiseshell'. The colours are very attractive ones, great use being made of brown, green and purple, which are under a clear glaze, as opposed to overglaze painted enamels used on later Staffordshire figures, frequently mistaken for Whieldon.

Two of the many apprentices that Whieldon took on were to become very important potters; Josiah Spode who later was to claim the invention of bone china which will be dealt with later, and Josiah Wedgwood.

Josiah Wedgwood was born in 1730 in Burslem. After being apprenticed to his brother at his late father's Churchyard Pottery, he went to Thomas

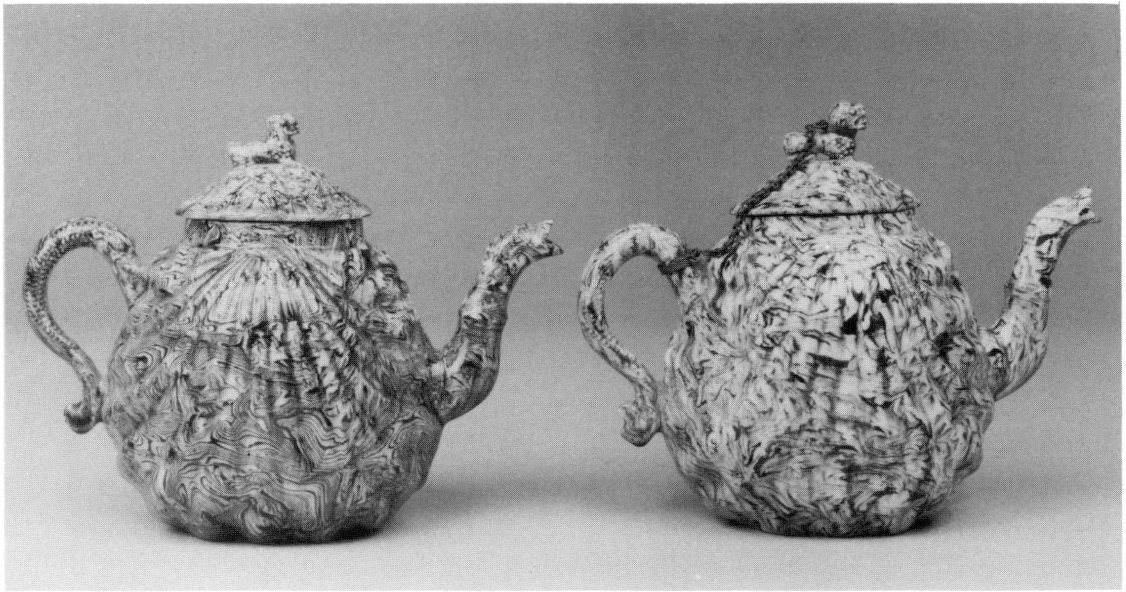

Plate 18. Two Staffordshire solid agate lead-glazed teapots of Astbury/Whieldon type in the shape of pecten shells. These agate wares are always superb in potting and form.

Christies

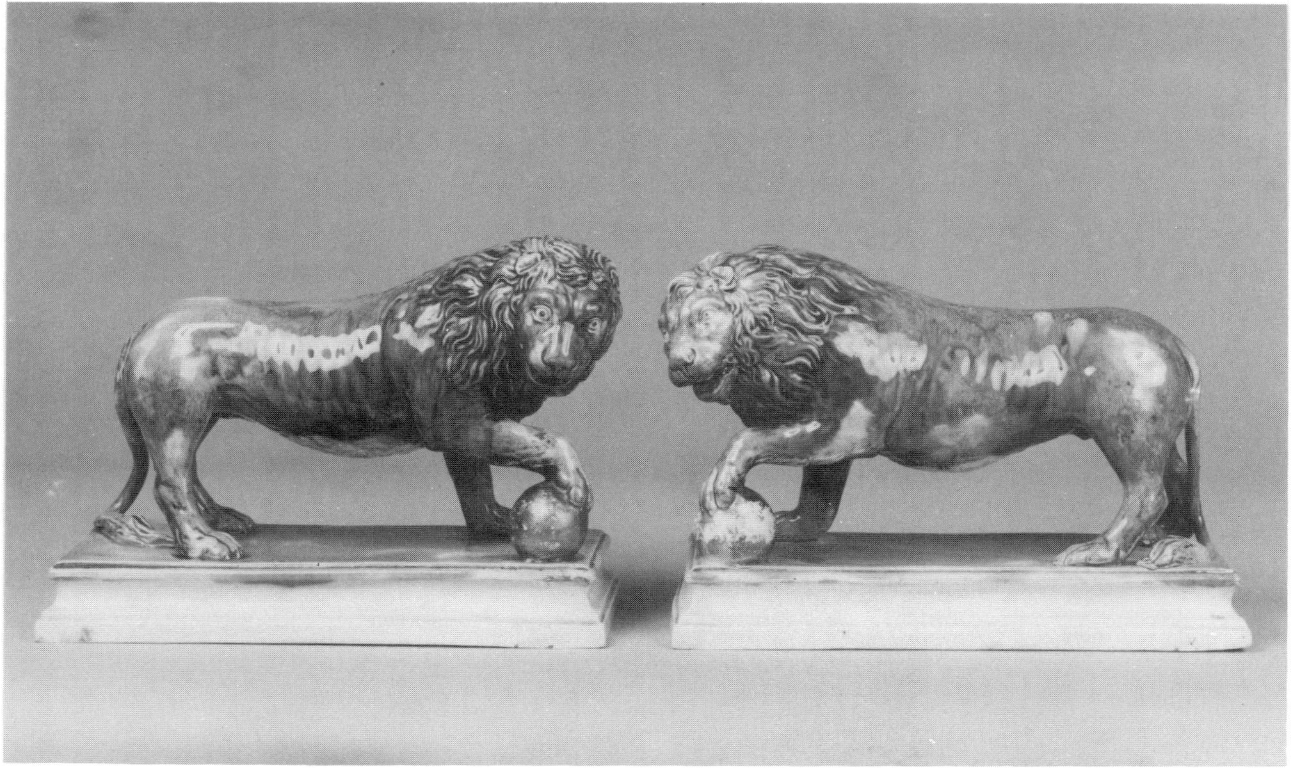

Plate 19. A pair of Ralph Wood/Whieldon models of lions typically decorated with running underglaze colours, *c.*1770.
Christies

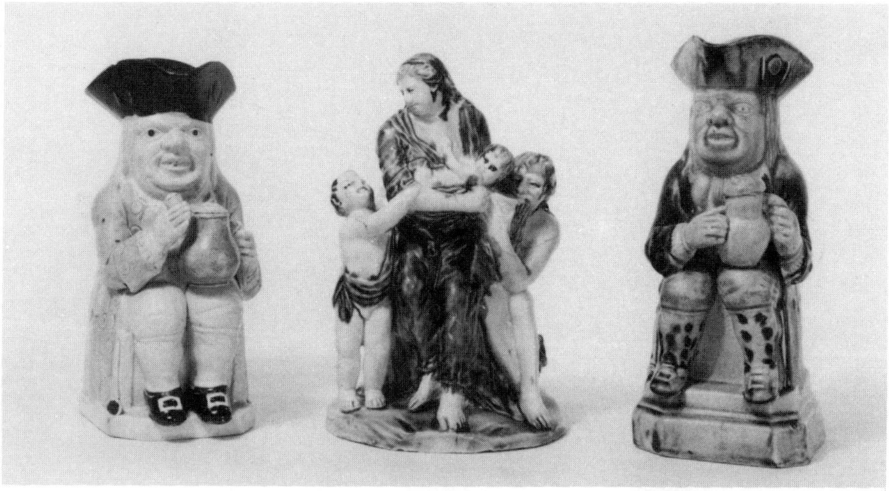

Plate 22. A Ralph Wood group of Roman Charity, and two Toby jugs, each with mottled coloured glazes, $6\frac{1}{2}$ in. and 10 in. This so-called usual model of Toby jug remained popular well into the present century.

Phillips

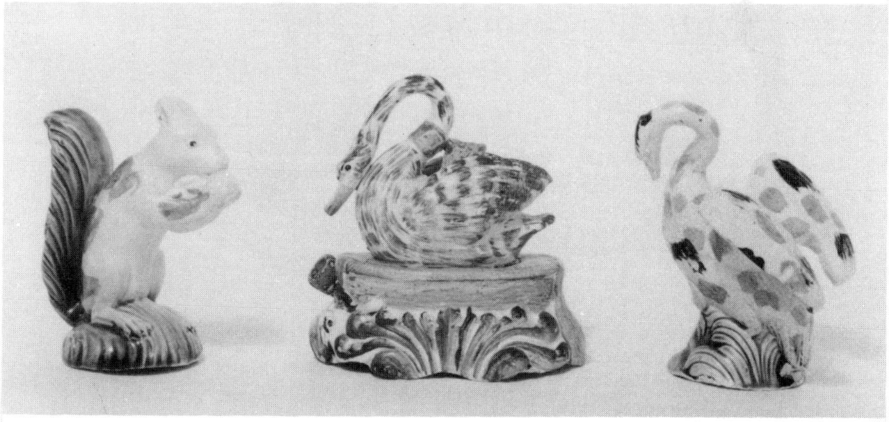

Plate 23. A Staffordshire pottery model of a squirrel splashed in ochre and green, and two Staffordshire swans with coloured enamels and glazes, 4 in. and $4\frac{1}{2}$ in., late 18th century. A large assortment of small animal models were produced at this period and although simply moulded, have a certain naïve charm.

Phillips

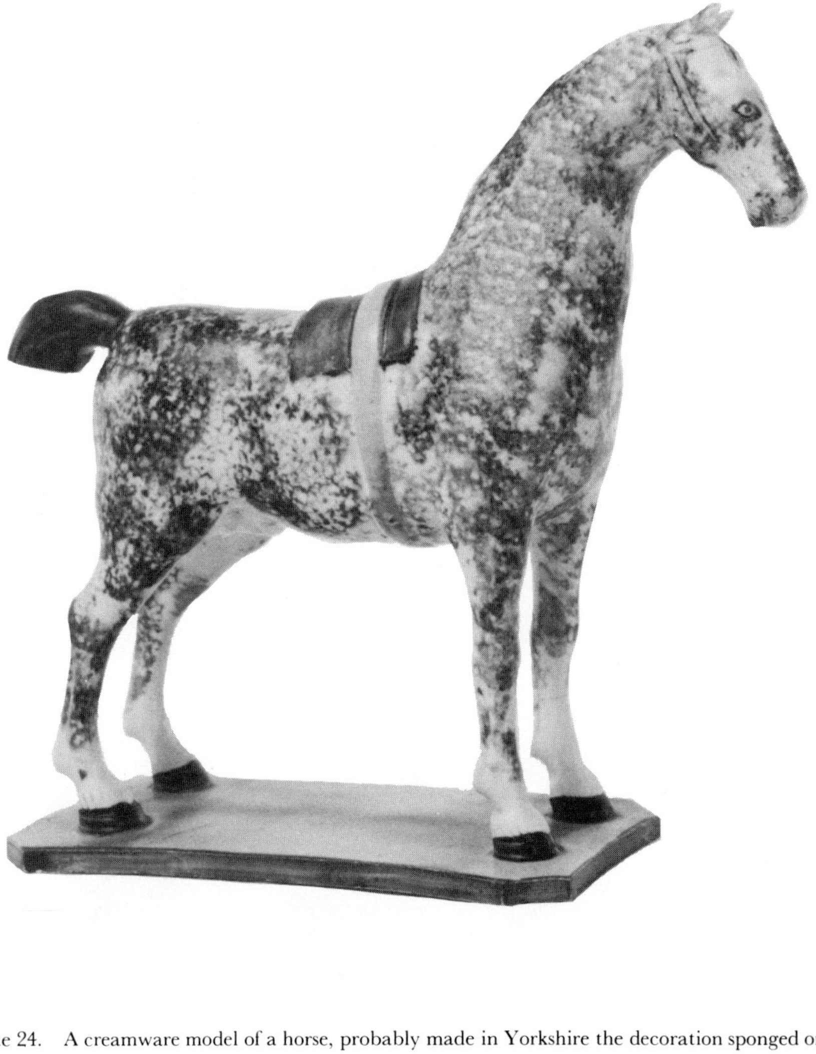

Plate 24. A creamware model of a horse, probably made in Yorkshire the decoration sponged onto the fired pottery before glazing, 6 in.

Phillips

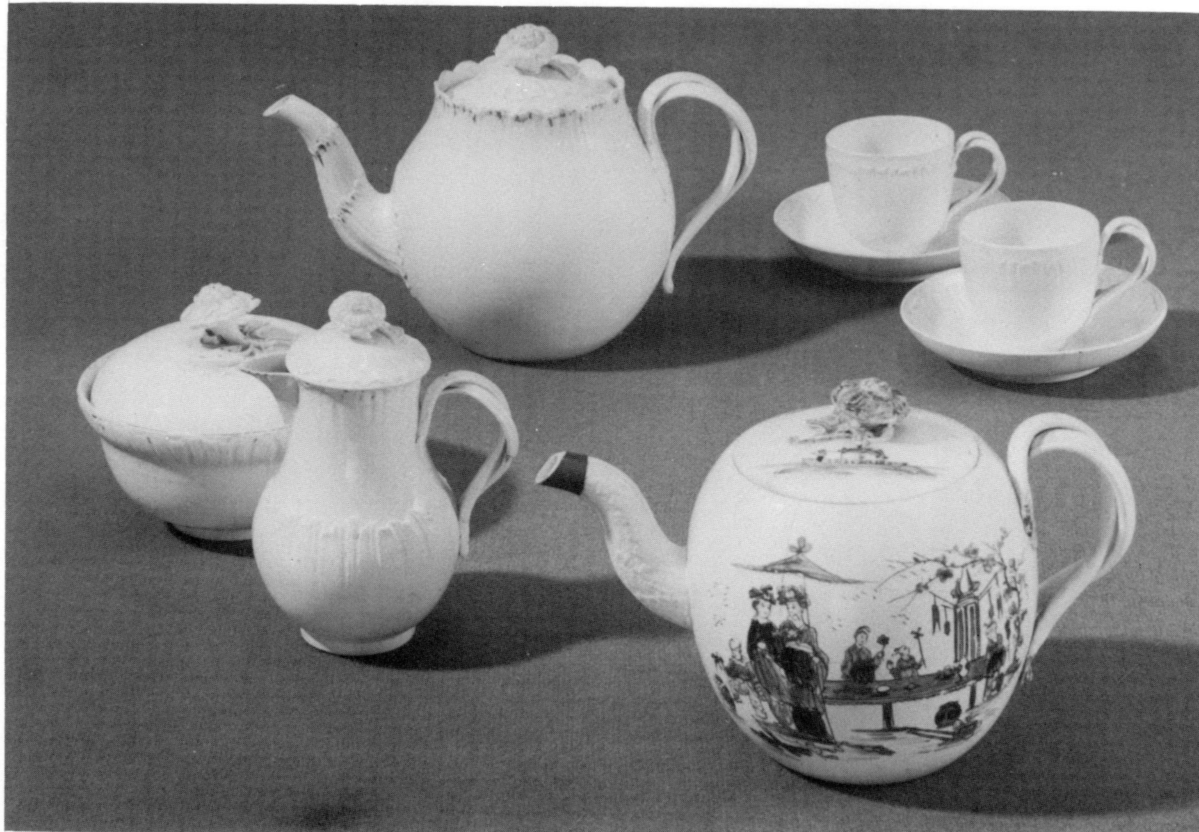

Plate 25. A Wedgwood 'Queen's Ware' tea service of shell edged shape with traces of oil gilding, *c.*1775, and a teapot and cover enamelled with a Chinoiserie subject, *c.* 1770.

Josiah Wedgwood & Sons Ltd.

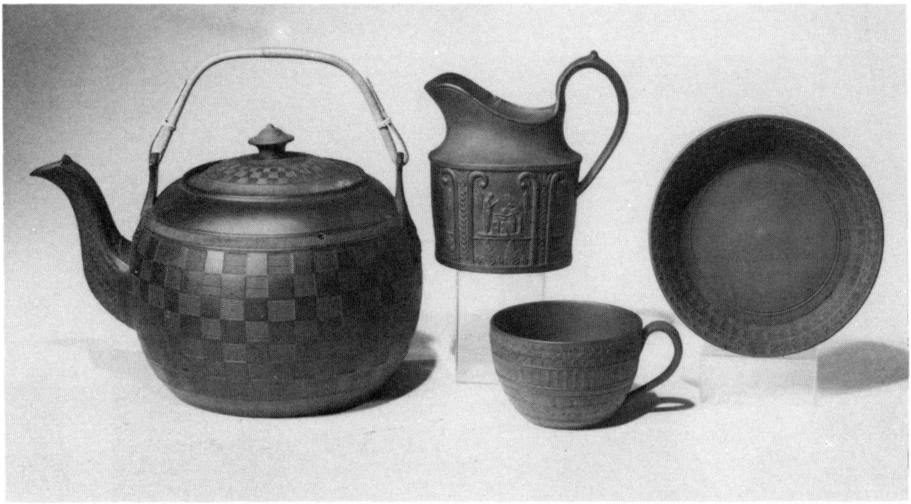

Plate 26. A selection of Basalt wares made by Leeds Pottery, the tea kettle and cup and saucer with engine-turned decoration produced by a moving lathe, tea kettle $6^{1}/_{4}$ in., marked Leeds Pottery impressed.

Geoffrey Godden, Chinaman

and are difficult to ascribe. They look much more ancient than the typical mid nineteenth figures, and of much greater quality, but are relatively quite rare.

John Turner. In a pottery at Lane End in Staffordshire he made fine jasper, basalt and cream wares from about 1762. After his death in 1787 the factory was continued by his sons until 1806, moving into the production of a hard earthenware similar to the later 'Ironstone'. A great speciality of the factory were mugs and jugs of a stoneware body decorated with hunting and drinking scenes in a raised ornament. These wares can often be fairly translucent, especially in their thinnest parts. Very few early wares are marked, although a number of later ones bear the impressed word TURNER.

Rockingham. At Swinton in Yorkshire made earthenwares in the Leeds style in the eighteenth century, but the wares are unmarked and very difficult to ascribe. *JAMES NEALE* took over Humphrey Palmer's Church Works at Hanley in 1776 and made wares of Wedgwood type often marked with the word NEALE. *JACKFIELD* in Shropshire is usually credited with all the many shiny black glazed red earthenwares in existence, but most of these were probably made by a number of Staffordshire factories.

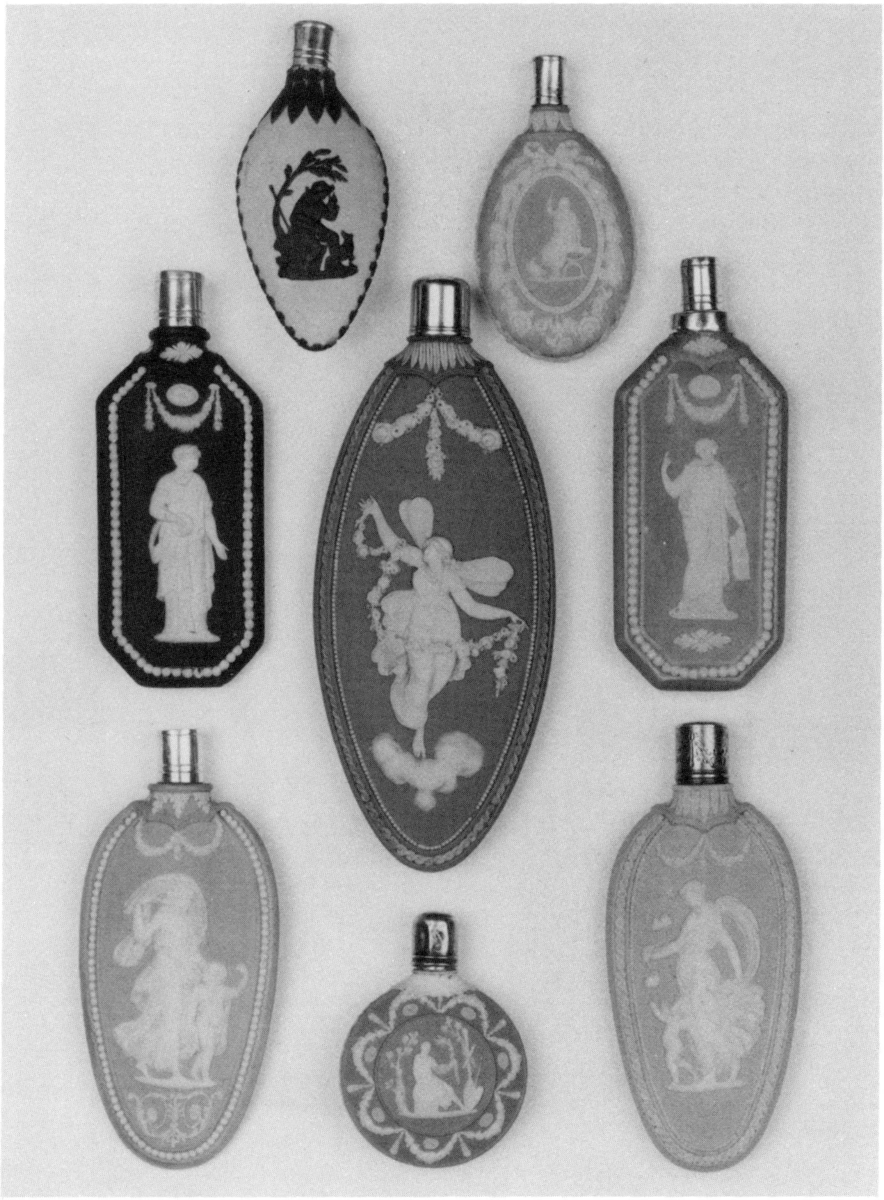

Plate 27. A group of Jasperware scent bottles from the late 18th/early 19th centuries. Bottles such as these were made by several manufacturers, principally Wedgwood, Neale and Turner.

Christies

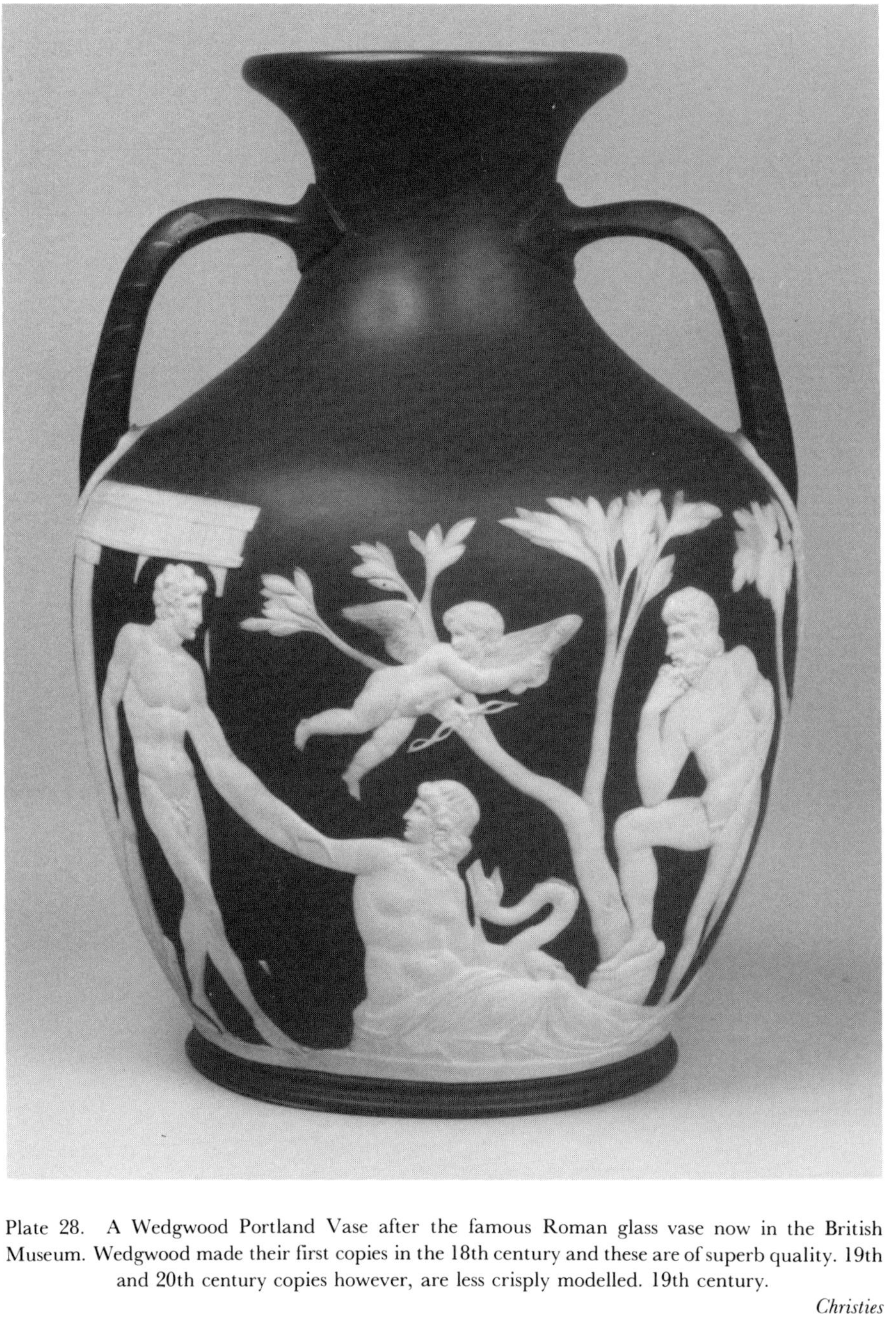

Plate 28. A Wedgwood Portland Vase after the famous Roman glass vase now in the British Museum. Wedgwood made their first copies in the 18th century and these are of superb quality. 19th and 20th century copies however, are less crisply modelled. 19th century.

Christies

William Adams and Son. This family of Tunstall in Staffordshire produced great quantities of pieces in the Wedgwood style, especially fine blue jaspers with white relief decoration from about 1769, and the firm is still in production to this day. A number of the early wares are marked with the impressed word 'ADAMS'.

Generally in the case of eighteenth century earthenwares it should be a case of thinking first of the quality of the piece and not worrying too much about who made it. There is still scope for acquiring good pieces, especially those of the 'Jackfield' type, which are very much undervalued.

7 Eighteenth Century Porcelain

It took England a long time to discover how to make porcelain, many years of striving to produce a white, translucent ware to equal the Chinese. When Meissen eventually achieved success in about 1708 the ware they produced was a hard paste porcelain; England still had nearly another 40 years of searching before they were able to bring forward soft paste porcelain.

Soft paste is strictly an artificial porcelain, made either from soft stone, such as soapstone and various other ingredients, or bone ash and fritted materials, as opposed to the 'true' porcelain of China made from China-clay (kaolin) and china-stone (petuntse) fired at a high temperature with a flux. The German, and most other European hard paste porcelain is a very different material to most of the English wares (apart from Plymouth, Bristol and New Hall who made a tolerably good hard paste body); the title 'soft paste' is a good description and the body glaze gave a much softer effect to the eye and hand, the *feel* of which can be quite easily acquired, which will avoid the damage caused by filing the piece with a triangular file—the common method given in so many books of deciding whether a piece is soft paste (a file will mark soft but not hard paste).

Although not so durable as hard paste and without the latter's ability to avoid surface scratches or cracking when boiling liquid was put in (apart from Worcester, whose wares never cracked nor crazed), English soft paste had one great artistic advantage in that the onglaze colours sank into the glaze producing a softer and more attractive appearance.

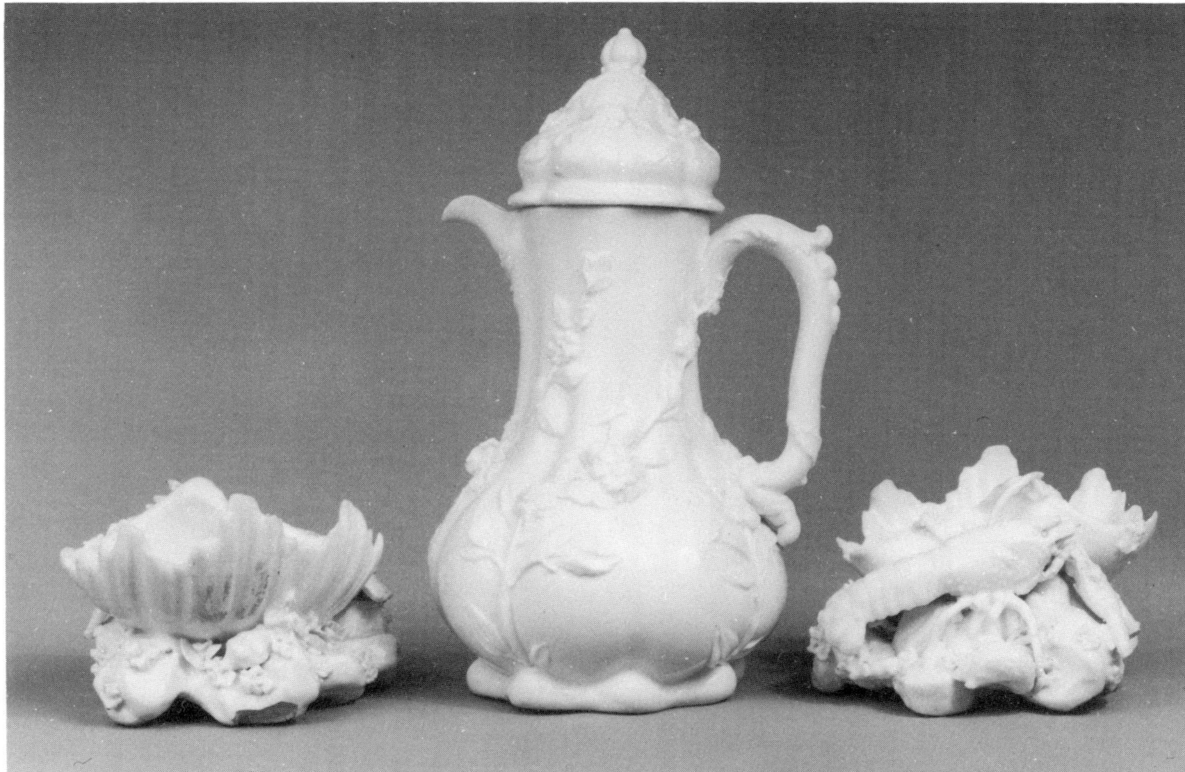

Plate 29. Chelsea porcelain of the Triangle period typically left in the white. The lobster and shell salts are based closely on silver shapes and show the influence of the silversmith who owned the factory, Nicholas Sprimont, marks of incised triangles.
Christies

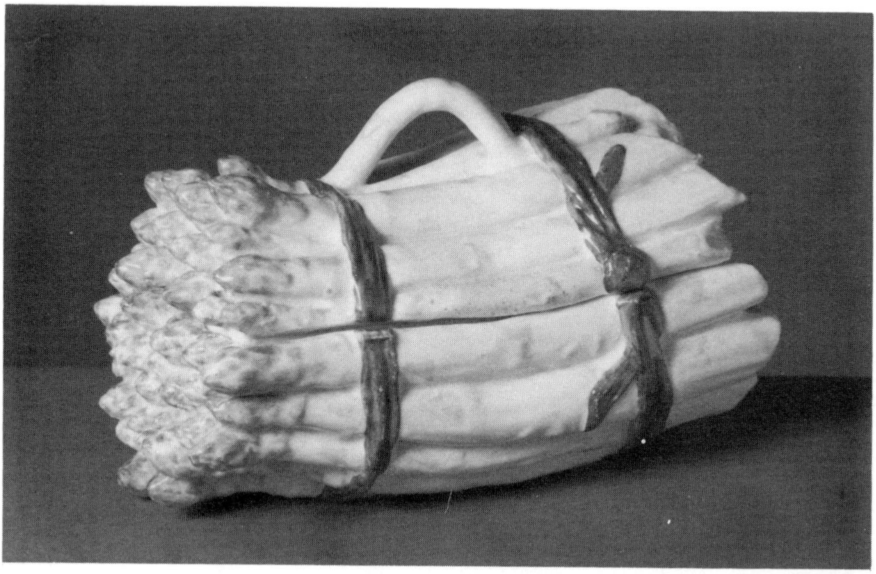

Plate 30. Chelsea porcelain tureen in the shape of a strapped bunch of asparagus, probably derived from a Meissen original and showing superb potting technique. Red Anchor mark and number 63 in red, $7\frac{1}{4}$ in. long.

Victoria & Albert Museum

The English factories are treated in chronological order of their starting to make porcelain.

CHELSEA AND CHELSEA/DERBY *c.*1745–*c.*1784

Chelsea, which was probably England's first porcelain manufactory, was certainly established by 1745. Its porcelain is always of the soft paste variety, although there are a considerable number of fakes, especially made on the Continent in the late nineteenth century, which are generally of hard paste. It is, therefore, essential to know the difference between the materials. Genuine Chelsea quite often shows small light spots or 'pin holes' and also the very characteristic 'moons'. Flat wares were usually fired on spurs which left three scars—rough points of glaze—arranged in a triangle in the centre of the base. The glaze is usually very glassy and footrims were usually ground flat and free of glaze. The history of Chelsea divides itself up into periods.

TRIANGLE PERIOD

The first dated pieces, curious vessels known as 'Goat & Bee' jugs, vessels modelled as a goat, sometimes have the date 1745, an incised triangle and the word 'Chelsea'. There are, however, a great number of fakes of this particular vessel made in the much whiter bone china body possibly by Coalport and Minton. The period 1745–9 is known as the 'triangle period' in view of the incised triangle, which on genuine pieces is always a very rough, crudely incised shape.

RAISED ANCHOR PERIOD

This period from 1749 to 1752 is referred to as the 'Raised Anchor Period' as the usual mark was the anchor moulded on a raised pad. The wares of this period, both ornamental and useful, are of very fine quality and good taste. Decoration tends to be simple and the pieces present a slightly milky white appearance through the addition of tin in the glaze, a feature which continued in the 'red' but not the 'gold anchor' period.

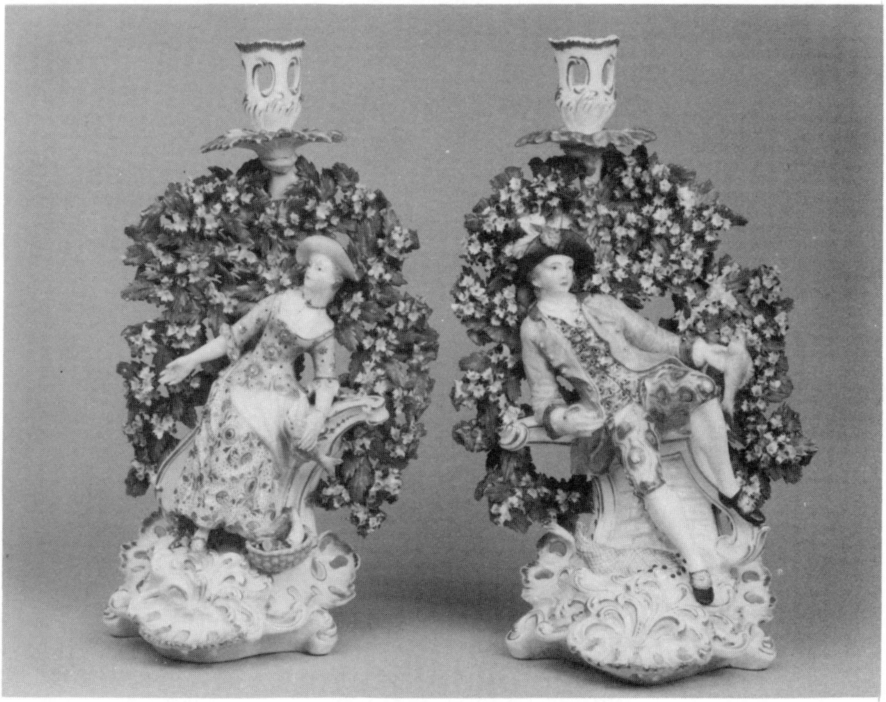

Plate 31. Gold Anchor period Chelsea figure candlesticks, typical of the high rococo of the 1760's and 1770's. As with most Chelsea figures of this period the costumes are elaborately coloured and gilt, Gold Anchor marks at the reverse.

Christies

RED ANCHOR PERIOD

In this period 1752-6 the anchor mark was painted directly on the glazed body in red enamel. This anchor is very small on genuine pieces rarely more than a quarter of an inch in height and on figures it is often placed in an unobtrusive spot. Very large anchors should be treated with great caution. The quality and taste of this period is again very high.

GOLD ANCHOR PERIOD

From 1756 to 1769 a mark of a *small* gold anchor was used and the wares of this period become much more ornate, vases frequently being too ornate in shape for good taste. Figures often have bocages and useful wares elaborate gilding, often with ground colours. The glaze in this period is now clear, thickly applied and with a tendency to craze. A number of small scent bottles and seals were made and are called 'toys'.

CHELSEA/DERBY PERIOD

Production of porcelain ceased early in 1769 and the factory was sold to James Cox in August 1769 and in February 1770 it was purchased by William Duesbury, the proprietor of the Derby factory. Duesbury used the Chelsea works mainly as a decorating establishment although some ware was probably made there, until 1784 when the premises were given up and some of the moulds taken to Derby. The years 1769 to 1784 are termed the 'Chelsea/Derby' period and the wares are generally very fine, thinner potted with uncrazed glaze. The gold anchor continued in use, but the most common mark is a script letter 'D' with an anchor running through the down-stroke. A crown above an anchor is also found, these marks being in gold. Figures and vases of this period often show three or four patch marks on the base, as are found on Derby wares. Shapes are often Neo Classical.

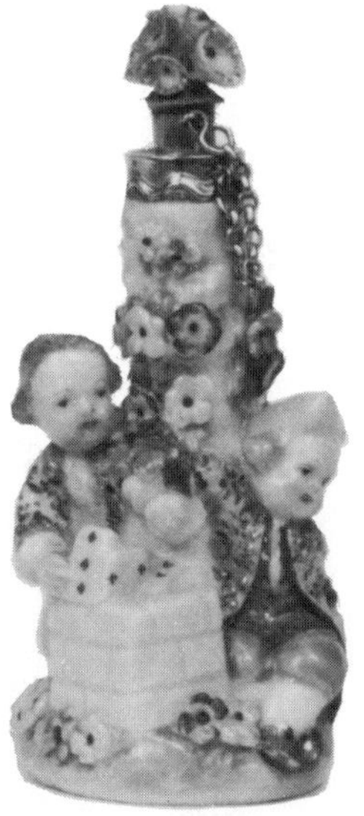

Plate 32. A Chelsea scent bottle modelled as two boys building a house of playing cards, the underside with gilt inscription 'Je Vous L'Adresse', gold mounts, $2\frac{1}{4}$ in., Gold Anchor period.
Phillips

These periods should not be regarded as hard and fast, considerable overlapping being found. It should also be realised that a considerable quantity of Chelsea porcelain is unmarked.

It is believed that a small group of unmarked

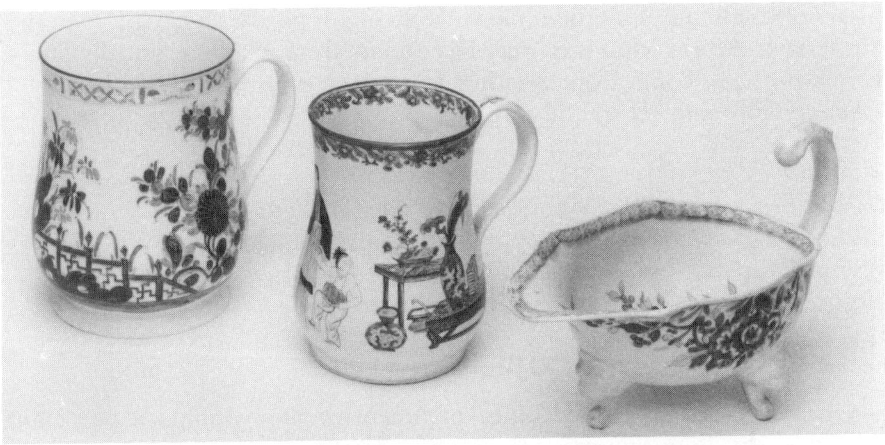

Plate 33. *Left:* A Bow bell-shaped mug painted in underglaze blue, onglazed red and gold, $5\frac{1}{2}$ in., *Centre:* a Bow mug with a bright polychrome Chinese subject $5\frac{1}{4}$ in., *Right:* A Bow sauceboat on lion-mask feet, after a silver shape, $8\frac{1}{2}$ in. long.

Phillips

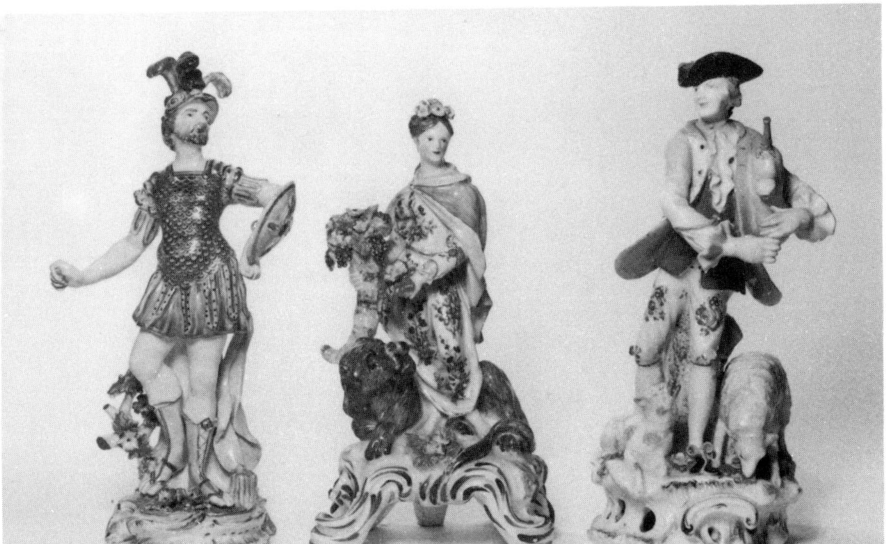

Plate 34. A group of Bow figures. *Left:* Mars, with richly gilt armour, *Centre:* Asia, from a set of the Continents, *Right:* A shepherd playing bagpipes, each on rococo bases.

Bonhams

pieces of Chelsea type, called 'Girl in a Swing' type after a key piece in the Victoria & Albert Museum, may have come from Chelsea, but they may very well have come from another factory or even have been made by Chelsea workmen off the factory.

FURTHER READING

Chelsea Porcelain, the Triangle and Raised Anchor Wares by F. S. Mackenna
Chelsea Porcelain, the Red Anchor Wares by F. S. Mackenna
Chelsea Porcelain, the Gold Anchor Wares by F. S. Mackenna
English Porcelain 1745–1840 by R. J. Charleston (ed)

BOW *c.*1746–*c.*1776

One of the earliest of the English eighteenth century soft paste porcelain factories, the Bow factory was actually in the Parish of Stratford near London, and although a patent for making porcelain was granted to

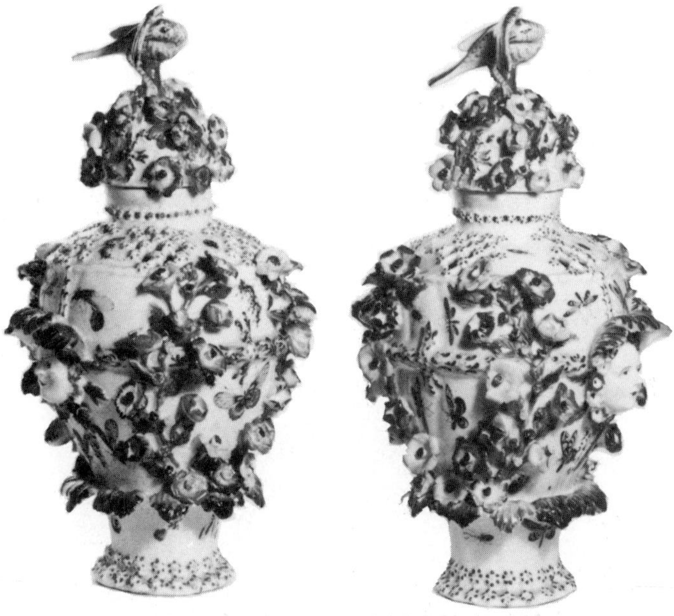

Plate 35. A pair of Bow 'Frill' vases and covers with pierced necks and encrusted masks and flowers. Such vases were also made by Derby and although impressive pieces of potting never command very high prices and are well worth looking out for.

Bonhams

Edward Heylyn & Thomas Frye in 1744 it is not thought that porcelain on a commercial scale was made until about 1746 or 7. All the wares were of a bone ash body, the shapes generally very good and a wide range were made, from useful wares to a large number of fine figure groups.

Few of the earliest wares are marked, apart from painter's marks. The first factory marks occur from about 1750 when the factory seems to have been known as New Canton, some rare circular inkwells being inscribed 'Made at New Canton' dated 1750 and 1751. Principal productions were blue and white painted wares and particularly fine powder blue was made.

Onglaze enamelled wares were made, the pieces being rather simply decorated, often after Chinese originals and generally of not as high a standard as Chelsea and although the figure groups from Bow are not as fine in quality as those from the other London factory, they are still very spirited. A major field of production was in transfer printing; however it now seems likely that credit for the first use of printing on porcelain must go to Worcester.

Bow pieces are fairly easy to tell from their contemporaries with frequent comparative handling. The basic body is frequently of a rather drab grey colour, rather heavy and not very translucent in the earlier period. Later on the body is of a more open texture, a creamy white colour and lighter. Quite often small cracks and tears in the body are to be found. The glaze is close fitting, very soft and easily scratched and quite often has a slight iridescent look. The blue has not quite the quality of the Worcester blue and is usually more blurred. The body stains brown where it is exposed when the glaze wears off. Often brown marks which look like chips on the rim are caused by staining - they seem to be chips but the glaze is not cut into. Onglaze colours are very strong on early Bow, especially a turquoise green. Footrims are very shallow, often too small for the bases, causing the centres of the base to touch the ground.

In 1776, the same year in which Dr. Wall of Worcester died, William Duesbury of Derby aquired Bow and the site became a manufactory for turpentine.

DERBY

The history of ceramic making at Derby causes a lot of confusion among ordinary collectors because of the number of different factories and changes of names involved. The fact that the present Royal Crown Derby Porcelain Company is not the direct successor of the original factory tends to make confusion greater in the mind. It is hoped that the splitting up of the history of Derby into the different centuries may help to make things clearer.

It is thought that the first production of porcelain in Derby were figures, which were being produced by 1750. Few of these early figures are marked

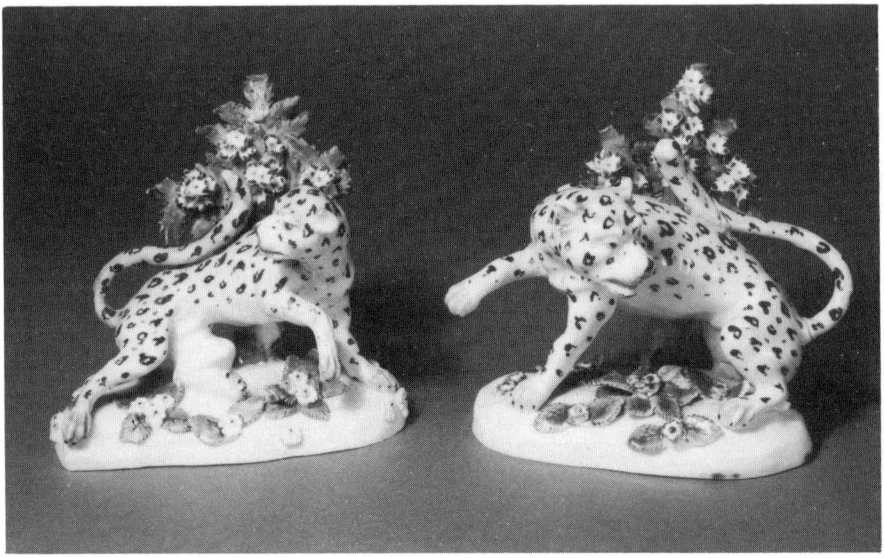

Plate 36. A pair of early Derby models of leopards preparing to combat, turning towards to each other and modelled with a great sense of movement. Typical flowering bocage behind serving also as supports to hold the figures steady in the kilns, $4\frac{1}{2}$ in.

Phillips

but they have some features in common, particularly the so-called '*dry edge*' figures, which have a glaze free edge around the foot.

In 1756 William Duesbury, who previously appears to have merely been a decorator in London, joined John Heath and Andrew Planche to manufacture porcelain in Derby. Planché quite quickly dropped out of the venture and as Heath was merely the financial support, Duesbury was virtually in sole charge. He was a good business man and quickly got Derby on a sound footing especially in the production of figures which often closely resemble Meissen originals, but lack the freedom of the pieces they were copying.

Derby's figures are more like those of Chelsea from about 1760 and although figures were the principle production, useful wares were also made. The early useful wares are of variable quality, quite often thickly potted and distorted in shape with glaze that sometimes shows pitting and has enamelled insects painted on to cover the blemishes. The figures usually have three or four 'patch marks' under the bases, round dark marks denoting where the figures rested on pads during firing.

After Duesbury's purchase of the Chelsea factory in 1770 there was a great improvement in the production and in 1771 the first announcement of figures in the biscuit. Biscuit figures cost more to purchase than glazed

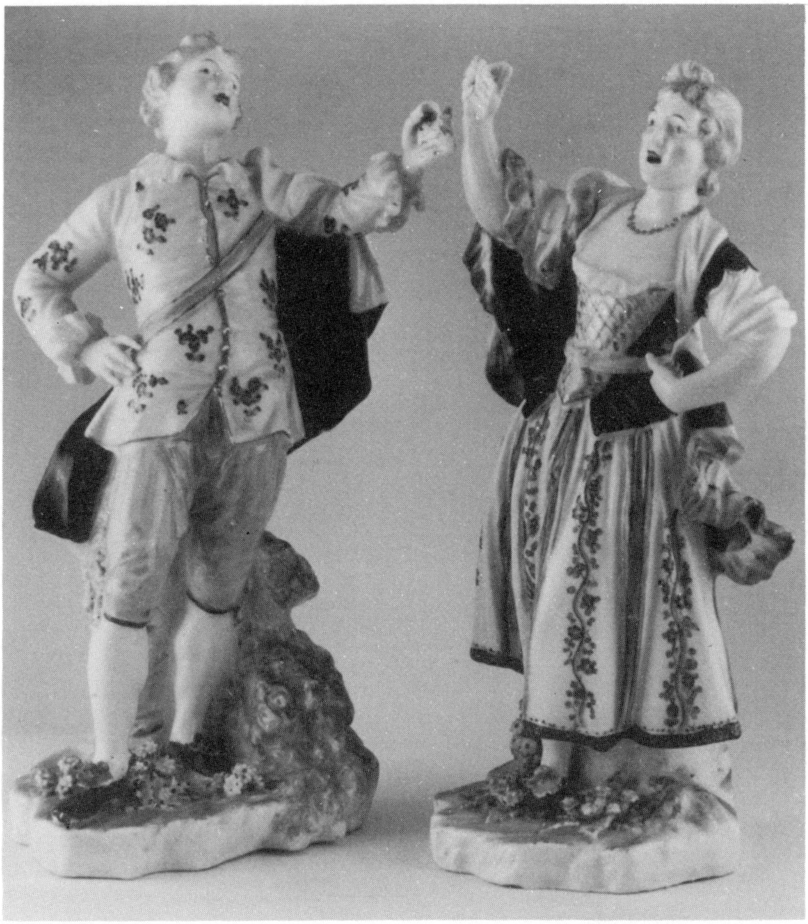

Plate 37. A pair of Derby figures of duet singers, well modelled and decorated in enamel colours, 'Patch' marks under the bases, *c.*1765.

Derby Museum

and coloured ones and this apparent anomaly is explained by the fact that only absolutely perfectly produced pieces could be sold in this state, whereas those with imperfections could be camouflaged by glaze and enamels. Huge numbers of figures were made, very few of them marked except for the incised number of the list of models on the base.

The last thirty years of the eighteenth century are noteworthy for the steady improvement in the production of useful wares, especially tea and dinner wares. A number of fine decorators worked for Derby; landscape painters such as Zachariah Boreman, Thomas (Jockey) Hill, and the

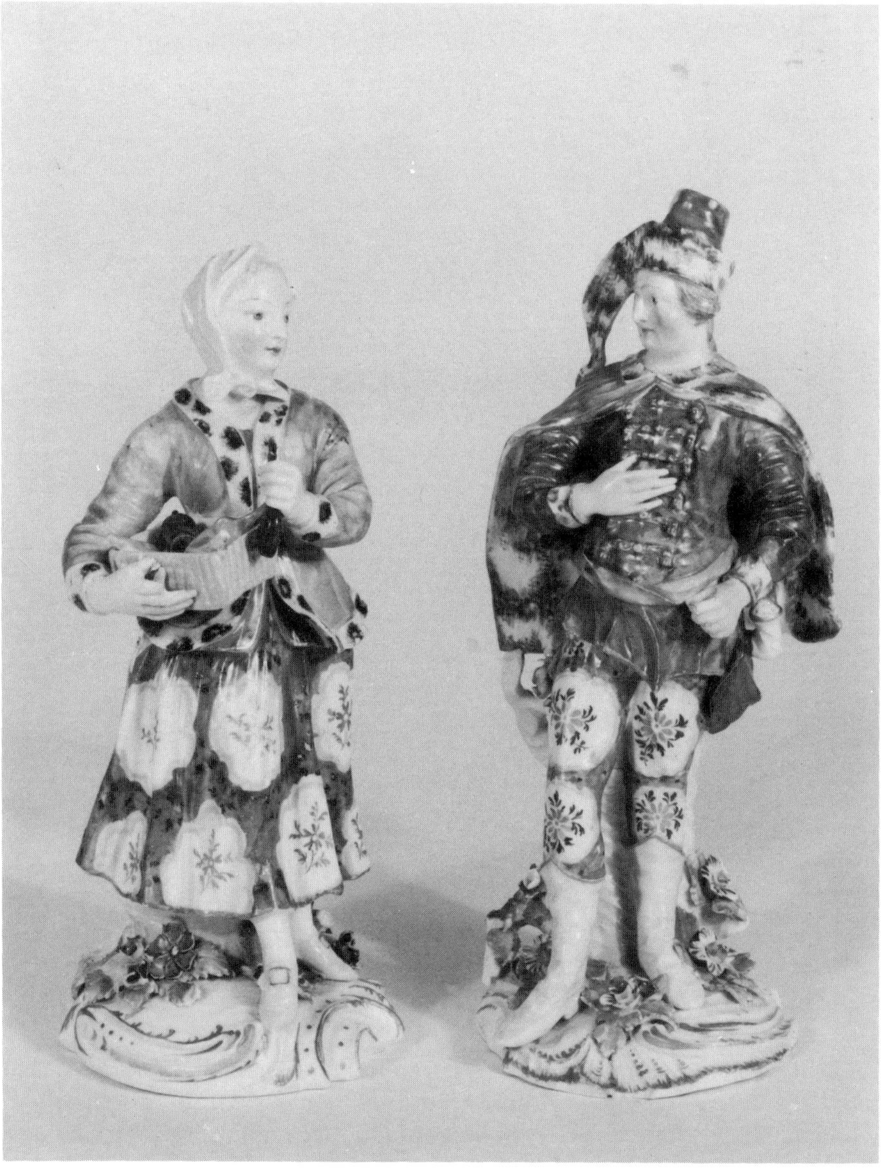

Plate 38. A pair of Derby figures of David Garrick as Tancred and an actress, probably Mrs. Cibber as a Vivandierè, both well coloured, $8\frac{1}{2}$ in. and 9 in., Patch marks.

Phillips

Brewer brothers, John and Robert, and George Robertson; figure painters such as Richard Askew and James Banford; George Complin, an especially fine fruit painter and William Billingsley whose subject was pink roses. Billingsley became the principal flower painter in 1790 until 1796 when he went to the newly found Pinxton factory. It should not be thought all small roses painted on porcelain were done by Billingsley, an impression that one sometimes gets when auction sale details are read, nor that Billingsley was the finest flower painter of all time.

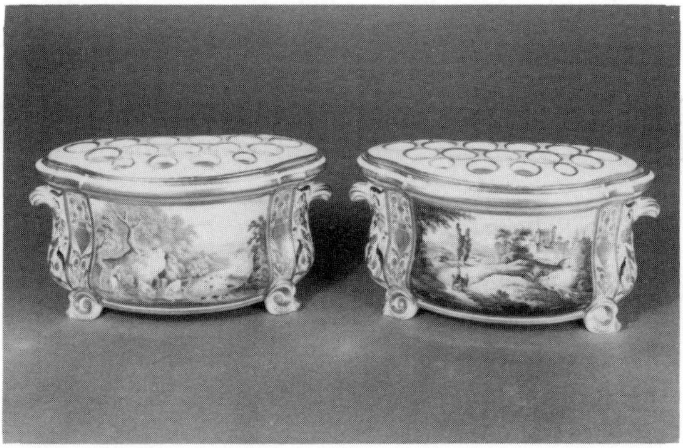

Plate 39. A pair of Derby Bough pots and pierced covers, the white ground with gold and coloured scrollwork with reserved panels, perhaps by Robert Brewer, with landscape scenes 'in Cumberland' and 'in Italy', 7½ in. wide, crown, cross baton and D marks in red.
Phillips

One of the finest Derby flower painters was William ('Quaker') Pegg who painted flowers with great freshness and spirit. Other fine Derby flower painters were Moses Webster and Thomas Steele. A number of these painters continued on into the nineteenth century.

It is possible to tell the names of the painters of a large number of Derby items if they carry pattern numbers, usually written on the base near the Derby factory mark in puce. By great good fortune two of the pattern books—a plate book and a cup book—plus a number of loose sheets, have been preserved to us through the action of R. W. Binns of Worcester who managed to rescue them from possible destruction in the mid nineteenth century. The books are of great importance because as well as enabling us to ascribe a pattern to Derby if it does not have a factory mark, the books frequently note the name of the painter, references such as 'flowers by Billingsley' or 'fruit by Compline' being frequent. This should not be regarded as an infallible method of ascription, as it should be appreciated that another painter could take over and paint the pattern in similar style if the original artist was no longer available.

The Derby pattern books, still carefully preserved by the Worcester Royal Porcelain Company, have been reproduced in colour by John Twitchett, a great Derby expert.

As well as pattern numbers, Derby pieces frequently carry painters' and gilders' numbers, which are usually written well away from the main mark and pattern number, generally near the footrim. These numbers were those given to the particular decorator and Haslem provides a list of them in his book, although, like pattern numbers, they cannot be regarded as infallible. Before leaving Derby in its glory at the end of the eighteenth century it is right to point out that the quality of gilding is generally of superb quality, a part of the overall decoration that is sometimes disregarded.

Some blue and white painted and printed wares were made, but the production was negligible in both quantity and quality.

Derby paste is generally creamy in look in the puce mark period and poorer in the red mark period. In the next - the Bloor period - it declines even further and Derby porcelain becomes less collectable.

FURTHER READING

The Old Derby China Factory by John Haslem
Old Derby Porcelain & its Artist Workmen by Frank Hurlbutt
Derby Porcelain by F. B. Gilhespy
Derby Porcelain by F. A. Barrett and A. C. Thorpe

LONGTON HALL

This factory was the first to bring the making of porcelain to the Potteries and while the production of the factory was of poor quality compared to the better factories, it did produce a few original things.

Longton Hall was founded about 1749 by a William Jenkinson who was to be joined and superseded by several partners, including one William Littler who has been credited with the distinctive bright blue colour found on some Staffordshire saltglaze ware and a rather similar, more messy looking blue on Longton Hall porcelain, both known as 'Littler's Blue'.

The factory had a perilous life and kiln losses were very great owing to the difficult material used which did not have the addition of either bone ash or soapstone to strengthen the soft paste glassy frit body. Production finally finished in 1760 when a great quantity of ware remaining unsold was sent to Salisbury for public auction. Littler managed to get hold of

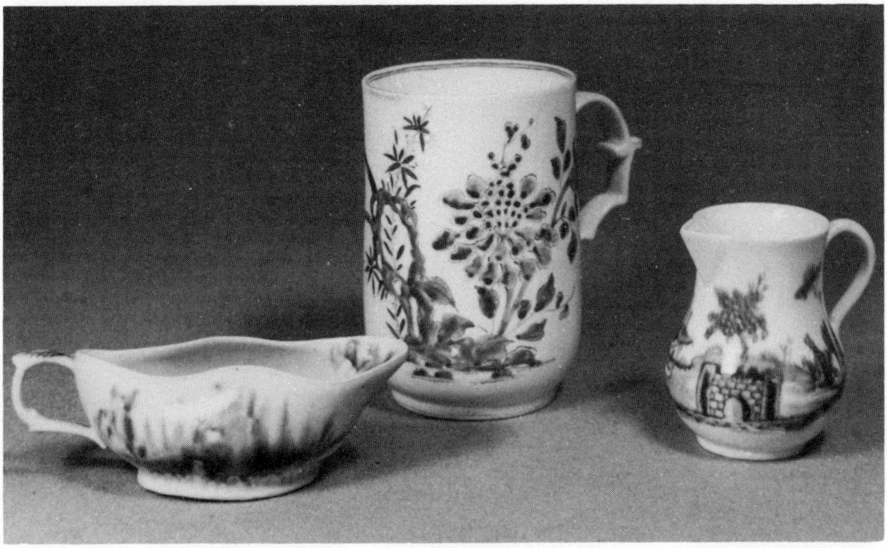

Plate 40. Longton Hall sauce boat, mug and milk jug, in shape and decoration of the primitive early style of about 1775, the sauceboat showing the typical running blue, the mug with famille rose enamels, 5 in. high.

Stoke-on-Trent City Museum

some ware and in 1764 he turned up at West Pans, near Musselburgh in Scotland decorating the pieces for local people.

Few wares are marked, but the marks most associated with early wares are forms of an L, usually crossed or with dots. Early useful wares are crude and generally thickly potted, a quantity of different shaped leaf dishes and stands were made and these are probably the best shapes of the first few years, better in quality than the larger pieces which are of poor shape, with awkward, thick handles. Most of these early pieces can be found decorated with 'Littler's Blue'—a bright and very runny blue.

Longton Hall is best known, however, for its production of figures, especially the 'Snowmen' of the first few years. The snowmen are so called because they are so thickly glazed that features are white and blank. These figures were made in great numbers, often based on Meissen, Chelsea or Oriental originals.

From about 1754 the standard of production was higher, the pieces were more thinly potted and the glaze and paste improved. A number of Oriental blue and white patterns were produced, usually without borders, and they sometimes have letters of the alphabet underneath the base. The biggest improvement was in the field of onglaze enamel decoration, which may be accounted for by the arrival of William Duesbury who stayed at

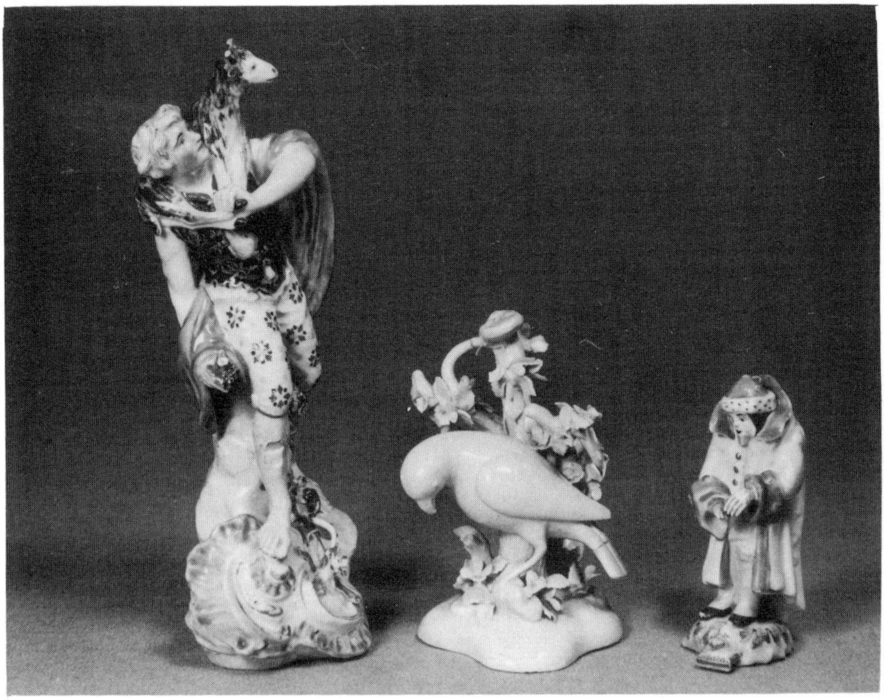

Plate 41. Longton Hall figures of the 1750's, the bird left in white glazed state, the others decorated in enamel colours, $10\frac{1}{2}$ in., $5\frac{1}{2}$ in. and $4\frac{1}{2}$ in.

Stoke-on-Trent City Museum

Longton for two years en route to Derby from London. Elaborate moulded shapes were produced for enamelled pieces, such as melon teapots, although these are still nowhere near the quality of their London prototypes.

Figures in this period normally have *rococo* scrolled bases instead of the simple flat or domed bases of the previous years and usually depict humans as against the earlier animals.

In the last two or three years of production the wares tend to become simpler, almost mass-produced in their simplicity and a number of pieces were transfer printed by Sadler and Green at Liverpool. The most important pieces made in this last period are large figures, such as the bust of the Prince of Wales, a large figure of Britannia and the mounted figure of the Duke of Brunswick.

Longton Hall pieces are relatively rare nowadays, although the prices are not too high, except for the finest pieces. Although the wares are somewhat crude they have a certain charm and should fetch more money than they do.

FURTHER READING
Longton Hall Porcelain by Bernard Watney

WORCESTER (AND LUND'S BRISTOL)

To Worcester goes the distinction of being the only English porcelain factory of the many founded in the middle of the eighteenth century to have continued to this day in an unbroken tradition. The reason is not hard to find—Worcester's formula using soapstone from Cornwall had the great ability of withstanding boiling liquids without cracking or crazing and it is an indisputable fact that no Worcester porcelain of the eighteenth century is found crazed. This led Worcester to concentrate on the production of useful wares and leave the making of figures and purely ornamental pieces to others. Another reason is that Worcester seems at all times in its long history to have had an instinctive sense of good style and taste.

The history of Worcester ceramics is a long one and with so many factories and different names of periods being involved it is rather difficult to comprehend, but the splitting up into centuries in this book may make things easier.

The first certain use of soaprock in making 'soft paste' porcelain was the short lived factory of Miller & Lund in Redcliffe Backs, Bristol. It is possible that the Bristol factory grew out of an earlier factory in Limehouse, London, as a certain Dr. Pococke in 1750 described a visit to what is generally called the Lund's Bristol factory by writing 'I went to see a manufacture lately established here by one of the principal manufacturers at Limehouse which failed'. Very little is known about the Limehouse factory, not even its site nor any of its productions are known and we are not on very much firmer ground when we consider Lund's Bristol. It was certainly in production by 1750 as a few rare figures of an old Chinese man have the date 1750 and the word BRISTOL embossed on them. A dozen or so sauceboats and cream boats of silver shape also have the word BRISTOL or BRISTOLL embossed under the base. In 1752 the Bristol factory was bought lock stock and barrel by Worcester and with it the valuable licence for soapstone from the Lizard. All the moulds in use at Bristol and some of the workers appear to have been brought up river to Worcester, as during the excavation on the Worcester site a great number of wasters of shapes similar to the Bristol marked pieces were found, proving that Worcester continued to make the earlier shapes for a number of years.

It is therefore very difficult to know for certain whether pieces of the years 1750 to 1752 are Bristol or Worcester and unless they bear the word Bristol it is only safe to refer to these wares as Bristol/Worcester. Large quantities of very charming useful wares date from this early period, a number of them being of silver shape and with Oriental style decorations, although many are influenced by Bristol delft painting.

DR. WALL PERIOD 1751-1776

On 4th June, 1751 a deed of partnership, still preserved by the Worcester Royal Porcelain Company, was signed by 15 partners to found what was first referred to as the Worcester Tonquin Manufacture and later the Worcester Porcelain Company. The 15 subscribers were all local men apart from Edward Cave, who was the Editor of the Gentleman's Magazine in London, and two of the partners are specially referred to as having invented the secret formula and their subscription money was paid for and they were to have a share in future profits. The two were Dr. John Wall, M.D., a surgeon and amateur artist, and William Davis, an apothecary in the town.

The period that runs from 1751 to 1776, the year of Dr. Wall's death, is now referred to as the Dr. Wall period, a period during which some of the finest porcelain produced in this country was made. We have learnt a great deal about the qualities of these wares from the results of the archaeological excavation on the site of Warmstry House, the house in whose grounds the factory was established. Both fine blue and white and coloured useful wares were made in huge quantities, in fact Worcester would appear to have been the most prolific of the eighteenth century factories to go by the large amount that still remains and by the fine quality of the material. So good a body was it that hardly any wasters showing bad firing features were found on the site.

By about 1755 most of the early silver shapes had given way to more ceramic styles, mask jugs with bodies formed of overlapping cabbage leaves, formed by jollying in moulds, or plain thrown shapes such as bowls and 'sparrow beak' jugs. One of the finest shapes is the teapot, always beautifully balanced and proportioned and often with a flower knob. Painters' marks—small symbols or initial like marks—appear on the bases or more rarely on other places on the vessel, usually in underglaze blue and it is not until about 1758 that the recognised factory marks of an open painted crescent in underglaze blue, or, less commonly, a blue painted W, is used.

As well as blue and white Oriental patterns and chinoiseries, Worcester also produced onglaze enamelled decorations which were often in the Meissen style of flower painting—the so called 'Meissner Blumen'. The

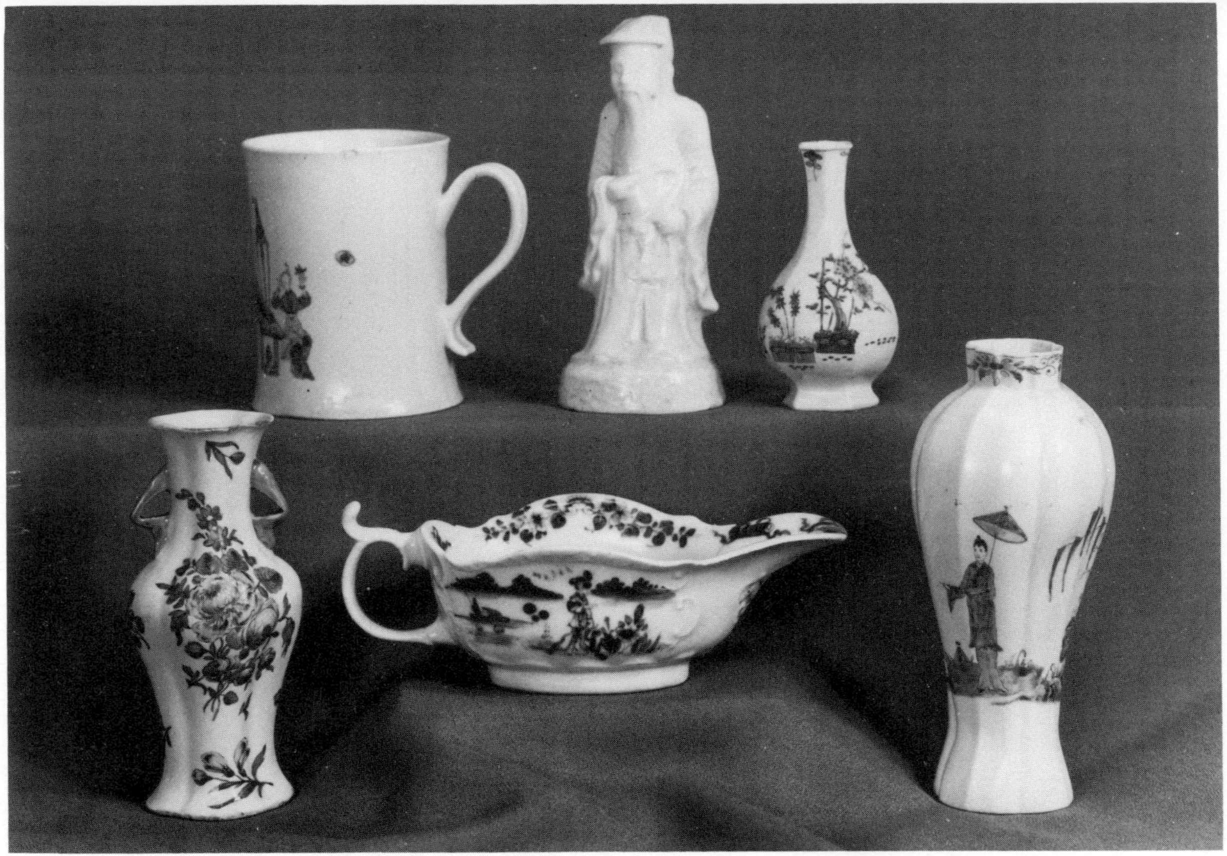

Plate 42. Lund's Bristol and Bristol/Worcester soapstone porcelain. *Top row:* a mug of 'Scratch Cross' type, figure of a Chinaman marked 'Bristol 1750', a small hexagonal 'Onion' vase. *Bottom row:* fluted vase with curious handles and Meissen type flowers, sauce boat painted in underglaze blue in Three-dot style, embossed 'Bristol', and an attractive fluted vase painted onglaze with a 'Long Eliza' figure, height $7\frac{1}{4}$ in., all *c.*1750–55.

Dyson Perrins Museum, Worcester

glaze is always close fitting and uncrazed, footrims are generally of triangular shape and translucency generally a strong green. It is not until after about 1760 that a glaze free margin (often wrongly called glaze shrinkage) is seen in the form of a ragged narrow strip, or patches, free of glaze just inside the footrim.

By 1757 transfer printing was in use at Worcester, probably brought from the enamelling works at Bilston and Wednesbury by Robert Hancock, who was later to be made a director of Worcester, onglaze at first, generally in black and more rarely in violet or lavender, the black being known as 'jet enamels'. The process was highly successful and great quantities of ware were produced, the scenes showing great heroes such as the King of Prussia, George III and General Wolfe, beautiful scenes of L'amour and the Tea Party or birds and Chinese subjects, some of them taken from the popular book of engravings 'The Ladies Amusement, or the art of Japaning made easy'. The earliest prints probably produced a year or so before the first dated one of 1757, are known as the 'Smoky Primitives' and are curious vignettes of squirrels and battleships. Outline prints were done which could be filled in in enamels to provide an easy way of producing effective coloured wares by young or inexperienced decorators.

Prints of this period should not be looked upon as cheap mass produced wares; the process was an involved, slow one and the results should be compared with hand painted porcelain in the same way as an orange with an apple, both different but equally effective in their own way.

Underglaze printing was first used at Worcester about 1760, these wares being generally marked with a printed crescent in blue, either an open or a hatched crescent, or with an additional letter or 'Man in the moon' face, the latter variant being rare. The first blue prints were floral scenes, apart from one showing a man in a pavilion watching boats, but underglaze printing rapidly developed and by 1770 had taken over from underglaze painting as the main production of the factory, although the elaborate borders, especially the cell borders, were still being painted by hand.

Fine onglaze painted wares were produced and although these were not the main production of the factory more coloured ware remains to us than blue and white; the reason being that the more expensive coloured wares were looked after and put in cabinets whereas blue and white was made for everyday use, broken and thrown away. In the late 1750's and early 1760's Chinese and Japanese styles were very popular, but from 1760 or so the introduction of blue and pink scale ground colours led the way towards a more European style of onglaze decoration and this was hastened by the arrival of a number of the Chelsea painters. A certain quantity of ware was bought in the white by outside decorators, especially by Giles in London, although it is very difficult to know with certainty whether a piece is

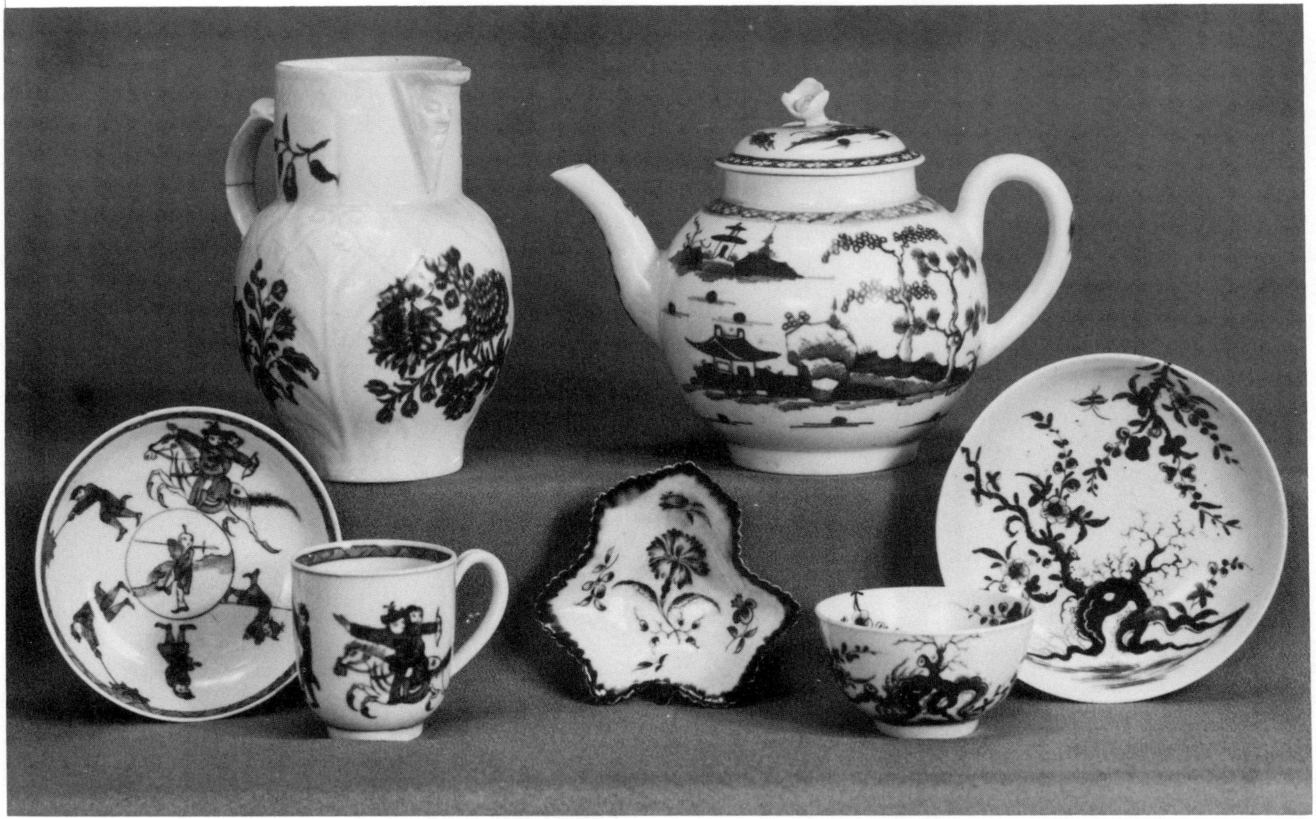

Plate 43. Worcester blue and white porcelain of the Dr. Wall period *c.* 1751–76, the 7 in. 'Mask jug' on the higher shelf is transfer printed with floral sprays, all the other pieces are painted, the 'Cannonball' pattern on the teapot and the 'Prunus Root' pattern on the teabowl and saucer are both fairly common while the coffee cup and saucer bears the much rarer 'Eloping Bride' pattern. The small leaf was for pickle.

Dyson Perrins Museum, Worcester

Worcester or London decorated. Where marked, the general mark used on the finest wares is a fretted square, especially on blue scale wares.

By 1770 the climax of onglaze decoration seems to have been reached at Worcester, most of the finest wares having paintings of flowers, fruit or 'fabulous' birds in panels left white after ground colours had been applied. The finest painters on Worcester at this period were John Donaldson, who specialised in copies of Continental style figure scenes, especially those of Boucher, and J. H. O'Neale, whose favourite subjects were Aesop's fables, animal subjects and scenes from the classics.

Very few figures seem to have been made, probably owing to the concentration on useful wares, but a few have been ascribed to Worcester. These include a Gardener and companion, a Sportsman and companion, a Turk and companion and 2 canaries in apple blossom. No fragments of any of these were found on the site, but a model of a figure group depicting Cupid at Vulcan's forge was found, a coloured group which has always been incorrectly ascribed to Longton Hall. Worcester figures of this period are undoubtedly the rarest examples of English porcelain.

DAVIS/FLIGHT PERIOD 1776–1793

In 1776 Dr. Wall died in Bath and he was succeeded as Manager of the factory by the apothecary William Davis. Davis died in 1783 and the factory was bought by the London Agent, Thomas Flight.

The period from 1776 to 1793 has been renamed by me the Davis/Flight period, a period that overlaps the old so-called First Period and Flight period. This was a time of great competition from the Caughley factory's blue printed wares, Wedgwood's Queen's ware and the cheap Chinese Nankin wares which were pouring into the country. Worcester had to compete or go under and compete they did with large quantities of fine blue printing in a violet-toned blue. Most of these late printed pieces have been ascribed to Caughley for over a hundred years and the finding of them on the Worcester site was one of the major surprises of the Excavation.

Although the crescent mark continued to be used, generally very small on painted and hatched on printed wares, a new mark seems to have been invented for some of the Willow Pattern type printed scenes that Worcester made in great quantities—the so-called 'disguised Chinese numeral' marks, which have always previously been ascribed to Caughley. In this Davis/Flight period it is possible for Worcester pieces to show a straw or orange translucency, especially in wares made after 1780, although the general translucence is still a green, varying to a green/yellow. A glaze-free margin is very common.

In 1788 the factory had a visit from King George III who ordered a

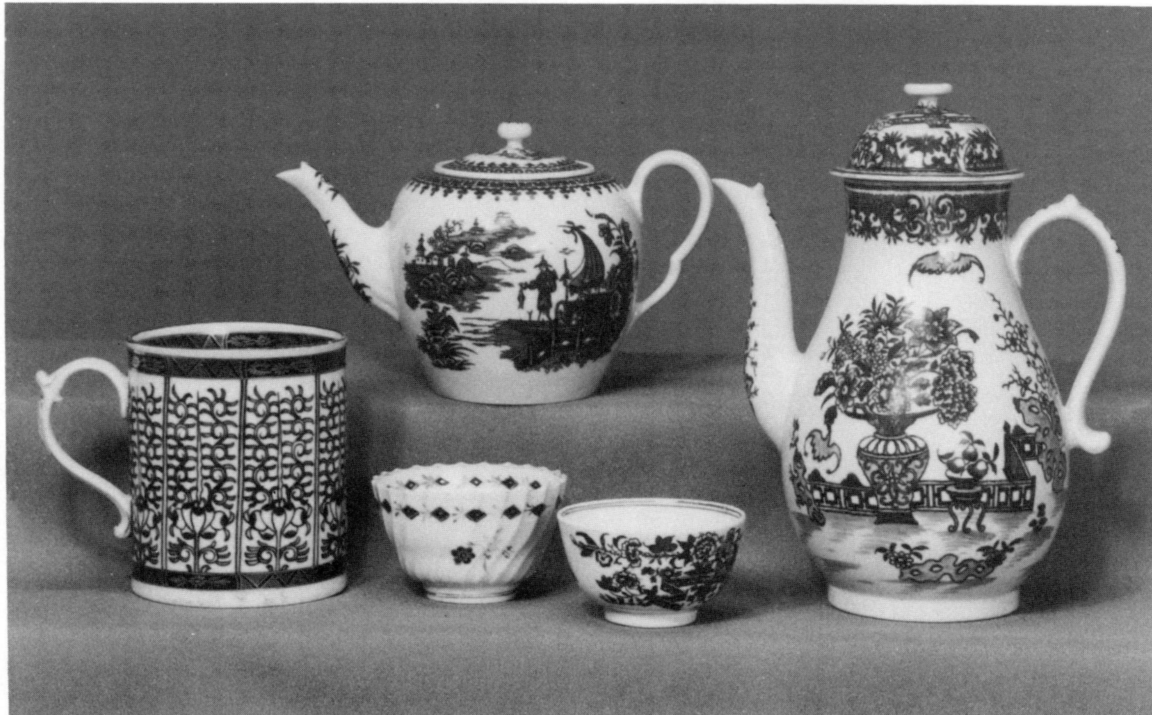

Plate 44. Worcester porcelain of the Davis/Flight period, 1776–1792, printed or painted in violet-toned blue; the teapot bears the Worcester version of the 'Fisherman' pattern (note the wiggly fishing line), the coffee pot, 9 in. high, is printed with the Bat pattern with hand shaded areas, a feature not used at Caughley, two typically shaped and decorated teabowls and a large mug painted with the Royal lily pattern, marks either crescents or disguised numerals.

Dyson Perrins Museum, Worcester

service of the Blue Lily pattern (the title was duly amended to Royal Lily) and the company was granted the Royal Warrant. Most of the non printed patterns were very simple, quite often just blue borders with purple or gilded decoration. Spiral fluted and ogee shapes were very common and some of the more splendid earlier blue scale patterns were done, probably as replacements.

FLIGHT & BARR PERIOD 1792–1804

In 1792 Martin Barr joined Flight and a steadily improving standard of fine quality painted wares were made. The words 'Flight & Barr' are sometimes used, but the most common mark is an incised 'B' of a rather distorted form, the upper loop of the B often being smaller than the lower, or less commonly vice versa.

CHAMBERLAIN'S FACTORY

In about 1786 Robert Chamberlain, who had worked for Dr. Wall as a decorator, started his own factory, at first merely buying porcelain in the white, painting and gilding it and selling it. He bought finished wares from both Thomas Turner at Caughley and Flight at the Warmstry House factory in Worcester and also dealt in glass. It is sometimes difficult to tell if a piece is Caughley or Chamberlain decorated at this period, unless the name Chamberlain is to be found on the piece.

Chamberlain had several difficult periods when he found it hard to obtain ware to decorate and sell and this possibly led him to make his own porcelain. The main consideration of Chamberlain will be dealt with later.

FURTHER READING

Illustrated Guide to Worcester Porcelain 1751–1793 by Henry Sandon
Caughley & Worcester Porcelains 1775–1800 by Geoffrey A. Godden
Flight and Barr Worcester Porcelain 1783–1840 by Henry Sandon

CAUGHLEY/COALPORT

The recent discoveries on the Worcester kiln site have helped to clear up a lot of previous misunderstandings about the relationship between Caughley and Worcester wares. It has always been thought that Caughley porcelains were inferior to those of most of the other English porcelain factories, but the regard in which the ware has been held has gone up greatly and it is now highly collectable. In the section in this chapter dealing with Worcester it has been shown that a large quantity of blue and white porcelain previously ascribed to Caughley is in fact Worcester,

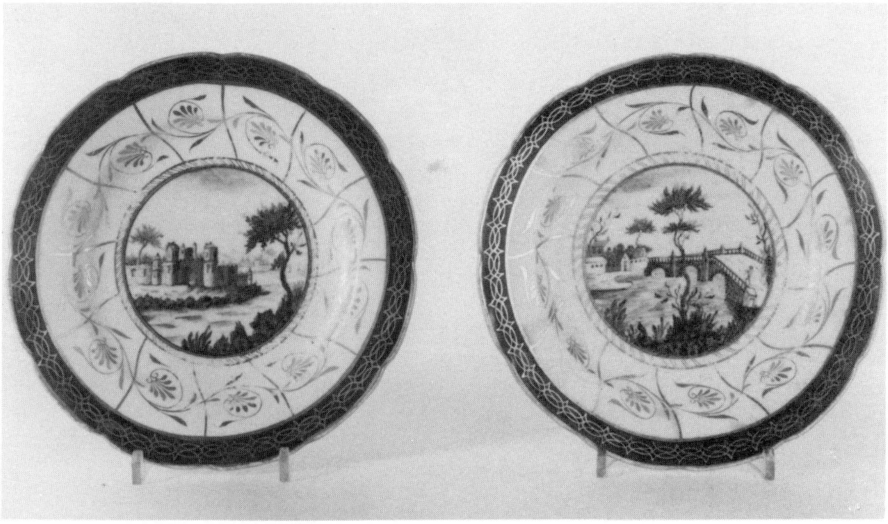

Plate 45. A fine pair of Caughley dessert plates decorated in underglaze blue with a style of landscape painting unique to this factory, the borders enriched with gold. 9 in., impressed SALOPIAN marks.
Private Collection

leaving the wares of the Shropshire factory very much rarer than previously believed.

It is believed that *pottery* making began in the 1750's at this small Shropshire village named Caughley (pronounced Carflee locally) which is about 2 miles south of Broseley, about a mile from the river Severn, and on the opposite bank of the river from the village of Coalport, to where the factory later moved.

In about 1772 Thomas Turner, who had been an apprentice at Worcester, particularly learning the art of engraving and transfer printing from Robert Hancock, went to Caughley to improve the standard of earthenware and begin producing porcelain. By 1775 production was well advanced and Turner was joined by Hancock, who had sold his shares in the Worcester factory. From 1775 until 1799 the factory produced mainly blue and white printing marking their wares with a C mark (quite different to the hatched crescent of Worcester), or an S which stood for Salopia, the Latin name for Shropshire. The impressed word 'Salopian' is also rarely found impressed, but this mark should not be confused with a late nineteenth and twentieth century Benthall or Broseley factory which impressed the word 'Salopian' in their earthenwares.

The factory also made some coloured wares, but these were not a major production. Shapes were often very close to Worcester, although generally

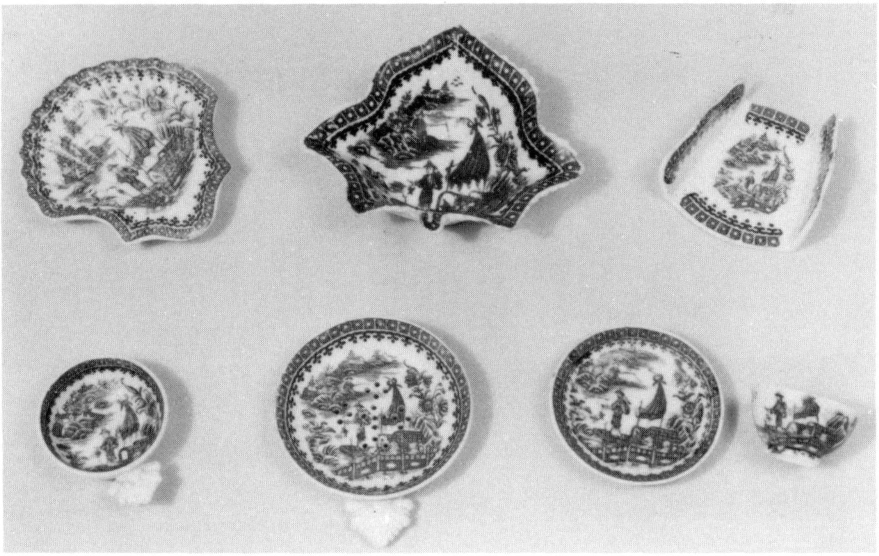

Plate 46. A group of small Caughley objects printed with the 'Fisherman' pattern, *top* from left, pickle shell dish, leaf pickle dish, asparagus server, *below*, taster, egg drainer and toy teabowl and saucer; pickle shell $3\frac{1}{2}$ in. *c.*1780–85.

John Sandon Collection

more heavily potted and with footrims generally of a rather square section as against the general triangular shape of Worcester. Some potting and firing techniques are similar to Worcester, in that a glaze free margin is common and early wares can show a green and later wares an orange translucency. Rims, especially those of bowls, are usually rounded, as against the generally chamfered outside edge of Worcester rims.

A number of printed patterns have versions which were done at both Worcester and Caughley and for the differences between these the reader is referred to the relative sections of my own book *Illustrated Guide to Worcester Porcelain 1751–1793* and to the book by Geoffrey Godden noted below. Prices and appreciation have risen rapidly in recent years.

In 1799 the factory was bought by John Rose, who had already established his main factory at Coalport on the other side of the river, continuing to use the Caughley site for some processes. The Coalport factory is dealt with later.

The Caughley site is at present part of a large gravel sand and clay workings and little remains of the original factory

FURTHER READING

Caughley and Worcester Porcelains 1775–1800 by Geoffrey A. Godden

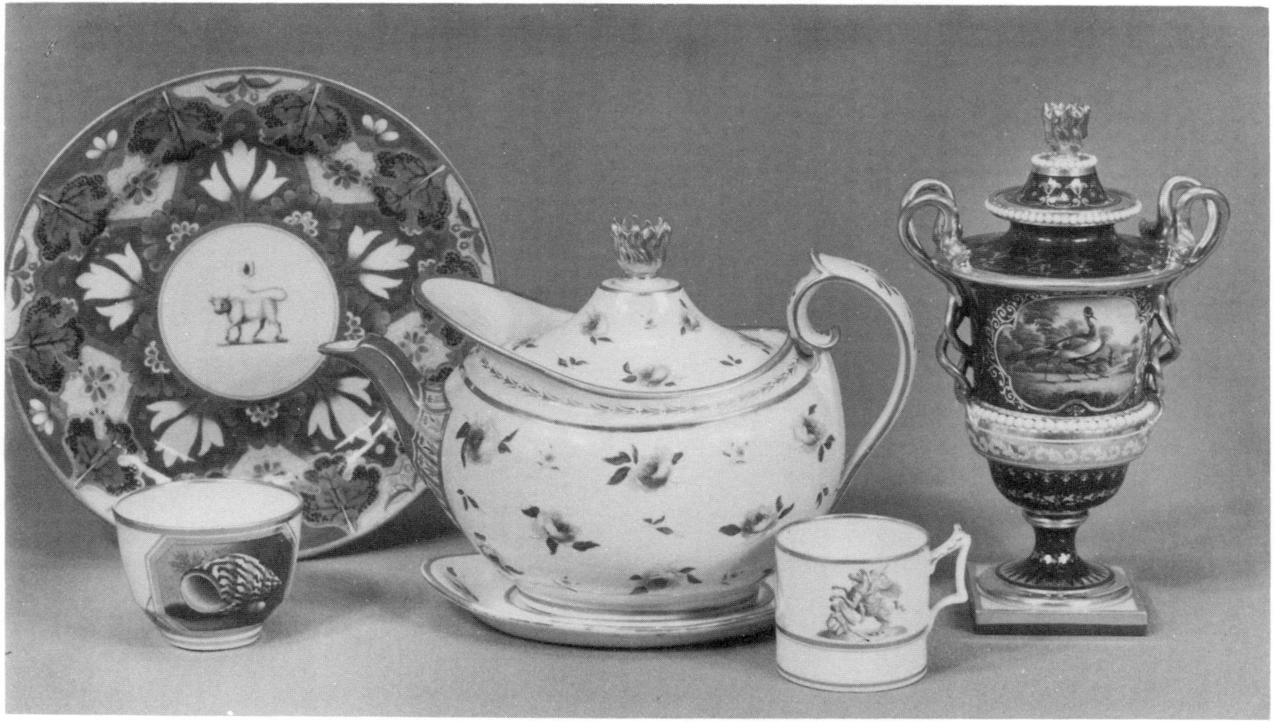

Plate 47. A group of Worcester porcelain from the Flight and Barr periods, the coffee can Bat printed with a classical subject, *c.*1800, the cup painted with keenly sought shells, Barr Flight and Barr, *c.*1810, the armorial plate with a splendid Japan pattern mainly in reds and greens, the teapot cover and stand of boat shape with roses, *c.*1810, and a vase with deep cobalt blue ground and painted exotic birds, twisted serpent handles and applied enamel pearls, Flight Barr and Barr, 9 in. high, *c.*1820.

Dyson Perrins Museum, Worcester

LIVERPOOL

The story of Liverpool porcelain is a very confusing one, there being so many short lived factories in the city, some of them within a stone's throw of each other and as hardly any of the wares are marked and many of them are rather poor copies of some of the other English factories, expert knowledge is generally required to sort out one factory from another or even make a firm ascription to Liverpool.

The usually suggested methods by which Liverpool pieces can be recognised—the chief ones being a translucency of a duck egg blue colour and footrings with an undercut shape on the inside—are too variable to be reliable. For instance a large number of undercut footrims were found on Worcester site wasters. In this general book it may be safer to merely list the various Liverpool factories and suggest that the enquiring collector builds up a collection of positive different pieces, which will do more than volumes of books can to help towards an understanding. Most of these factories we have already met in the chapter on delft.

Richard Chaffers (*c.*1754–65). This was in Shaw's Brow, now William Brown Street and probably made both bone ash and soapstone porcelain. Both blue and white and coloured wares were made and some pieces were printed by Sadler of Liverpool and sometimes bear his name.

Philip Christian (1765–76). Christian was Chaffers partner and following the death of the latter in 1765 continued to make soapstone porcelain. Wares are very similar to the earlier period but handles are often of a more ornate shape and shortly before Christian sold his lease of a Cornish soapstone mine to Worcester in May 1776 some rather poor copies of Hancock type underglaze blue prints appear to have been done.

Seth Pennington (*c.*1769–99). In 1776 he took over Christian's factory, making phosphatic porcelain, but some earlier dated pieces are known, some of mask jugs, which suggests that they were made elsewhere, possibly at a china works run by Seth's brothers John and James. Wares are generally blue and white, both painted and printed. On early pieces the glaze is very wet looking and often pools under the base, forming the so-called 'thunder cloud' effect. The wares were usually poorly painted.

Samuel Gilbody (*c.*1754–61). This factory was close to Chaffer's and made more distinctive porcelain than most of the other Liverpool factories. Early wares often have an underfired glaze which tends to craze and a very common form of decorating is in blurred underglaze slaty blue with onglaze iron-red and gilding, resembling 'clobbered' pieces. A quantity of onglaze transfer printing was done by Sadler. Cracks in the ware tend to stain brown and the translucency of later pieces is almost colourless.

William Reid (*c.*1755–61). Probably the first of the Liverpool porcelain

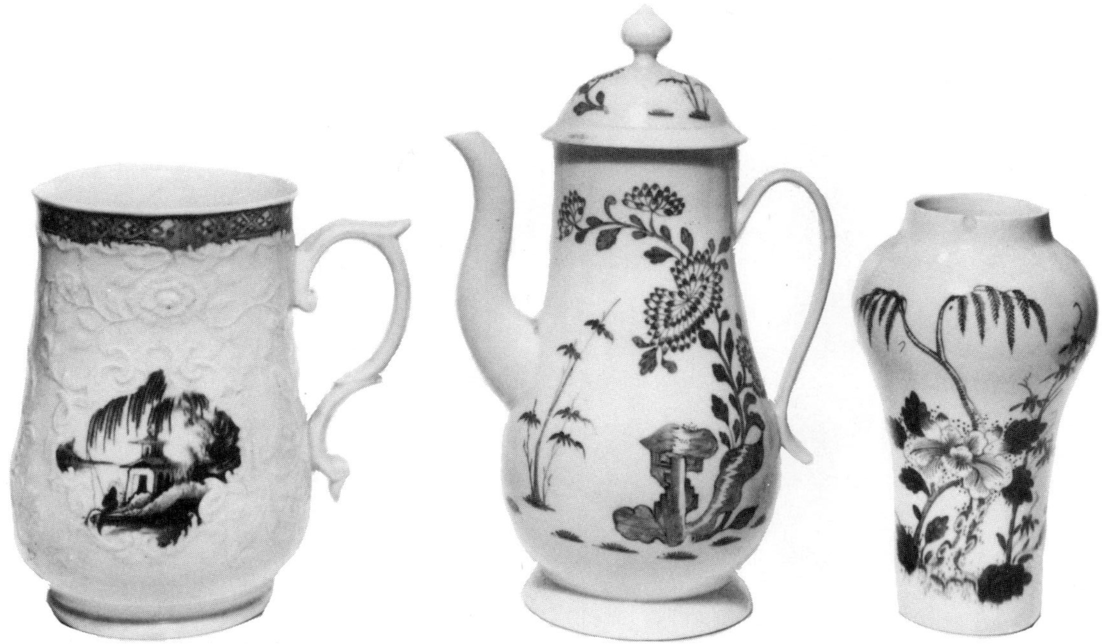

Plate 48. Group of Liverpool porcelain, a bell-shaped mug from Christian's factory and a coffee pot vase by Chaffer's factory, each painted in underglaze blue and frequently mistaken for Worcester. However, note the somewhat unbalanced proportions of the shapes.

Sothebys

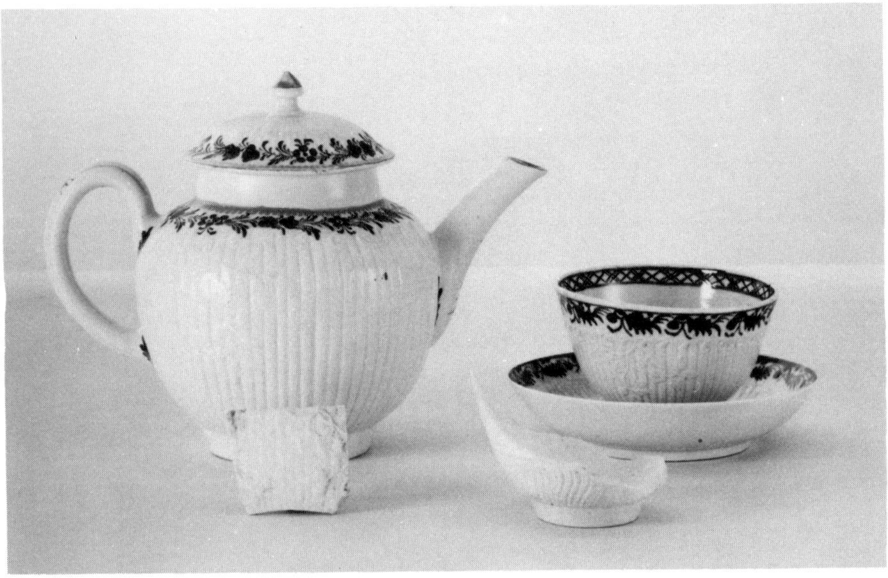

Plate 49. Liverpool porcelain teapot and teabowl and saucer of fluted and moulded shape, from Seth Pennington's factory, shown with matching wasters found on the site; it is the finding of such wasters on factory sites which can now teach us so much about what wares a factory made; the decoration is in underglaze cobalt blue, *c.*1770.

City of Liverpool Museum

makers, Reid's factory was on Brownlow hill. Most of the wares are blue and white and have some afinity in shape to Lund's Bristol and Bristol/Worcester pieces and a number of pieces are steatitic.

William Ball (*c.*1755–69). This factory was in Ranleigh Street and the wares were also steatitic. One range of wares produced were polycrome prints, transfer prints in two or three colour outlines, usually pink, brown and black, frequently over-painted in enamels. Cobalt blue has a very sticky look.

Thomas Wolfe (*c.*1790–1800). Wolfe had Staffordshire connections and his wares have a distinctively Staffordshire look, many of them having similarities to New Hall. A number of pieces are decorated with prints resembling those on Liverpool tiles in a variety of colours, such as black, brown and purple. Potting is rather poor and translucency often of a greenish-white colour.

FURTHER READING

Liverpool Porcelain by K. Boney

English Porcelain 1745–1850 by R. J. Charleston

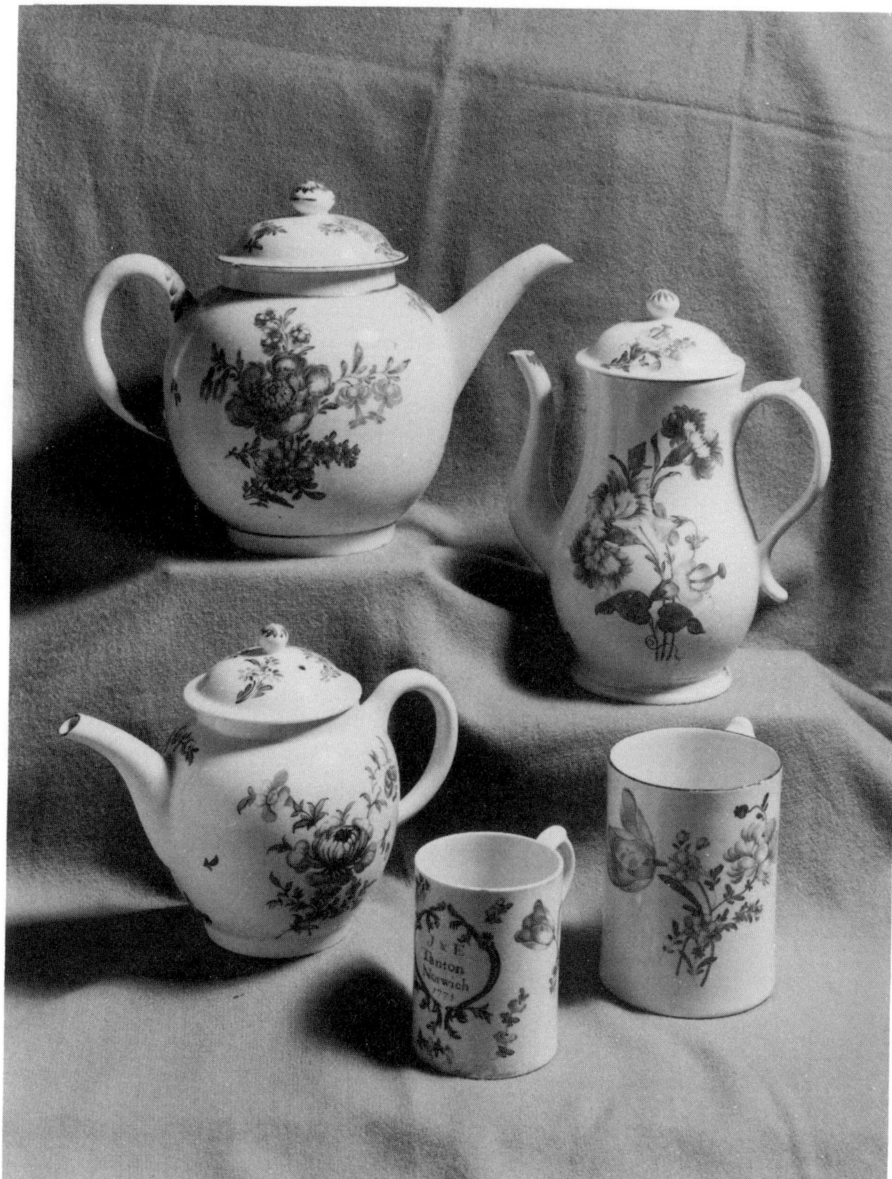

Plate 50. A range of typical Lowestoft porcelain wares finely painted in the distinctive style of the so-called 'Tulip' painter. Although the shapes are quite good the balance and positioning of handle and spout should be compared with the more perfect ones of Worcester (Plate 43).

Norwich Museum

LOWESTOFT

Lowestoft was yet another factory which made a great amount of wares in imitation of Worcester, even going to the extent of using an open crescent mark after about 1771. There is no actual Lowestoft mark as such, although it used the marks of Meissen and other factories. A number of blue and white pieces have painters' marks in the form of numerals painted just inside the footrims, the most frequently found being 3, 5, & 8.

Porcelain making started in about 1757 and finished in 1802. At first blue and white painted wares were produced but after 1771, when Robert Browne Junior succeeded his father as Manager, underglaze blue printing and onglaze enamel decorating was done. The wares are of a bone ash body, generally well potted, although the shapes are not quite up to the standard of the Worcester ones they are imitating. The body is very soft and underglaze blue, usually of a very dark colour, sinks in like blotting paper. Footrims tend to slope on the inside and were straight on the outside.

Of all shapes, the round, thrown teapot is the most like Worcester, although the geometric precision of the arrangement of the draining holes and the presence of glaze on the underside of the teapot cover flange are non Worcester characteristics.

The factory was very much a local one and a number of inscribed and dated pieces for the local trade around Lowestoft were produced, in particular round birth tablets and mugs with 'A present from Lowestoft' or some other local town on them. These were the forerunners of the 'present from' wares which reached their zenith in the late Victorian period. You should beware of imitations of the Lowestoft inscribed wares—fakes and reproductions made by Samson of Paris and by other French firms mainly in the late nineteenth century in hard paste porcelain.

FURTHER READING

The Illustrated Guide to Lowestoft Porcelain by G. A. Godden
Lowestoft Porcelain in the Norwich Castle Museum by Sheenah Smith

PLYMOUTH AND BRISTOL

The history of these two factories was continuous, Plymouth running from about 1768 to 1770 and the manufactory then being transferred to Bristol, where it lasted until about 1781. All the wares were hard paste porcelain, the earliest English hard paste made and the Bristol factory should not be confused with the earlier Miller & Lunds soft paste manufactory.

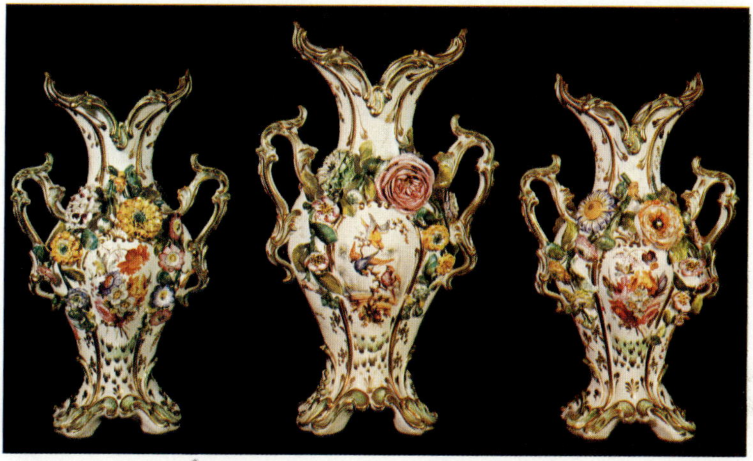

Plate IX A garniture of three Coalbrookdale vases applied with a mass of colourful modelled flowers. Whilst many factories made flower encrusted pieces, those made at Coalport are perhaps the best known.

Phillips

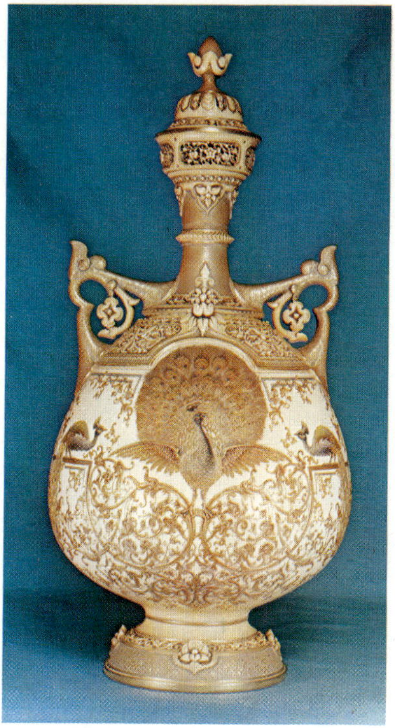

Plate X A superb Royal Worcester large vase showing the Persian influence of the 1880's, the peacock portrayed in thick tooled gold built up over many kiln firings.

Sothebys

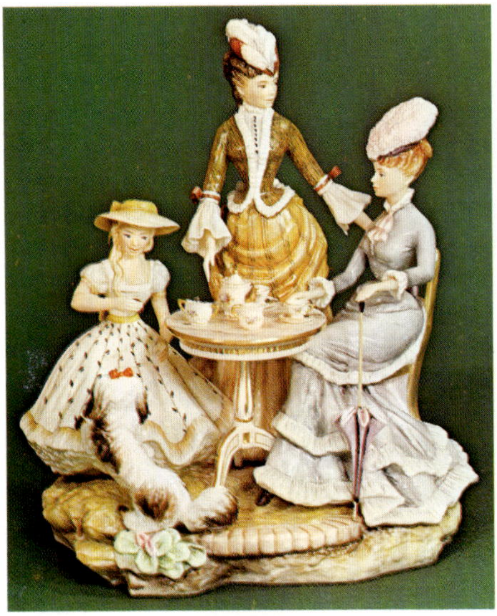

Plate XI The Tea Party, a fine Royal Worcester figure group modelled by Ruth Van Ruyckevelt and produced in 1968 in a limited edition of 250.

Royal Worcester Spode Ltd

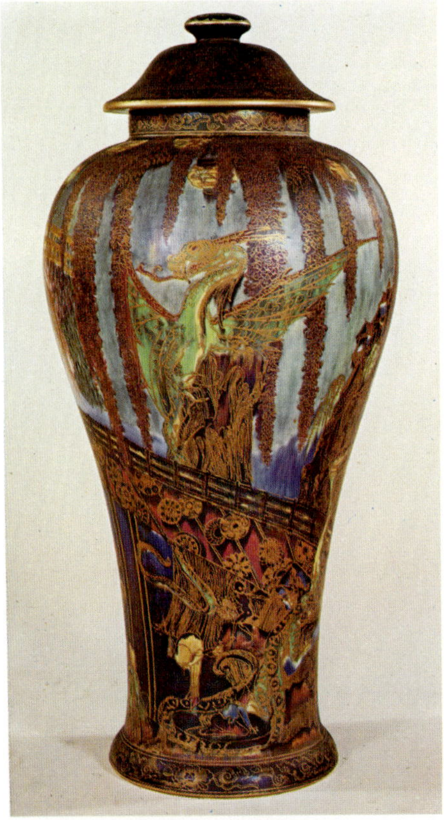

Plate XII A Wedgwood 'fairyland' lustre vase designed by Daisy Makeig-Jones with dragons, scrolls and lanterns concealing fairy folk, 14 in. high.

Sothebys

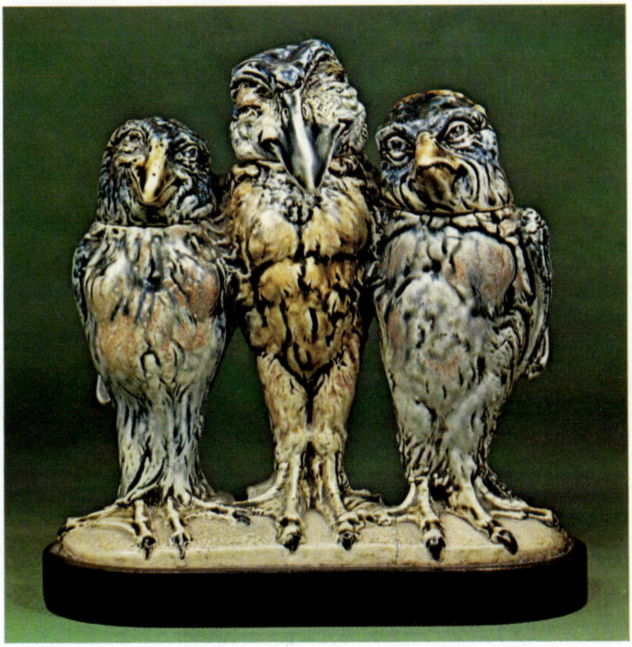

Plate XIII A group of three Martinware birds titled 'Three's Company', modelled by Robert Wallace Martin, the loose heads designed to be displayed in a large range of amusing positions, the base fully signed and dated.

Sothebys

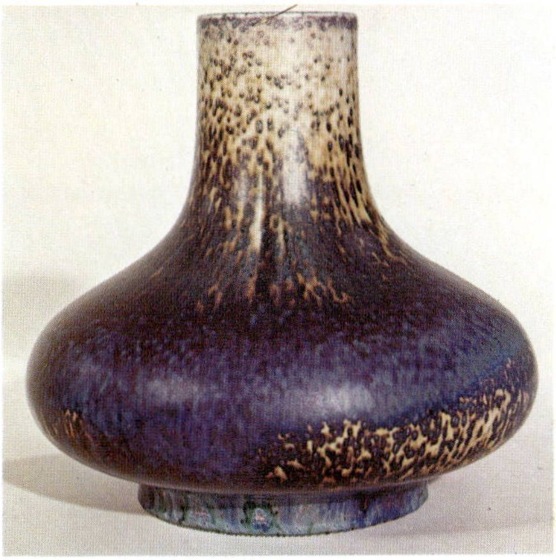

Plate XIV A good Ruskin pottery vase by William Howson-Taylor, brilliantly glazed in the 'Red Kiln' with a high-fired mottled glaze in rich colours.

Sothebys

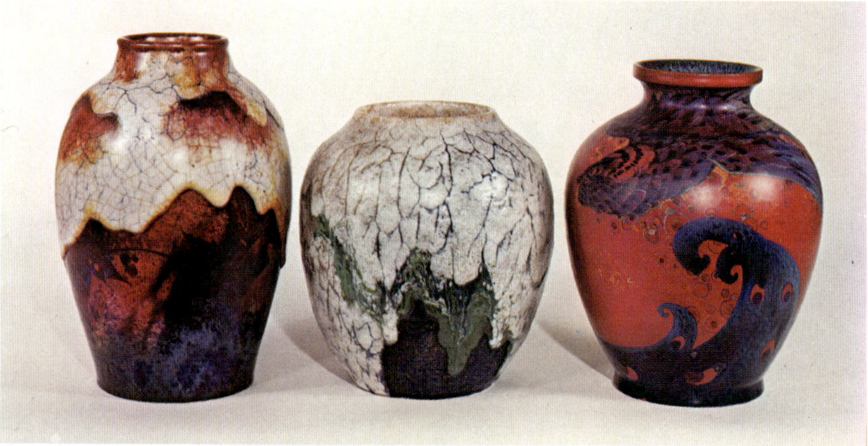

Plate XV Two Royal Doulton 'Chang ware' vases by Charles Noke and Harry Nixon, together with a 'Sung' vase painted with a bird and waves in rich flambé.

Sothebys

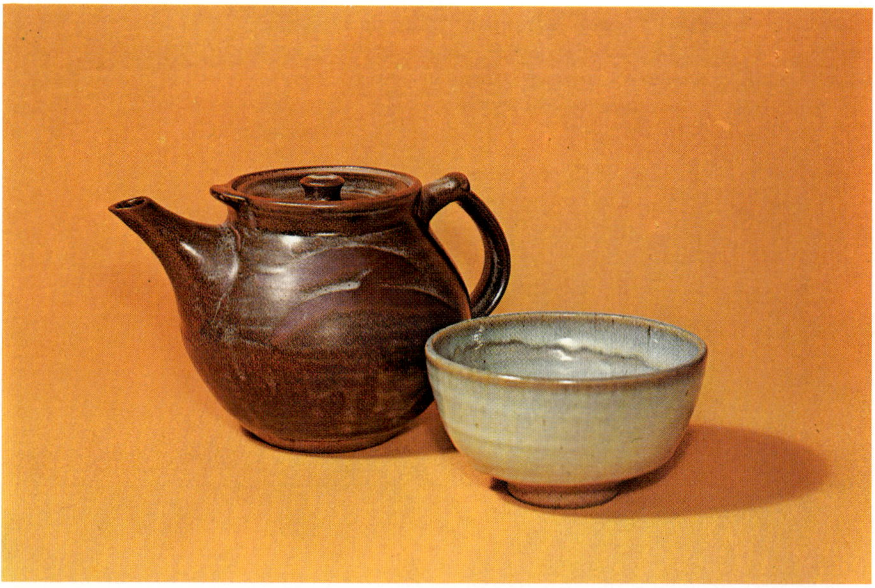

Plate XVI A stoneware teapot and bowl by Geoffrey Whiting with Tenmoko glazes inspired by oriental ceramics, typical of the products of a large number of leading contemporary potters whose work can be bought quite reasonably.

Geoffrey Whiting

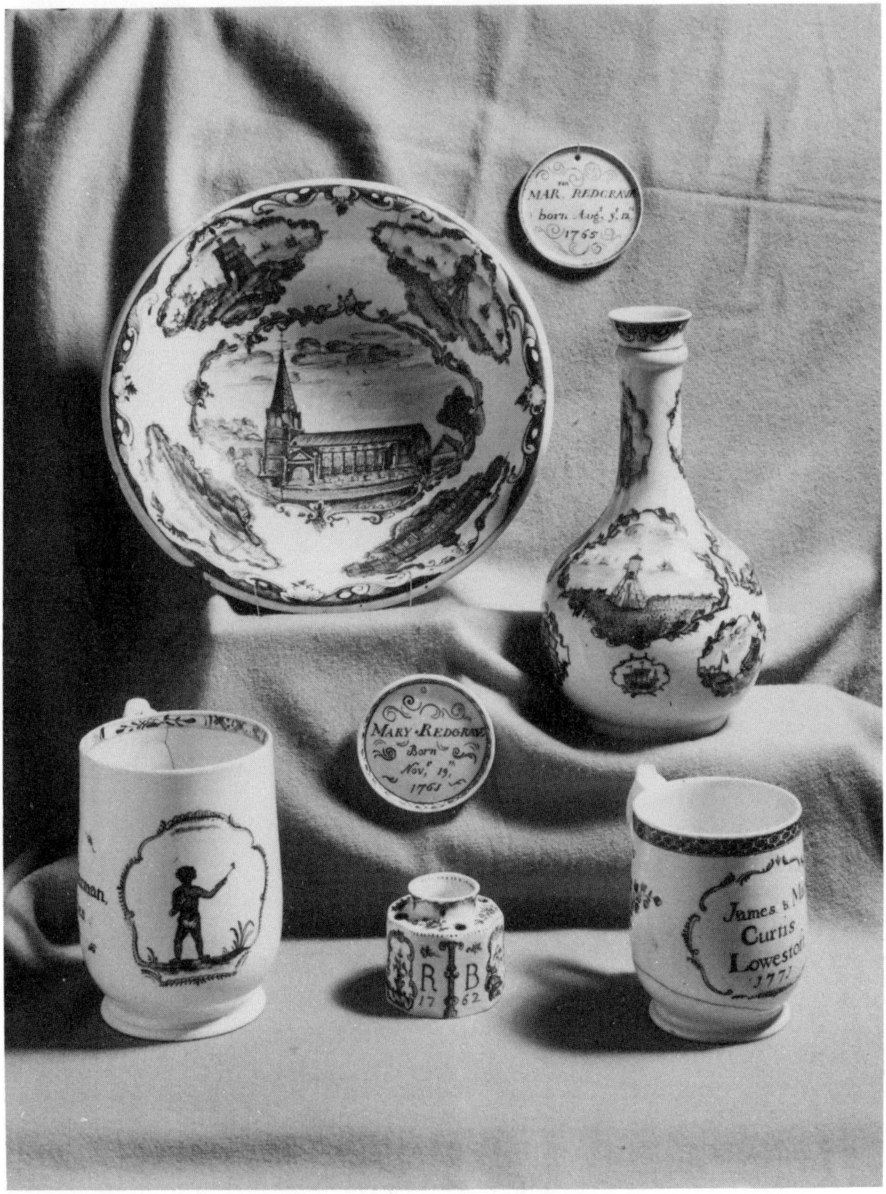

Plate 51. Group of Lowestoft porcelain painted in underglaze blue, including a wash bowl and water bottle with local views, an ink pot and two of the charming birth tablets that the factory made. Lowestoft specialised in pieces made for local people with their names and the date on them.

Norwich Museum

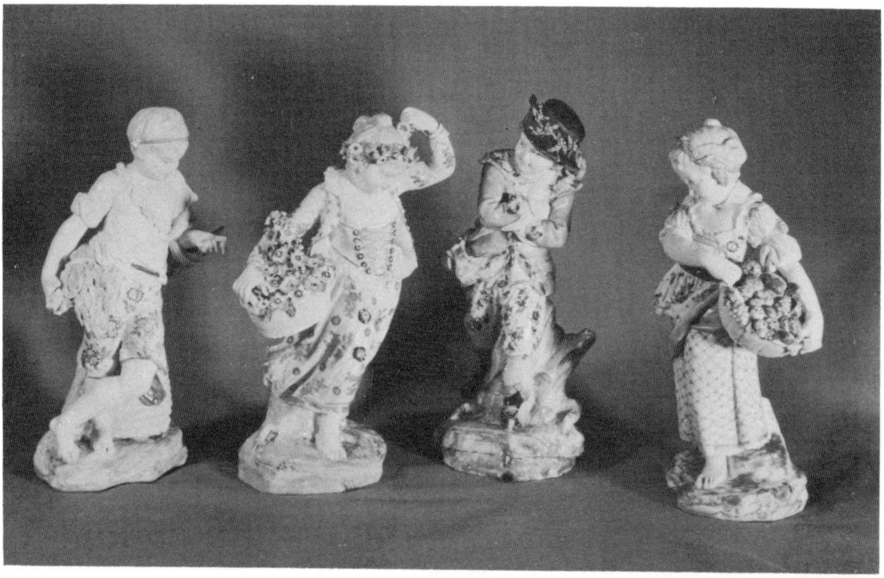

Plate 52. A set of four Champion's Bristol hard paste porcelain figures representing the 'Rustic Seasons' decorated with onglaze enamels; unmarked, height $10\frac{3}{4}$ in., *c.*1775.
Bristol City Art Gallery & Museum

The Plymouth factory was established by William Cookworthy, an apothecary and ardent Quaker. The early wares were mainly blue and white and as the factory seemed to have great difficulty with flat wares the best pieces were mugs of either straight sided or characteristic bell-shape and sauce boats. Some rather primitive animal figures were made, but around about the time of the move to Bristol fine large figures were produced typified by the 'Continents', which depict a female figure with animals. Plymouth blue is usually a very grey tone.

The mark used at Plymouth was like the apothecary's mark for tin and this mark possibly carried on for a short while at Bristol. Cookworthy was joined by Richard Champion, also a Quaker and a Bristol merchant, and increasing production of useful wares, especially tea and coffee wares, was a noteworthy move. A characteristic feature of Bristol handles is that usually they seem disproportionately large. Figures continued to be made and also hexagonal vases, very charmingly decorated with birds and flowers. Also made were small, oval, unglazed plaques with modelled flowers.

The usual Bristol mark is a small painted cross, sometimes associated with a painter's number. Also used was an initial 'B' with a cross and a copy of the Meissen cross swords. One characteristic feature of wheel turned

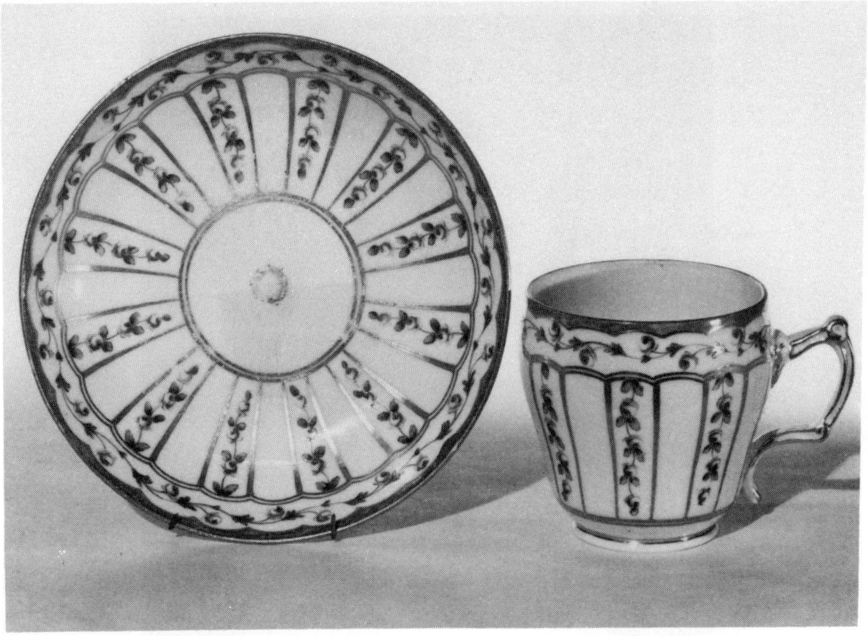

Plate 53. A Bristol coffee cup and saucer in hard paste porcelain, painted in French style with festoons of roses, diameter of saucer 5 in., marked with a cross and number 5 in blue enamel.
Geoffrey Godden, Chinaman

wares is the so-called 'wreathing', spiralling low ridges. Bristol hard paste porcelain can now command very high prices.

FURTHER READING
Cookworthy's Plymouth and Bristol Porcelain by F. Severne Mackenna

NEW HALL

The New Hall factory had its origins in the Bristol factory as Robert Champion's patent for making hard paste porcelain from china clay and stone was bought by a group of Staffordshire potters in 1781, when the patent had 15 years to run. At first the factory was at Tunstall, but the next year it was transferred to premises in Shelton, also in Staffordshire, eventually called New Hall.

New Hall's production falls into two broad periods; in the first, to about the year 1812 they made hard paste type porcelain very like the Bristol body; from 1812 to 1835, when the factory closed, they made bone china, and this period will be dealt with later.

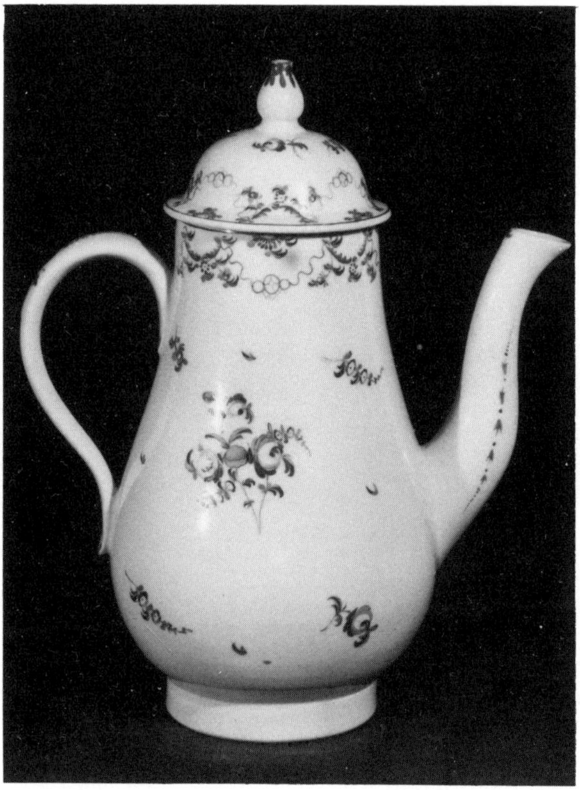

Plate 54. A New Hall porcelain coffee pot of the popular pattern number 195, these simple floral sprigs and borders, inspired by cheap imported Chinese wares, proved very popular in the late 18th century, 9¾ in. high.

Geoffrey Godden, Chinaman

There are no factory marks associated with early New Hall hard paste type porcelain and the early wares are very like those of Bristol, the main difference being the glaze which on New Hall pieces generally gives a softer appearance, has a rather oily look, pools in bubbles and sometimes leaves small areas unglazed. The principle wares made were tea and coffee sets and these are generally very simply and charmingly decorated and of good, although unexciting form, one peculiarity being an original handle having a curious twisted 'clip'.

Early pattern numbers were usually written in large red, puce or black figures, often with prefix N or No. It is now realised that many wares that

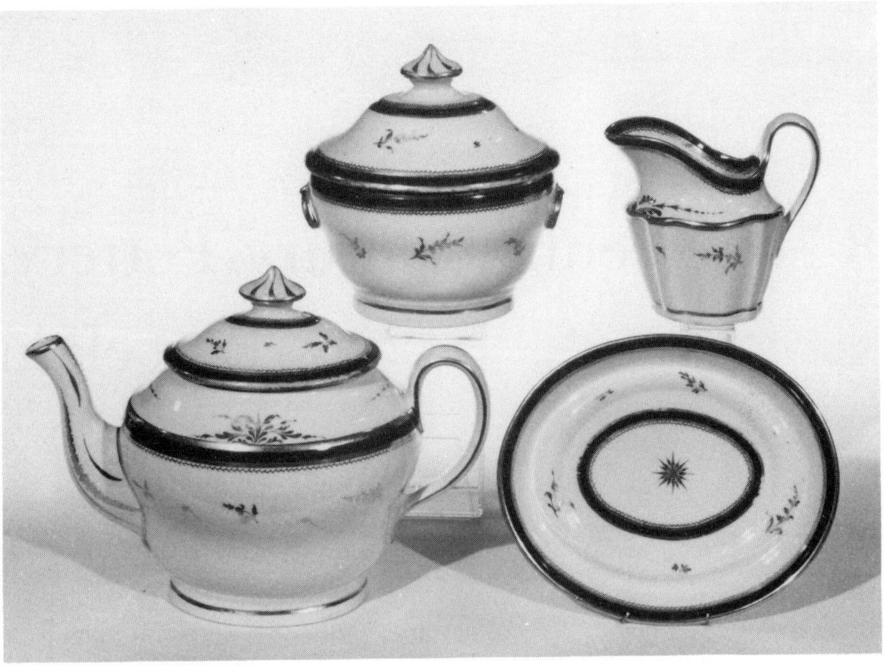

Plate 55. New Hall hard paste teawares *c.*1805, simply decorated with pattern No. 257, the teapot 6½ in. high.

Geoffrey Godden, Chinaman

used to be called New Hall are in fact from other Staffordshire factories who were imitators; their names are not yet known and they are called X, Y and Z.

FURTHER READING
New Hall and Its Imitators by David Holgate

8 Nineteenth Century Pottery & Porcelain

In this chapter porcelain and pottery are dealt with together as so many of the factories made both types of material. The nineteenth century was a very prolific one for ceramic manufacture and it should not be thought that everything made is necessarily collectable. A great quantity of very cheap, mass produced wares poured out of many factories and age does not automatically add value to them. Even fine factories made their pedestrian wares for cheaper, competitive purposes and the trade mark of one of the better factories on an example of their cheaper nineteenth century productions should not blind the mind to the necessity of using judgement. Printing in this century was very variable, some superb and some dreadful, and in general it is safe to say that good quality painting is more valuable than good quality printing, but a good printed piece is better value than a poor painting.

The most commonly made ceramics in the century were bone china and stone china and there was a great deal of difference in their material. Fine bone china has animal bone as the main constituent of its body and produced ware of great beauty, strength, fineness and, in particular, of incredible translucency, although some wares described as bone china that have little bone in them cannot be compared with their better relations. Ironstone china was not china in the sense of bone china, nor did it have any iron in it, but it was a highly vitrified earthenware made from felspathic stone, and was of such hardness and durability that ironstone was a very apt description. It was, of course, opaque.

Great quantities of porcelain were still being made in the early years of the century, although the quality was tending to decline. In fact the invention of bone china gave a much needed boost to fine quality translucent ware. Porcelain made one dying kick through the highly translucent beautiful wares produced by William Billingsley at Swansea and Nantgarw and Chamberlain at Worcester with his 'Regent China' body, but kiln losses were so ruinous—the ware coming so close to glass—that the last ditch fight failed. A porcelain body of a sort was to be used from the 1840's, called Parian, but the main story of the nineteenth century is that of bone china, the English material that is still made.

Other interesting movements were in the field of chimney ornaments, lithophanes, lustre wares, colour printing and the art pottery of the late nineteenth century and the art nouveau movement. Not all the ceramic work of this century is to everyone's taste and this applies especially to the very ornate wares of the Victorians who had a distressing habit of sometimes going too far in the addition of bits and pieces onto the basic shape.

One most interesting feature about the wares of this century, is that a number of factories used an elaborate system of year mark datings by which the exact year of manufacture and sometimes even the month and day, can be ascertained. These marks, used by such factories as Minton, Wedgwood and Royal Worcester, are given in full in the *Encyclopaedia of British Pottery and Porcelain Marks* by Geoffrey Godden (published by Barrie & Jenkins). Many wares also carry the diamond shaped registration mark that indicates the day, month and year when the design was *registered* at the Patent Office in London and does not indicate the date the actual piece was made, which could be up to some considerable time after the registration. These marks, which date from 1842 can also be found in the above mentioned book but it may be of help to indicate these here.

There are two forms of the system; from 1842 to 1867 the year appears in the top section of the diamond, directly underneath the Roman numeral that indicates the class of wares (IV for ceramics), and from 1868 to 1883 the year letter appears in the right hand section; thus:-

1842–1867			**1868–1883**	
1842 - X	1852 - D	1862 - O	1872 - I	1882 - L
3 - H	3 - Y	3 - G	3 - F	3 - K
4 - C	4 - J	4 - N	4 - U	
5 - A	5 - E	5 - W	5 - S	
6 - I	6 - L	6 - Q	6 - V	
7 - F	7 - K	7 - T	7 - P	

1842-1867		1868-1883	
8 - U	8 - B	8 - X	8 - D
9 - S	9 - M	9 - H	9 - Y
50 - V	60 - Z	70 - C	80 - J
1 - P	1 - R	1 - A	1 - E

The month letter is the same in each series:-

January	- C	May	- E	September	- D
February	- G	June	- M	October	- B
March	- W	July	- I	November	- K
April	- H	August	- R	December	- A

Details of the factory who registered designs before 1909 are held at the Public Record office, Ruskin Avenue, Kew, Surrey and members of the public may undertake a search in person for no charge. Postal requests for a search should be accompanied by *full* details of the mark and a £10 fee.

The wares of many factories bear printed, painted or impressed pattern and shape numbers, usually under the bases of figures and useful wares. These are internal factory numbers that help a lot if they are quoted in full if an enquiry is made to the particular factory about the piece but it does not give much information to an outsider. The numbers certainly do not generally indicate the year of manufacture, a mistake that is frequently made. Some other marks cause confusion sometimes, such as the date 'AD 1750' below the modern mark of Coalport, which indicates the date when they claim production probably began at Caughley and not the date of production of the piece.

One helpful indication of the date of a piece is that if the word 'England' appears with the Trade Mark it would not have been made before 1891, as to conform with the MacKinley Tariff Act all wares imported into the United States of America had to have the country of origin clearly marked. It therefore follows that any piece thus marked must have been made in or after 1891 and this knowledge would save a lot of confusion.

The main factories are dealt with alphabetically and this applies to the main ranges and styles not dealt with under the various factories. Not every worthy factory could possibly be indicated and it is hoped that the pieces illustrated will inspire the search for other items of comparative quality.

SAMUEL ALCOCK & CO. *c.*1828-59

The firm made fine unglazed china and Parian busts, moulded Parian vessels and blue printed wares. A notable feature was the production of

Graeco-Roman style vases decorated with classical subjects. The wares are often marked with the initials 'S. A. & Co.'. They also made pottery.

C. J. C. BAILEY—FULHAM POTTERIES 1864-89

A continuation of the Fulham Pottery in London, the wares are becoming collectable.

BARGEWARE

Wares used by the canal folk or bought as presents, often glazed with the so called 'Rockingham' treacle brown and with slip decoration in simple style based upon the seventeenth century. Many were made at Church Gresley.

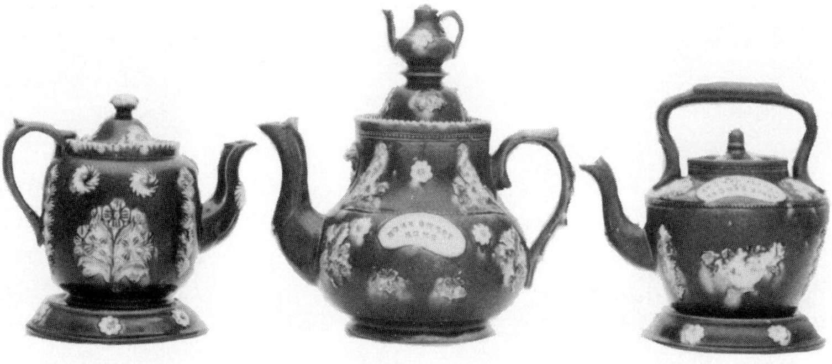

Plate 56. Group of three Bargeware teapots of contrasting shapes, each embossed with typical coloured motifs on running brown glazed grounds.

Sothebys

BELLEEK 1863-

The Belleek factory was founded in County Fermanagh in Ireland in 1863 after exhaustive searches to find a useful stone for making porcelain in the country. Experiments in firing the various bodies were carried out at the Worcester factory and the very characteristic look of Belleek ware with its glossy, iridescent pearl glaze, contrasting with unglazed areas, had Worcester counterparts in the 1860's.

Figures, ornamental and useful wares were made in both parian and porcelain, the most typical having quite elaborate pierced and strip basket work and applied flowers and the addition of shells and other marine effects. The Company is one of those extraordinary ones which, like Wedgwood, still produce wares which are virtually unchanged from the

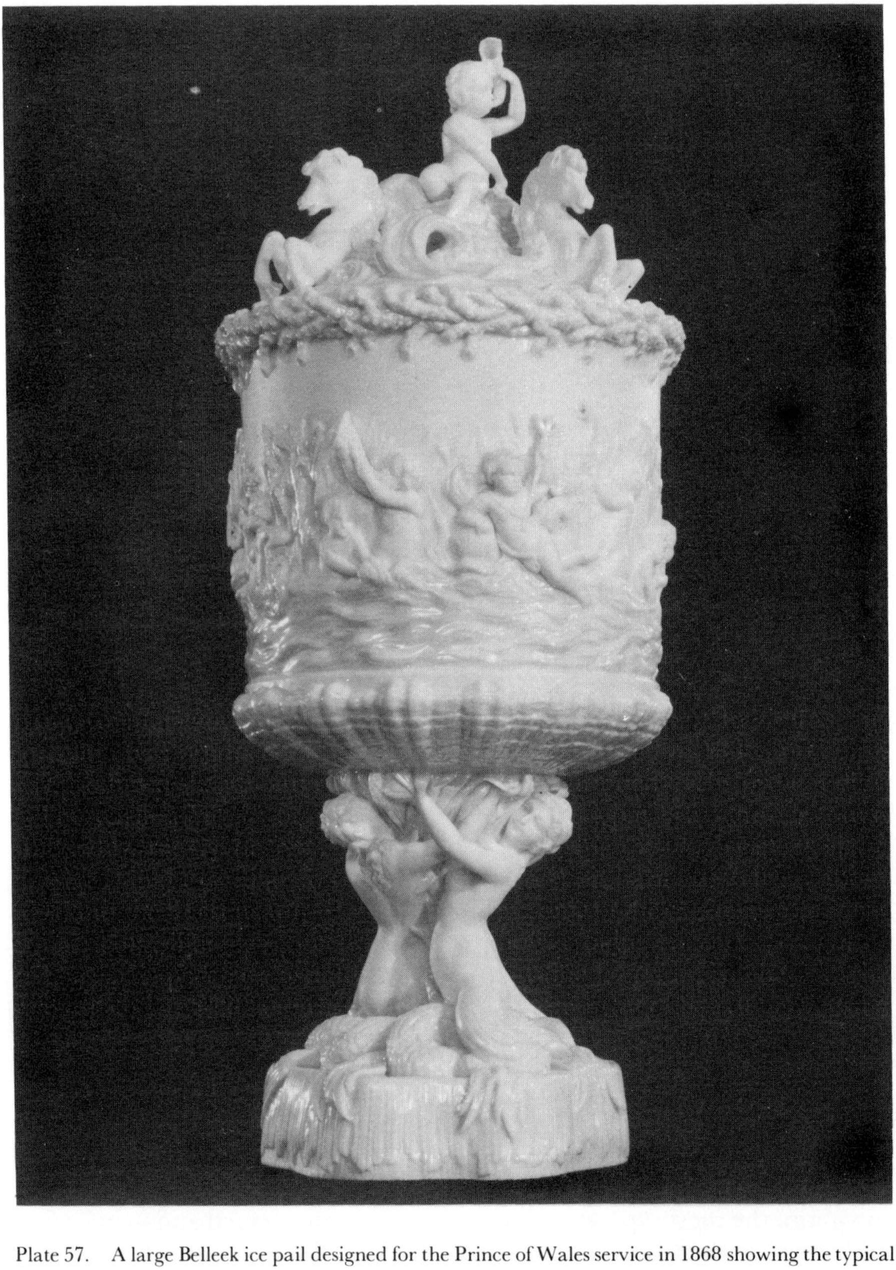

Plate 57. A large Belleek ice pail designed for the Prince of Wales service in 1868 showing the typical use of both glazed and unglazed parian and emphasis on marine motifs, 18 in. high.

Geoffrey Godden, Chinaman

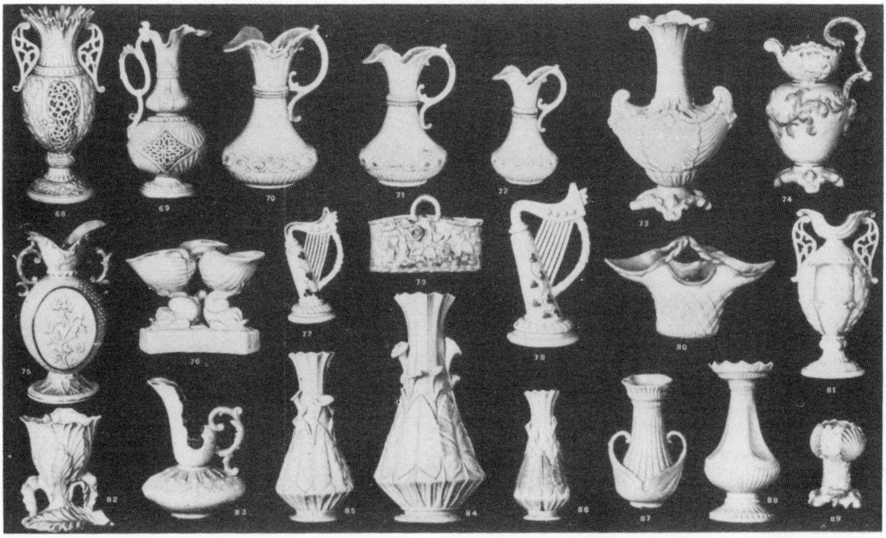

Plate 58. A page from the Belleek Catalogue of 1904 showing a range of ornamental wares, such pieces seldom have enamelled decoration and rely on their lustrous pearl glaze.
Photograph *Geoffrey Godden, Chinaman*

originals and which are as popular today as ever. Early pieces generally have the standard printed or impressed mark showing a tall, printed tower with a wolfhound on the left and a harp on the right and underneath the word BELLEEK. Later versions after about 1891 are not so detailed and have an addition of CO. FERMANAGH IRELAND under the word Belleek. Rare early marks are the impressed BELLEEK CO. FERMANAGH or FERMANAGH POTTERY, the latter sometimes found on Lithophanes, and an impressed or printed crowned harp.

BEVINGTON & CO. 1817-1821

This firm produced creamwares and porcelain of a good standard in Swansea. The impressed mark BEVINGTON & CO. SWANSEA is rarely found on earthenwares.

JOHN BEVINGTON 1872-1892

A Hanley factory that produced porcelain figures in the Dresden style, using a Dresden type mark looking like crossed swords with a letter B at the bottom in underglaze blue. Reproductions of eighteenth century English porcelains were also done and although not of great quality they are referred to here as a warning of their existence.

CHARLES BOURNE 1817-1830

This Fenton (Staffs) firm, although little known or regarded as yet, produced painted porcelain of a very high quality and of such a standard that the wares are usually confused with Coalport, Derby or Chamberlains, the patterns usually being floral or of late Imari type. One way of correct ascription is the frequent use of the initials CB above the pattern number, although this may only occur on key pieces of a service. Bourne wares are of highly collectable quality.

BRANNAM OF BARNSTABLE 1879-

Produced very individual pottery, often with slip decoration and inscribed poems, incised names under the base. Not yet collected, but of good quality and must become appreciated.

BRETBY (TOOTH AND CO.)

Art pottery made from 1883 near Burton-on-Trent in Derbyshire, the most interesting pieces being in an Art Nouveau form.

BRISTOL POTTERIES

A number of earthenware factories flourished in this great ceramic centre, the main one—The Bristol Potteries—still in existence to this day although a move away from the City to the West Country has removed the connection with the City of Bristol.

BURMANTOFTS 1882-1904

Art pottery with interesting glaze effects—a so-called faience—and vigorous shapes, made at Leeds.

CARTER AND CO. 1872-1921

Made interesting earthenwares, art pottery and tiles in Poole in Dorset. Subsequently became Carter, Stabler and Adams and Poole Pottery, which exists to the present day.

CASTLEFORD *c.*1800-1820

A number of moulded stoneware jugs and teapots are ascribed to this factory, owned by D. Dunderdale & Co., but very few pieces are marked 'D. D. & Co.' and the name 'Castleford' is often given to a style of white stoneware with moulded floral and figure decoration with blue painted enamel lines.

CASTLE HEDINGHAM 1864–1901

Wares made by a rather strange artist potter named Edward Bingham at the Castle Hedingham Pottery in Essex are nearly always of a very ancient look, copies of old slip and moulded wares in the Wrotham style and often with seventeenth century dates upon them. The wares are usually marked with a castle above a scroll containing the name E. BINGHAM or an incised signature mark. Although the pieces are anachronisms they have great charm, like the best Bargeware, and although not yet expensive they will undoubtedly be keenly sought eventually and should be seriously considered.

COALPORT 1797–

Originally started by John Rose at the village of Coalport on the banks of the River Severn near Broseley in Shropshire, where two of the original bottle kilns may still be seen. Rose is believed to have been apprenticed to Thomas Turner at the Caughley factory, a few miles from Coalport and on the other side of the river and Rose bought Caughley as a going concern, running both factories until 1814.

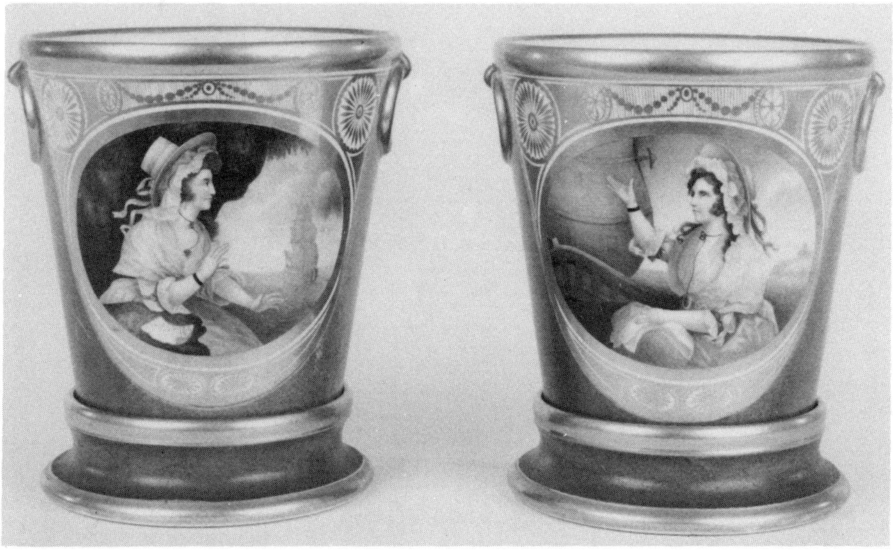

Plate 59. A fine pair of early Coalport jardinieres and stands, the mid-blue ground reserving panels painted, probably in the studio of Thomas Baxter, with portraits of a lady (possibly Lady Hamilton), 6 in., S marks in red enamel.

Phillips

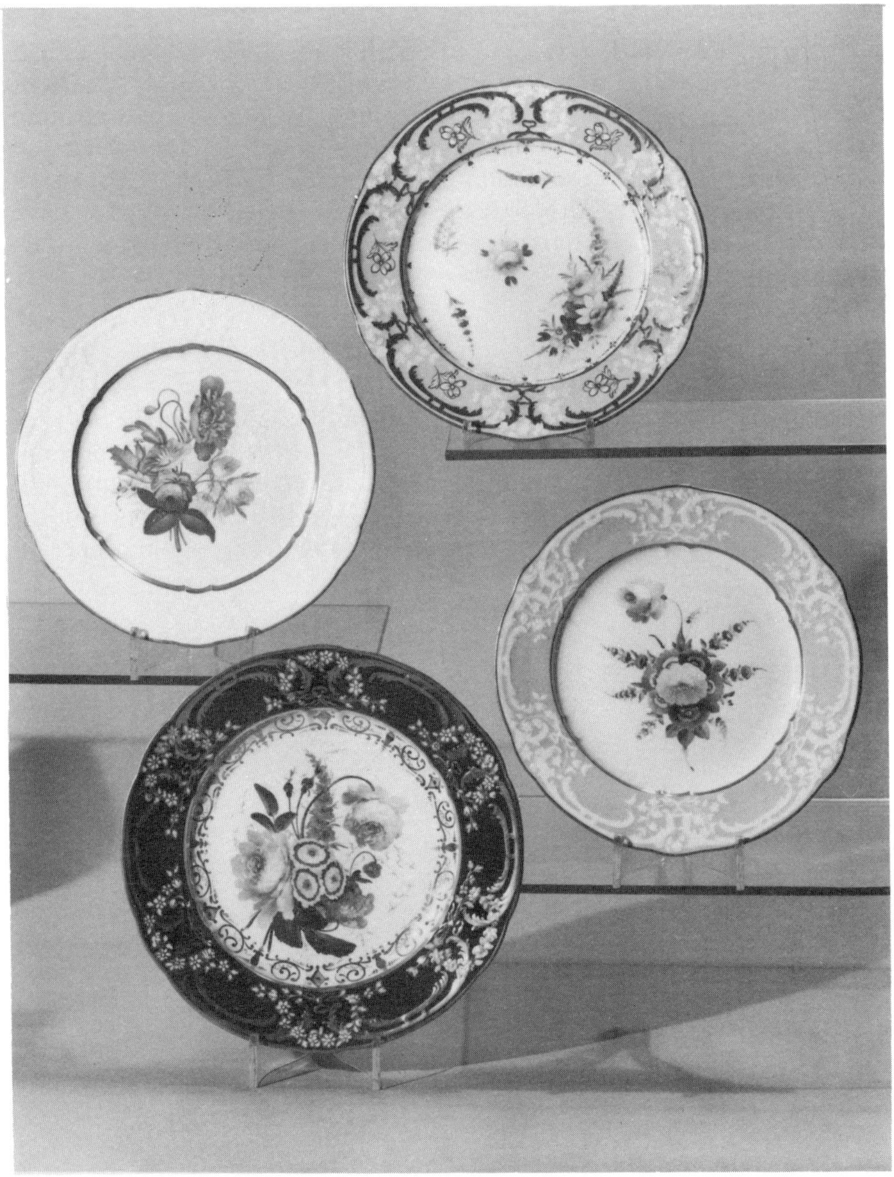

Plate 60. A selection of four Coalport bone china plates of the 1820's with moulded ribbon borders and delicately painted flower sprays, notice the many ways the same border moulding can be decorated to produce quite different effects.

Geoffrey Godden, Chinaman

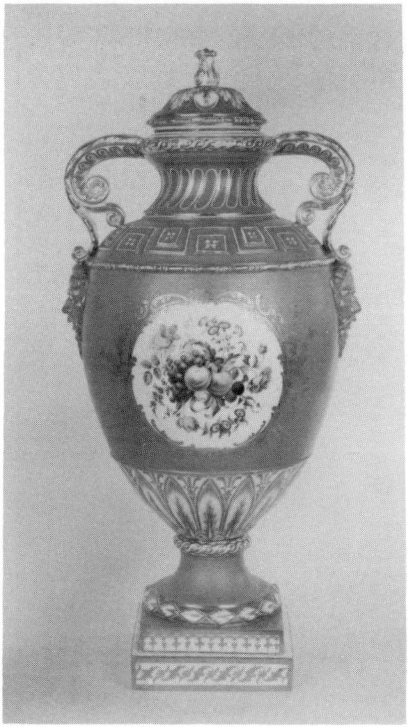

Plate 61. A very large Coalport vase dating from the mid 19th century, the turquoise ground reserving panels painted with fruit and flowers almost certainly by William Cook, 22 in. high, marked in blue CBD for Coalbrook Dale.

Phillips

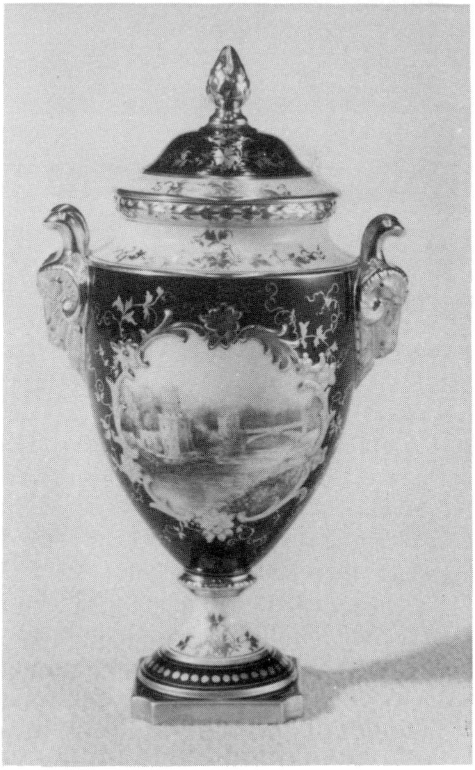

Plate 62. A 20th century Coalport vase utilizing deep blue and creamy-yellow grounds frequently found in conjunction on Coalport, the reserved landscape panel is again typically Coalport in style.

Coalport China Ltd.

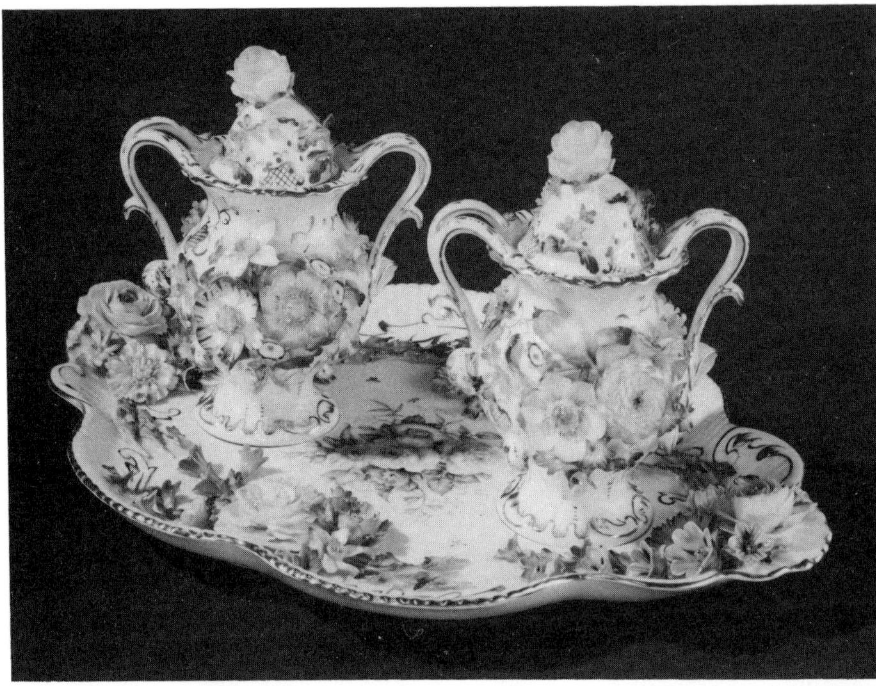

Plate 63. A Coalport tray and two pot-pourri with modelled and painted flowers. Flower encrusted pieces are often called 'Coalbrookdale' although similar pieces were made by many other factories. *Coalport China Ltd.*

The early Coalport wares are generally unmarked and very similar to Chamberlain, Worcester, with whom they are frequently confused. Some early wares have the very rare mark 'Coalbrookdale' painted and this name is frequently used to refer to Coalport wares, especially the florally encrusted vases of the 1820's and 30's, which are produced by the present Company to this day. Some of the early pieces in this style are marked 'C. D. and 'C. Dale', but most are unmarked. A number of the plates and dishes produced during this period have impressed numerals in the base, in particular a curious top heavy '2'. The earliest series of pattern numbers was 1 up to 1000 in various colours then fractional numbers 2/1 to 2/1000, 3/1 to 3/1000 written in gold, the number never exceeding 1000.

From the 1840's strong ground colours were used and imitations of ornate Chelsea and Sévres wares were made. The present Coalport company is now in Staffordshire and although it has changed hands a number of times the standard mark from about 1875 has included a reference AD 1750, referring to a claim for the first making of pottery at

Caughley. It should not, of course, be taken as referring to the year of manufacture of the particular piece, although this is quite a commonly held misconception.

FURTHER READING
Caughley & Coalport by F. A. Barrett
Coalport & Coalbrookdale Porcelains by Geoffrey Godden

H. & R. DANIEL *c.*1826–1841

Makers of fine quality porcelain and pottery in Stoke. Only a proportion of the wares are marked, usually with the full name H. & R. Daniel or H. Daniel & Sons, but are well worth seeking.

DAVENPORT *c.*1793–1887

Davenport started at Longport in Staffordshire when John Davenport took over Brindley's pottery. Only earthenware was made at first, to be followed by porcelain and a stone china body. Both fine printing and painting were done, mainly on useful wares and many services of excellent quality were made.

The mark usually found is the word Davenport sometimes associated with the anchor mark, which can be found on its own.

DELLA-ROBBIA COMPANY 1894–1901

Pre-Raphaelite styles produced by sgraffito process, now becoming collectable.

WILLIAM DE MORGAN *c.*1872–*c.*1911

One of the best known of the late nineteenth century craftsmen potters, William De Morgan was born in 1839 and studied painting at the Royal Academy School. He was influenced by his friend William Morris and produced painted tiles and plaques as blanks from firms and then in 1872 at his small pottery and showroom in Cheyne Row, Chelsea he made and decorated his own earthenware.

He had a great interest in old lustre ware and strange floral, fish and animal patterns, often in a resist process, are a great feature of his art. In 1882 he moved to Merton Abbey, then in 1888 to Sands End Pottery in Fulham. De Morgan had a number of skilled decorators such as Charles and Fred Passenger, J. Hersey and J. Juster and their initials may be found on many pieces, especially the larger vases and plaques.

De Morgan retired in 1907 but the firm was continued by the workmen until about 1911. Few of the early wares are marked but the later pieces are either marked with the name of De Morgan in various forms, or the situation of the pottery. Characteristics of the ware are the very soft bodies, a general heavy crazing of the glaze and the use of soft greens and blues in patterns resembling those on ancient Italian and Moorish lustrewares.

DERBY 1878-

The Derby Crown Porcelain Co. Ltd., formed in 1876, changed its name to the Royal Crown Derby Porcelain Co. Ltd. in 1890 and has produced some fine bone china vases and wares. These were a great improvement over much of the wares made during the Bloor period (1830-40) which produced a running down of the finer qualities of the earlier Derby factory. Some of the most collectable wares are those decorated with their traditional Imari type pattern in blue red and gold (the gypsies call it the

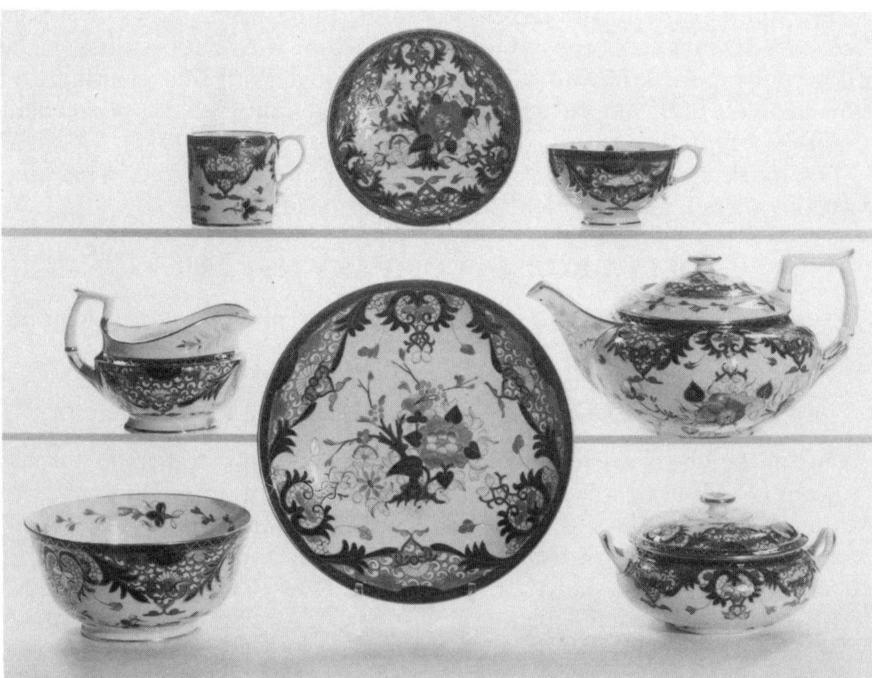

Plate 64. A range of Derby teawares of the 1820's painted with an Imari design basically in red, blue and gold. Derby have, up until the present day, specialised in such brightly coloured Imari patterns, the earlier examples well worth seeking as they cost no more than the corresponing modern piece, diameter of plate, $8\frac{3}{4}$ in. Red mark.

Geoffrey Godden, Chinaman

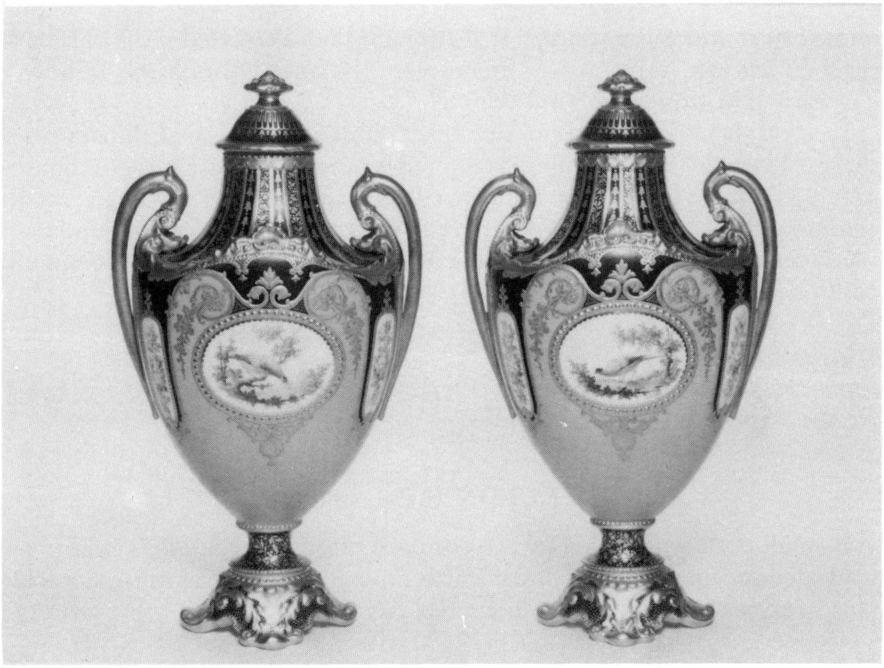

Plate 65. A pair of Royal Crown Derby vases in Sévres style, the panels painted by Desiré Leroy with exotic birds reserved on turquoise and deep blue grounds richly gilt, 7¾ in.
Phillips

'Cigar pattern' after the border pattern shape) and especially desirable are the miniatures. Among the most collectable painters are Rouse, Dean and Leroy.

FURTHER READING
Royal Crown Derby by John Twitchett

DOULTON *c.*1815-

Production started in Lambeth in London under the name of Doulton & Watts and mainly useful earthenwares were made including quantities of moulded stoneware bottles. It is not until the 1871 South Kensington Exhibition that the factory really started making the fine decorated stonewares—vases and jars—that are now beginning to be so highly regarded. One of the most interesting features of these pieces is that they generally bear the marks of the decorators, such artists as George Tinworth who did fine sculptural work and Hannah Barlow and Florence, her sister, who did incised bird and animal subjects. Although the salt glazed stonewares are the best known, other wares made were 'Faience', 'Impasto', 'Silican', 'Carrara', 'Marqueterie' and 'Chiné'.

In 1882 the manufacture of fine bone china was started at Burslem and this is still made. Perhaps the best known products are the character figures and jugs, a large variety of which have been produced during the twentieth century. These have seen a very marked increase in price recently and with the incentive of the book by Richard Dennis and Desmond Eyles should continue to rise.

FURTHER READING
Royal Doulton Figures by Desmond Eyles and Richard Dennis
Doulton Pottery by Richard Dennis

ELTON 1879–1930

A small pottery founded by Sir Edmund Elton at the Sunflower Pottery, Clevedon, Somerset. The finest wares have a gold and platinum crackle glaze and are very under-appreciated.

FAIRINGS

Literally, small things bought as presents at fairs. Most of these—small figure groups and ribbon plates, were German and beyond the scope of this book.

W. H. GOSS 1858–1944

The title Goss China is nowadays used to describe the huge quantities of holiday mementos, usually on a thin parian body, with the name and crest of the town on it, the shape often in the form of ancient Greek vessels. Most of these are of poor taste, although being quite keenly purchased in junk shops, but some of the Stoke-on-Trent firm's early productions of figures and busts in an ivory body very similar to that of Belleek can be very fine. These will be marked with the impressed or printed W. H. GOSS or W. H. G. Especially collectable are the early replicas of buildings, such as Ledbury Old Market House, Shakespeare's House, models of ancient crosses and churches.

FURTHER READING
Goss China Cottages by Hella Regnard
Price Guide to the Models of W. H. Goss by Roland Ward

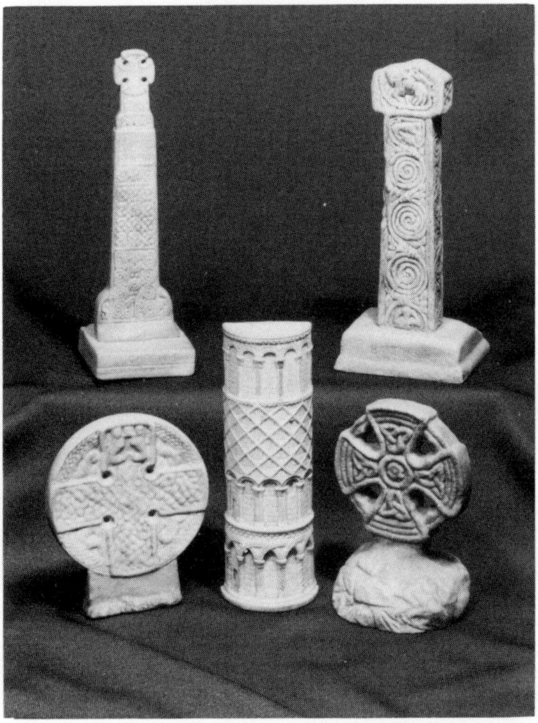

Plate 66. A group of W. H. Goss miniature models of monuments, the matt surface resembling stone. These are typical of the large range of souvenir pieces made by Goss, frequently bearing hand-coloured crests of popular towns.
Phillips

FREMINGTON

A family of potters named Fishley, the most important of whom was George, potted at Fremington in Devonshire from the late eighteenth to the nineteenth century and through the Fishley Hollands into this century. The early speciality was fine Devon harvest pitchers with amusing floral and animal designs.

FROG MUGS

One- or two-handled beer and cider mugs, often covered with a treacly brown 'Rockingham' glaze and made at Church Gresley. They usually have a modelled frog or lizard climbing up the inside poised to frighten the life out of the drinker who would think it was ready to jump down his throat. Such amusing pieces, used in the tavern, were the nineteenth century successors of the fuddling cups and puzzle jugs, the latter continuing to the present day. Other amusing vessels were chamber pots with frogs or a naughty rhyme or a portrait of Napoleon in the bottom—pointing to the rumbustiousness of the early nineteenth century.

HERCULANEUM POTTERY, LIVERPOOL *c.*1793-1841

Fine stonewares were made, typified by moulded jugs and figures and some basalt wares, although the latter are not of such good quality. The word 'Herculaneum' is often found impressed.

FURTHER READING
Liverpool Herculaneum Pottery by Alan Smith

HOWELL & JAMES

One frequently finds large dishes, plates, and plaques with a sticker underneath marked with the above name, often giving the original price in guineas. These are generally the work of the amateur artists, usually female, caught up in a short lived craze for 'do it yourself' painting in the last quarter of the century. These paintings were done on ware bought in the white from well known factories, sometimes carrying their impressed marks, but the mark should not blind the eye to the generally poor amateur effect of the work, although, of course, some painters could be more talented than others. Exhibitions held by the firm sold huge quantities of these pieces.

GEORGE JONES & SONS 1861-

This firm was established at the Trent Pottery in Stoke by George Jones, who had worked for Mintons. The wares are often very Minton like and a speciality was Majolica, some good pâte-sur-pâte was also made. Most pieces have a monogram mark with the initials GJ, sometimes above a crescent.

LINTHORPE POTTERY 1879-89

Interesting earthenwares with different glaze effects. A highly collectable ware at its best, with designs by Christopher Dresser.

MARTIN BROTHERS 1873-1914

The Martin brothers—Robert Wallace, Walter, Edwin Bruce and Charles are undoubtedly one of the most interesting family groups of potters and could be regarded as the first of the Studio Potters movement. Working as a team they designed, made and sold salt-glazed stoneware of a unique quality and standard ranging from miniature utilitarian pots to extraordinary grotesques such as jars in the shape of birds with removable heads. The design and modelling is faultless and the vessels are often incised with beautiful fish, animal and plant forms (Edwin Martin's speciality). A very interesting feature is the elaborate incised marking of every piece with the name of the firm, place of production (Fulham 1873-4, London 1874-8 and Southall 1878-00) and generally the months and year of manufacture—eg. 6/93 for June 1893.

The serious collecting of Martin ware has already begun and the major salerooms frequently feature some of the larger and rare items, such as the birds with removable heads, or with open mouths for use as spoon warmers, or the jugs with a face on each side, the earlier pieces tending to be more expensive. However these must be a good investment, as well as providing great pleasure with their robust earthiness, a curious mixture of Medieval English pottery and German stoneware.

MASON

This famous firm was started by Miles Mason who produced good quality porcelain up to 1813, including fine printing, Marked pieces are rare—sometimes the name of the firm, sometimes a mock Chinese square

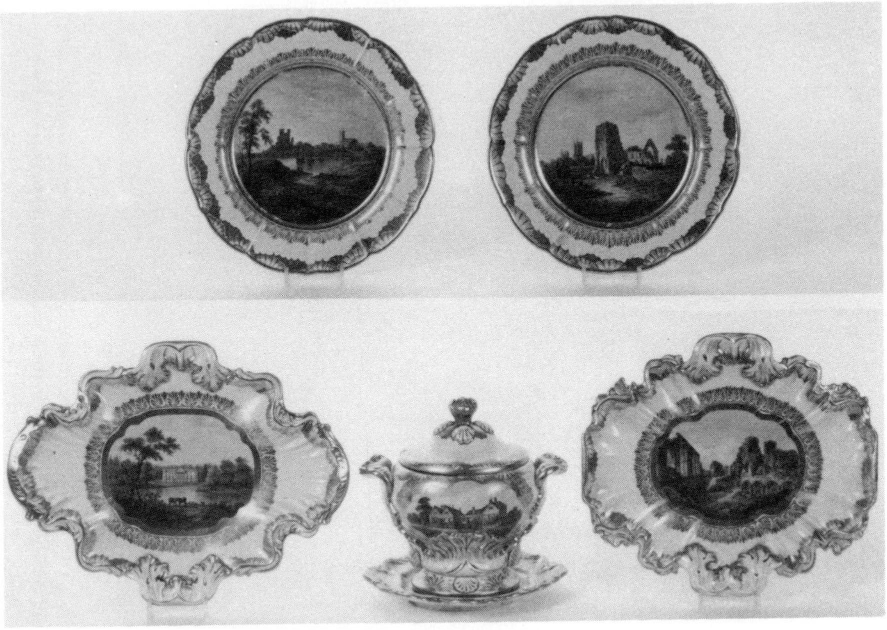

Plate 67. A Mason's 'Patent Ironstone' dinner service painted with named landscapes probably by Samuel Bourne. It is unusual to find such fine painting on Mason wares, the flamboyant shapes usually decorated with formal Japan patterns, various impressed marks.

Phillips

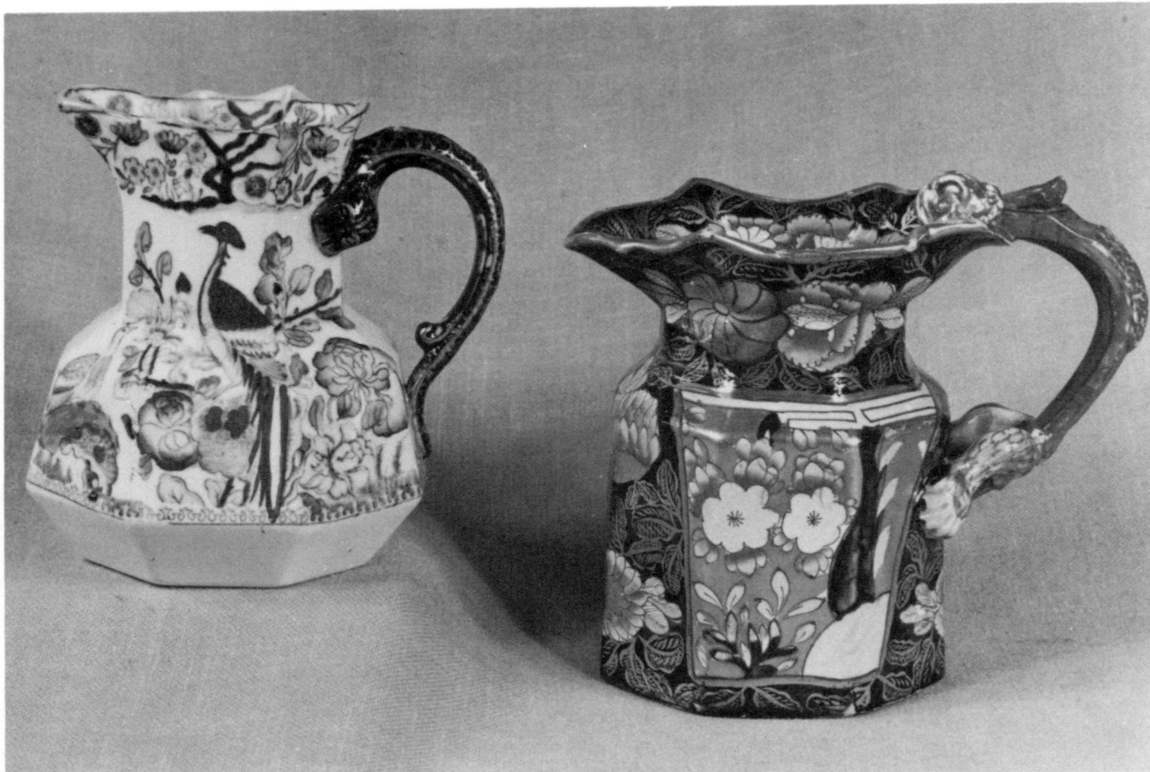

Plate 68. Two Mason's 'Patent Ironstone' jugs painted in onglaze colours over underglaze printed outlines. Ironstone was relatively cheap and jugs such as these served to brighten up the dismal cottages of the day, *c.*1830.

Mason's Ironstone China Ltd.

seal mark. In 1813 Miles' son Charles James Mason took out his patent for Ironstone. The ware was very durable and great quantities survive at very low cost considering the colourful character and good shapes of the ware. The colours and patterns used were bold, in the Japan style, with reds and greens predominating. In 1848 Mason became bankrupt and his moulds and patterns were purchased by Francis Morley of Shelton eventually coming in to the hands of Messrs. G. L. Ashworth & Brothers of Hanley who still produce Mason-type wares to this day. C. J. Mason had a second shot at manufacturing from about 1849 to 1852 and exhibited at the Great Exhibition of 1851.

A word of warning on dating—the mark used on Mason is identical to that used later by Ashworth.

FURTHER READING

Mason Porcelain and Ironstone 1796–1853 by Haggar and Adams

MAW & CO. *c.*1850–1970

Began making tiles at Worcester then moved to Broseley making tiles and art pottery in the style of de Morgan, nowadays becoming collectable.

MINTON 1793–

Although this firm started in the eighteenth century it is being dealt with in this chapter as it is basically thought of as a nineteenth and twentieth century factory. Minton's is one of the many factories whose best wares have often been confused with other factories and it is only with the publication of the book noted at the end of the section that the record has been corrected.

Thomas Minton was born in 1765 and apprenticed to Thomas Turner at Caughley where he must have had instilled into him the realisation of the potentialities of underglaze transfer printing from copper plates, many of the engravings being of a 'Willow Pattern' type. These were adapted by various factories into the production of *the* Willow Pattern print, the famous design that must rank as the most commonly used ceramic pattern in the world. Everyone must know the pattern of two birds flying towards each other, three Chinese figures crossing a bridge under a willow tree which leads away from an island on which is a large Chinese building under a tree having characteristic round blob leaves. The earliest versions of these patterns are of very fine quality and would well repay collecting even if it is not possible to know from which factory they come.

Thomas Minton's first business venture was as an engraver supplying coppers to pottery firms, Josiah Spode among them, but in 1793 he started

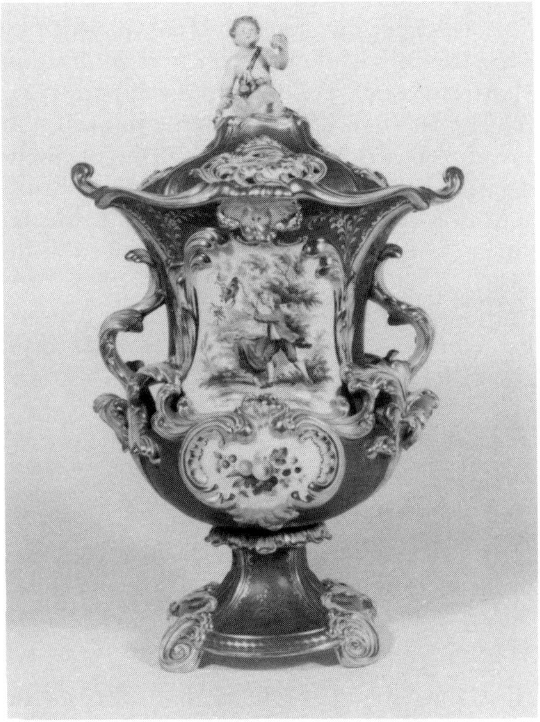

Plate 69. An elaborate Minton 'Dresden' vase and cover although in the most favoured French style, the finial on the cover is formed as a putto figure and painted panel represents Autumn, again very much influenced by 18th century French art, 14 in., *c.* 1835.

Phillips

his own manufactory in Stoke, producing blue printed pottery. In 1798 a semi-porcelain was produced, abandoned in 1811, restarted in 1821 and china was produced shortly afterwards, which has continued to the present day.

The earliest pieces often bear only a painted pattern number, often prefixed by the 'N' or 'No'. The first pieces bearing the factory mark of the crossed L mark (similar to the mark of Sèvres) probably date from about 1805 and the finest examples are painted by some of the ex-Derby painters, in particular Thomas Steele, the great flower painter.

The early pieces are usually of rather restrained, Spode like shape in the years from the 1820's to the 1840's, a great quantity of florally encrusted

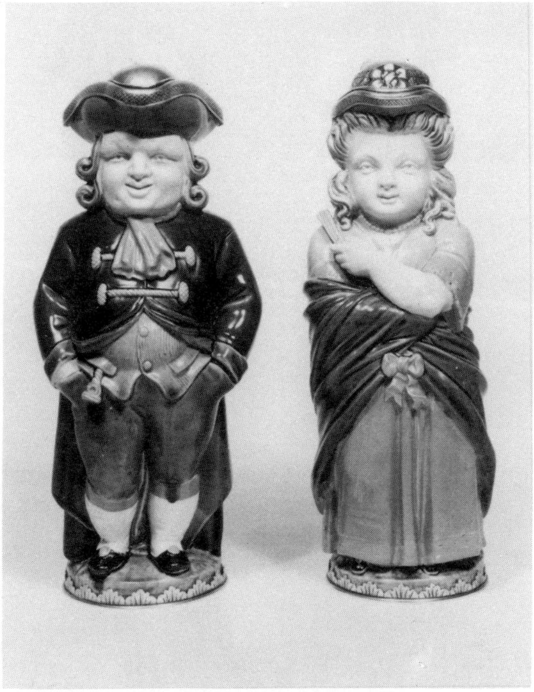

Plate 70. A pair of Minton 'Majolica ware' Toby jugs depicting a fashionable lady and gentleman, the strong colours produced under the running glaze, Majolica ware was manufactured by a great number of firms, but not usually of such high quality and with silver mounts by leading maker George Fox, impressed marks, *c.*1870.

Phillips

ornamental pieces of high quality were made, which are often wrongly called Coalbrookdale or Coalport. Enamelled and white biscuit figures were also made in the chalky body. From the 1840's very fine Parian figures were made; in fact Minton's were one of the three finest producers of Parian figures, the other two being Copeland and Worcester. Minton's Parian is usually of a creamy body with a slight glossy surface and is generally unmarked, except for some pieces which have an ermine-like mark. A series of moulded ware in a coloured hard earthenware was also made often marked with an initial M in the bottom right hand corner of a moulded or applied scrolled device, often with the shape number above it.

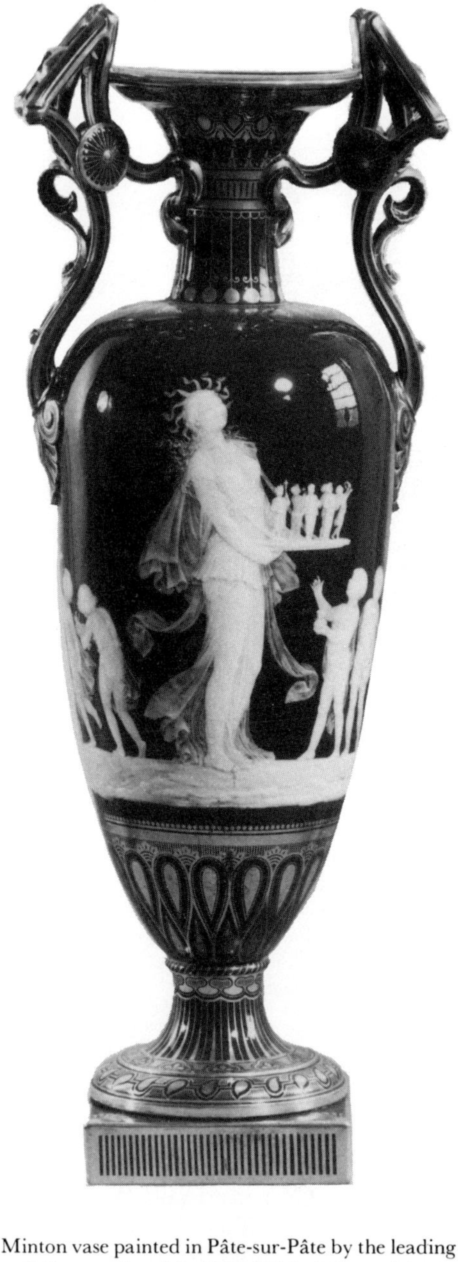

Plate 71. A magnificent Minton vase painted in Pâte-sur-Pâte by the leading exponent M. L. Solon, with the subject of the Toy Seller, produced in 1899. While Minton Pâte-sur-Pâte commands high prices, examples made by the Worcester and Staffordshire firm of George Jones, can still be acquired quite reasonably.

Minton (Photograph copyright of 'Pottery Gazette')

Thomas Minton died in 1836 and was succeeded by his son Herbert who traded as Minton & Boyle (marks often include the letters M &B) and from 1845 to 1868 as Minton & Hollins (mark of M&H). The ware became more ornate, but generally of high quality.

In 1850 the factory started producing majolica of very fine quality. In this period also the painting was of a high standard.

Some of the finest and most expensive Minton pieces were those produced in the form of decoration known as *pâte-sur-pâte*, the greatest exponent of which was M. L. Solon, who had been trained at Sèvres. The best quality work in this form fetches the highest prices for Victorian ceramics and while all Solon's personal work is signed and the price is likely to be in the hundreds of pounds the best work of his contemporaries may sometimes be found for more reasonable amounts.

From 1842 to the present day most of Minton's wares will carry code marks which date the exact month and year of manufacture and a list of these may be seen in Godden's *Encyclopaedia of British Pottery and Pottery Marks*. Most marks embody the word MINTON in various forms, often across a globe.

From 1868 Minton Hollins & Co. have made huge quantities of pottery floor tiles, both for church and domestic use and although the church tiles do not have the medieval like quality of the versions made by Chamberlain at Worcester, the domestic tiles can be very charming and grouped into sets to build up large patterns, can be bought quite cheaply, and should be sought. This firm, however, should not be confused with the main Minton Company and most tiles will be found marked either with Minton Hollins & Co. (Ltd. added in about 1928) or M H & Co.

FURTHER READING

Minton Pottery and Porcelain of the First Period 1793–1850 by Geoffrey Godden

MOORCROFT

Late nineteenth to twentieth century earthenwares, among the most collectable being the early Macintyre wares of which the best known is 'Florian'.

MOCHA WARE

Mocha is the name given to mugs and other simple wares often intended for public house use, decorated with bands of coloured slip and the characteristic 'trees' which were produced by a dark pigment mixed with an infusion of tobacco and hops which spread in the shape of a tree on the

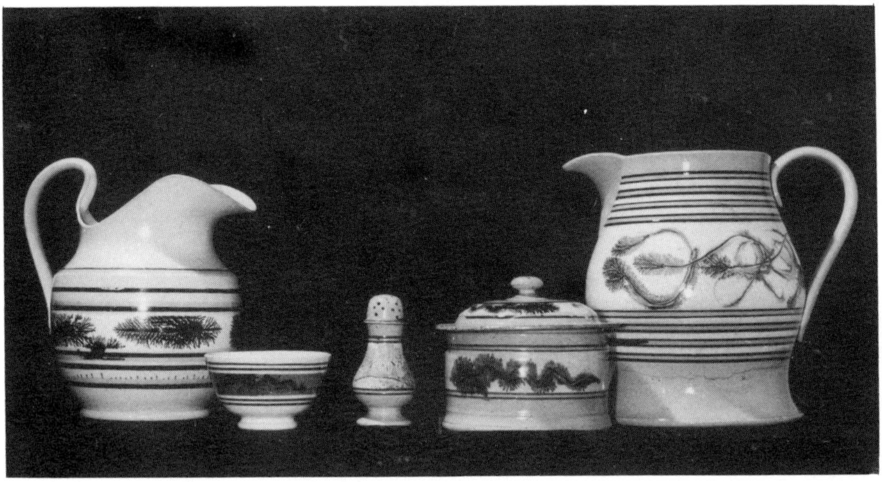

Plate 72. A range of Mocha Ware decorated with typical 'trees' and bands of colour, giving some idea of the collecting possibilities of this material, all 19th century.
Collection of K. A. Raybould

surface of the vessel. Many of the mugs made for pubs have the excise mark of the Weights and Measures applied on a pad. It is likely that the ware was first made in the late eighteenth century and their simple shapes and interesting decoration merit much greater attention than they have so far had. Similar wares without the 'trees' were made throughout the century and in this, only early examples being collectable. The wares were made in a large number of places throughout most of England and Wales and shapes are much more varied than might be imagined.

MOORE BROS. *c.*1872-1915

Some fine pieces were made by this firm up to 1905 and continued by Bernard Moore up to 1915. Most pieces are marked with the word Moore. Particularly interesting are the small ornamental figures such as figures holding bowls and the later vases with different coloured glazes, such as flambé. The early pieces can sometimes be of equivalent quality to such contemporaries as Worcester, and can be obtained at much lower cost. Some fine artists worked for the factory, notably Boullemier, who painted cupids and cherubs and Sieffert who was trained at Sèvres and did figure paintings in the French style. The body has a habit of staining rather badly.

NANTGARW

This Welsh Factory has the distinction of having made probably the most beautiful porcelain body ever produced. William Billingsley, who had done some experimental work on highly translucent porcelain at Worcester, took his knowledge to Nantgarw but had great difficulties with manufacture. Dillwyn, of the Swansea factory, was called in to give a report and found that 'the body was too nearly allied to glass to bear the necessary heat, and observed that nine tenths of the articles were either shivered or more or less injured in shape by the firing'. In September 1814 production was moved to the Swansea factory, but Billingsley returned to Nantgarw in about 1817 continuing production until 1820.

When correctly fired the wares had an astounding beauty and translucence. Examples are nowadays relatively rare and very expensive, those decorated at Nantgarw being, in general, more expensive than those

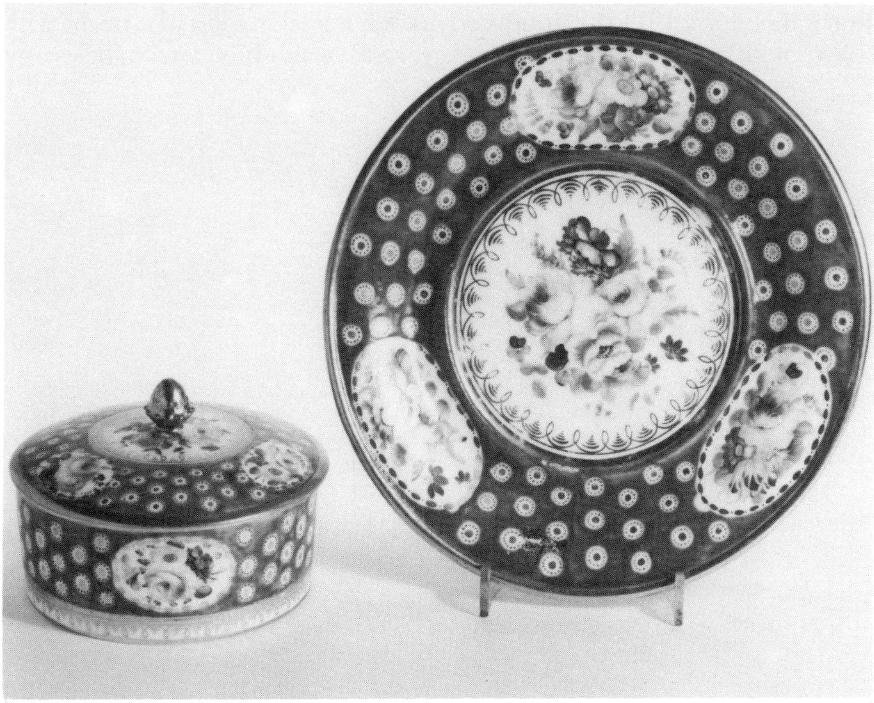

Plate 73. A Nantgarw butter dish, cover and stand from the celebrated 'Duke of Cambridge' service with flower panels on an *Oeil de Perdrix* ground.

Bonhams

by outside London decorators. A number of later Continental copies are in existence but once a genuine piece has been seen and handled there should be no possibility of confusion.

FURTHER READING

Nantgarw Porcelain by W. H. John

The Pottery & Porcelain of Swansea and Nantgarw by E. M. Nance

PILKINGTON (ROYAL LANCASTRIAN)

The manufacture of ornamental ware, mainly vases, began in about 1893 and continued until March 1938. The decorative effects were often similar to those of William De Morgan, especially the different lustre and resist decorations. The wares were quite expensive in their own day, being high class art pottery, but are at present very under-valued except for the lustres. The earliest pieces are seldom marked but from 1904–14 the standard impressed mark was an illuminated capital letter P set with two butterflies; from 1914 the impressed mark is a P set in a circular frame with a leaf motif below, with the word Royal above and Lancastrian below. In

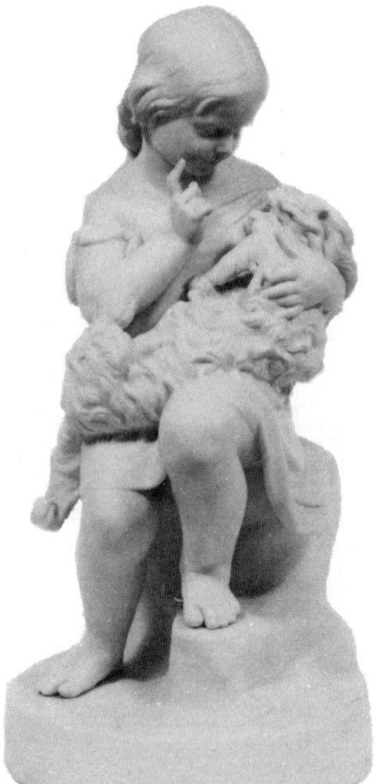

Plate 74. Parian figure by Copeland, entitled 'Go to Sleep', typical of Victorian sentimentality.

Sothebys

addition the marks of the various artists are usually on the piece, such as the curious figure of a crane to denote the work of Walter Crane.

FURTHER READING
Royal Lancastrian Pottery by A. Lomax

PINXTON 1796-*c.*1813

The factory at Pinxton in Derbyshire was founded by William Billingsley, on leaving the Derby factory, and John Coke to make porcelain. Wanderlust took Billingsley on to start a decorating establishment at Mansfield in 1799 but the factory was continued by Coke and later by John Cutts. Very few wares are marked—marks known are a painted crescent and star, an arrow-like device and the word 'Pinxton'—but they are generally of good quality, rather like puce-marked Derby and often have fine landscape and floral patterns.

FURTHER READING
The Pinxton China Factory by C. L. Exley

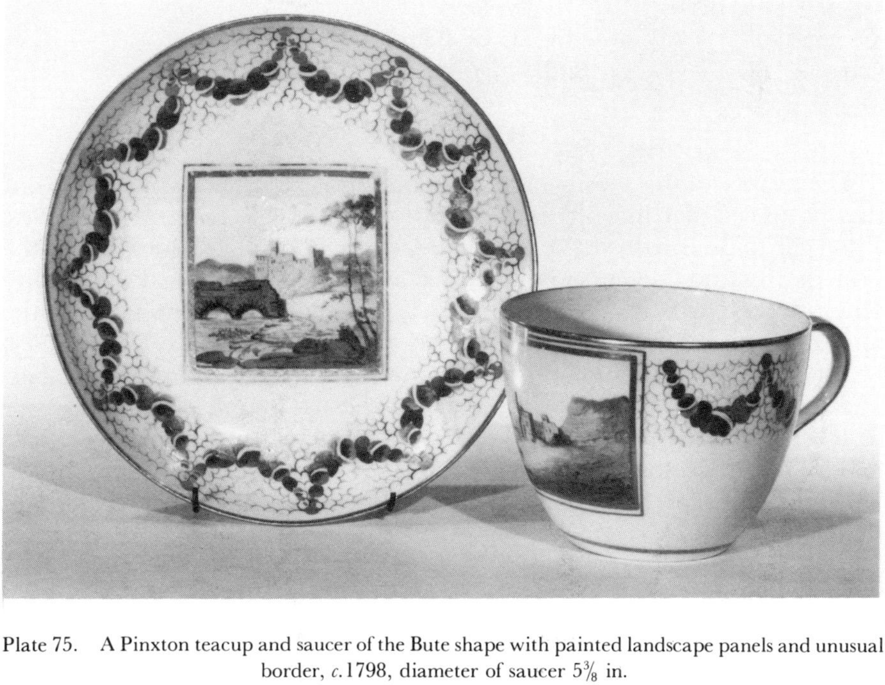

Plate 75. A Pinxton teacup and saucer of the Bute shape with painted landscape panels and unusual border, *c.*1798, diameter of saucer 5⅜ in.

Geoffrey Godden, Chinaman

POT LIDS

See Pratt and Company.

F. & R. PRATT & CO. 1810-

This firm should not be confused with the earlier eighteenth century so called Pratt Wares—relief moulded figures, jugs and teapots named after Pratt of Lane Delft. William's son Felix founded his own works in 1810 which continued into this century, very few of the early wares such as Etruscan decorated earthenware vases and jugs, being marked. From 1840, when '& Co.' was added to the firm's title, printed marks were used which include the name or initials of the firm. The later use of the term 'Pratt Ware' is used to refer to the use of multicolour printing used on pot-lids and useful wares. Such as can be seen in Plates 76 and 77. The wares are very colourful and the more common pot lid subjects can be purchased for around £20 while very rare designs, particularly of American subjects, can range up to £2,600, a price recently realised at Phillips in London. Beware of modern imitations printed by means of a photographic process.

FURTHER READING
The Pictorial Pot Lid Book by H. G. Clarke
Collecting Pot-Lids by A. Ball

RIDGWAYS

The history of this family of Shelton potters is a rather involved one but they produced such fine pieces that they long deserved a book to themselves. This will undoubtedly have a marked effect upon the value put on the firm's wares and they must be regarded as highly collectable. Fine quality blue printed earthenwares, stone china, porcelain and china were made, some of the wares up to 1830 being marked 'J. & W. Ridgway', or 'J. & W. R.' or 'J. W. R.' although most are unmarked except for pattern numbers and are frequently confused with such factories as Chamberlain, Worcester or Rockingham. John Ridgway was appointed potter to Queen Victoria and his mark was the Royal Arms with 'J R' below the central arms motif. The name finished in 1862 when Brown-Westhead, Moore & Co. bought the factory.

FURTHER READING
Ridgeway Porcelains by Geoffrey Godden

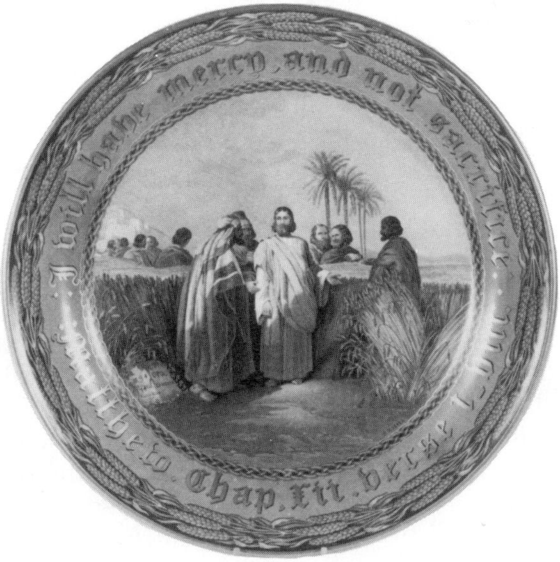

Plate 76. Pratt Ware circular dish painted in colours with Christ in the Cornfield after H. Warren, engraved for Pratt by J. Austin and produced in 1851 for the Great Exhibition.

Phillips

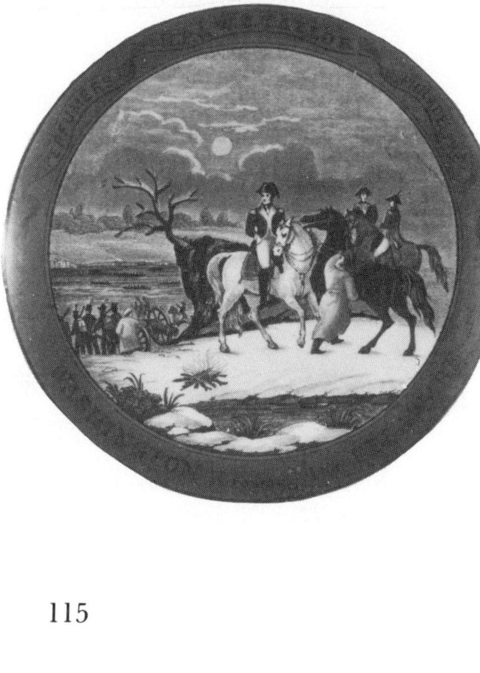

Plate 77. A Pratt Ware pot lid depicting Washington crossing the Delaware, produced for H. P. and W. C. Taylor, Perfumers, Philadelphia.

Phillips

ROBINSON & LEADBEATER 1864–1924

The Stoke firm specialised in the production of vast quantities of cheap, moulded Parian figures and ornaments, the majority of which are unmarked, although rare examples have the initials R & L within an oval. Although their poorest wares are hardly above the level of 'fairings', the best exhibit qualities of modelling and manufacture that make it imperative to look at such wares with care.

ROCKINGHAM (or SWINTON)

Although earthenware was made here from about 1745 ascription is difficult. It is not until the Leeds firm was broken in 1806 that John & William Brameld began to use the impressed word 'Brameld' as a mark. The firm ran into financial troubles and became insolvent in 1825. The following year Earl Fitzwilliam gave financial assistance, production restarted and the Earl's crest of a Griffin and the name Rockingham were used as marks and also the manufacture of porcelain started. Useful wares and great quantities of ornamental pieces—figures, animals, vases and baskets—were made as well as biscuit porcelain busts. Poor management led to the final closing of the factory in 1842.

The name Rockingham is often very loosely used, there being not only large numbers of later copies of the wares either in continental hard paste porcelain or English bone china bearing *printed* Griffin marks but also great quantities of period wares wrongly attributed to the factory. It is safe to rely

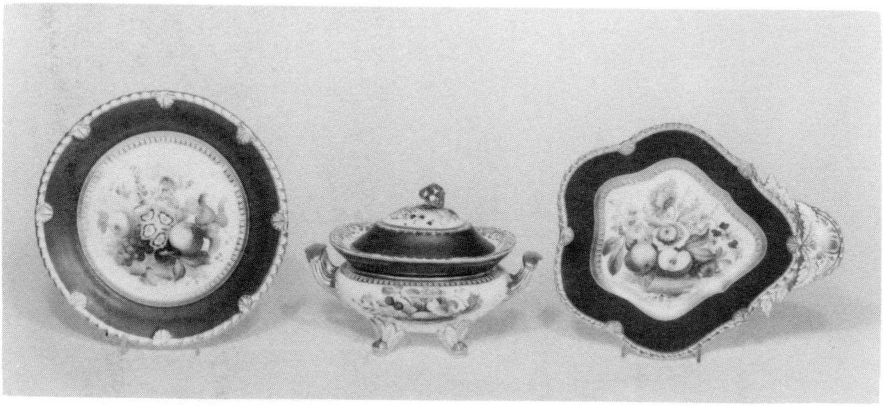

Plate 78. A Rockingham part dessert service with a claret ground and finely painted floral and fruit groups. However, wares in this style were made by a great number of factories and collectors should ensure that shapes and pattern numbers tie up before attributing wares to this factory.

Bonhams

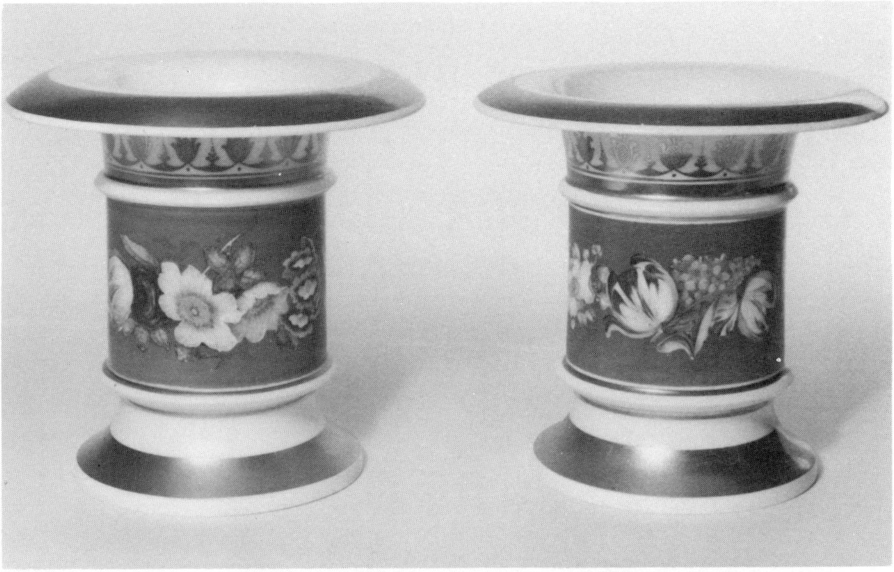

Plate 79. A pair of Rockingham vases with overhanging lips and painted bands of flowers on blue and green grounds, 5½ in., Griffin marks in red and CL 10 in gold; this not very well proportioned shape proved popular at Rockingham and these examples show the typical bright gold bands used as borders on many Rockingham pieces.

Phillips

only on genuinely marked pieces or on unmarked pieces that lie within the pattern number series known to have been used by the factory. Patterns run up to 1559 and then a series of 2/1 up to 2/78. Some figures and vases can be marked CL 1 to C L 14. The attribution to Rockingham of cottages or poodles and other animals with added clay to represent fur is on tradition rather than fact.

FURTHER READING

The Rockingham Pottery by A. A. Eaglestone & T. A. Lockett
Illustrated Guide to Rockingham Porcelain by Dr. Rice

SPODE, COPELAND & GARRETT 1770–

The firm of Spode was established by Josiah Spode in 1770. Reference is made in the earlier chapter to the eighteenth century wares but one of the most important developments in English ceramics, the invention of bone china, is usually credited to the firm just before the end of the century.

Early Spode wares are invariably of high quality. A new 'Stone China'

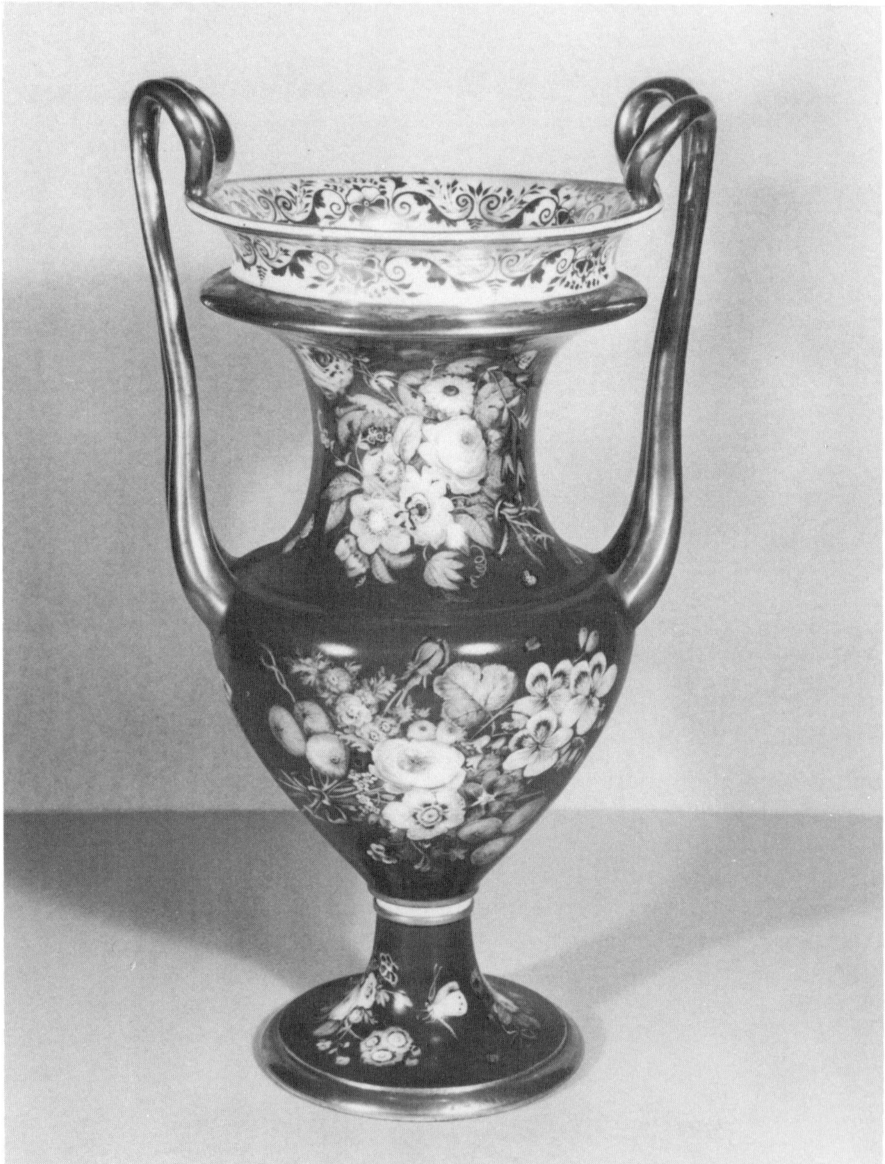

Plate 80. A Spode 'felspar porcelain' vase painted with bright flower sprays on a dark stone background, height 13¾ in., marked SPODE in red, *c.*1822.

Spode

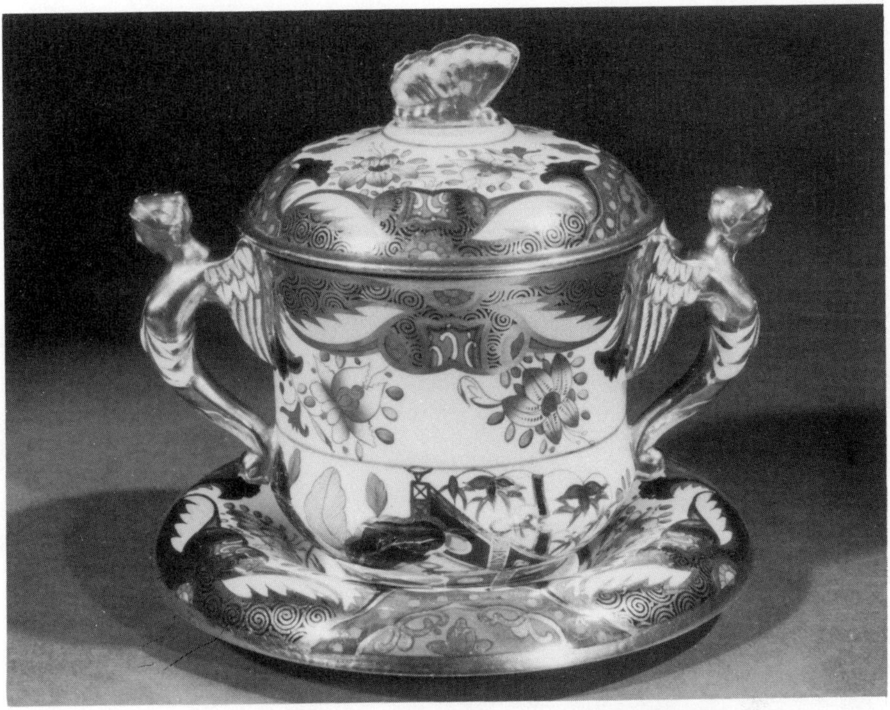

Plate 81. A Spode 'Image Handled' bowl, cover and stand painted in bright Japan colours and gold with the popular pattern 967, *c.*1815, 4½ in. high, marked SPODE and the pattern number in red.

Geoffrey Godden, Chinaman

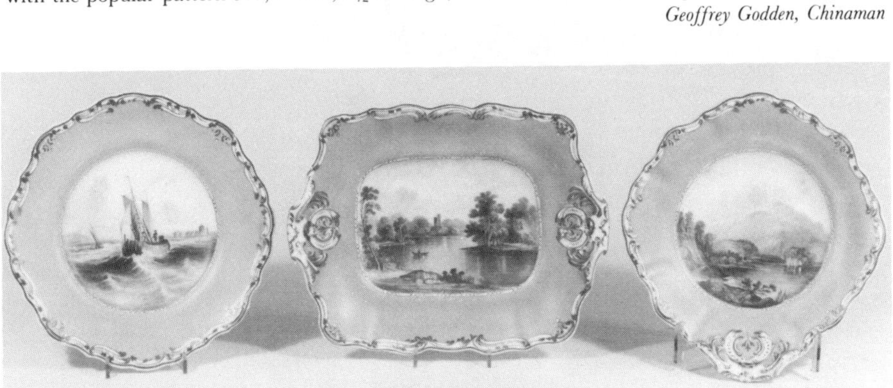

Plate 82. A Copeland and Garrett dessert service painted with named landscapes and seascapes on a lime green ground, Copeland and Garrett made a number of such services and although the painting is of good quality the shapes and ground colours are usually very much weaker.

Bonhams

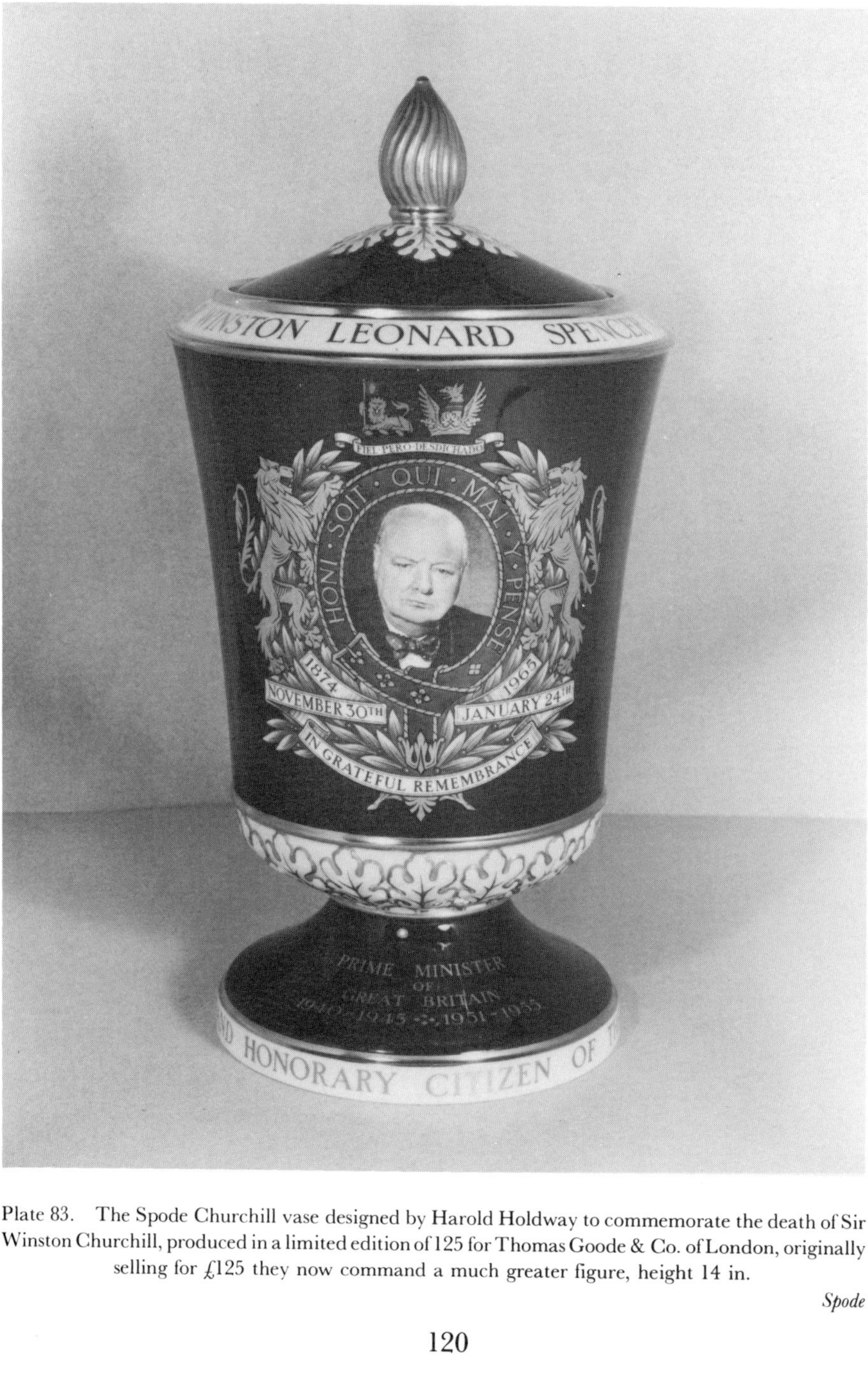

Plate 83. The Spode Churchill vase designed by Harold Holdway to commemorate the death of Sir Winston Churchill, produced in a limited edition of 125 for Thomas Goode & Co. of London, originally selling for £125 they now command a much greater figure, height 14 in.

Spode

body was introduced in 1805 and compares favourably with the later Mason's 'Ironstone'. Wares could be blue printed and these are of a fine standard and should be looked for.

In 1833 William Taylor Copeland bought the business and was joined by Thomas Garrett to establish the period of Copeland and Garrett until 1847. Early wares continued the fine standards of Spode and introduced some large animal models and plaques but among the most important pieces were the magnificent figures and groups in a parian body, the so called statuary porcelain, in the production of which Copeland & Garrett excelled, although they had their imitators. The highest quality parian figures of the 1840's–60's must surely rank as the most collectable of ceramics; they are terribly under-valued and are usually marked.

The partnership finished in 1847 and was continued by Copeland. They exhibited with great success at the Great Exhibition of 1851, large quantities of parian continued to be made and other fine wares. Most Copeland is clearly marked and in the late Victorian period often has impressed month and year marks.

FURTHER READING
Spode and his Successors by A. Hayden
Spode by Leonard Whiter

STAFFORDSHIRE FIGURES *c.* 1835–1920

Various Staffordshire firms produced huge quantities of chimney ornament type Staffordshire figures and Toby jugs right through the Victorian period and into the present century. A fresh view has recently been taken of these figures and they are now quite collectable, but care should be taken in looking at them as the quality is variable. Made from moulds, the more complicated and expensive ones are those with separate limbs and objects, which have to be produced from more than one mould as against the complete figures made in one mould, such as dogs. Named figures, especially of the rarer sort, such as prize fighters or cricketers, generally fetch more than un-named figures, but beware of modern reproductions.

SUNDERLAND

There were several potteries in the Sunderland area producing earthenwares, often decorated with splash lustre of characteristic irregular shapes, on a pale pink ground. The local Wearmouth Bridge was frequently featured in prints. Most wares are unmarked and modern reproductions of lustre have been and still are being made. Collectors should beware of

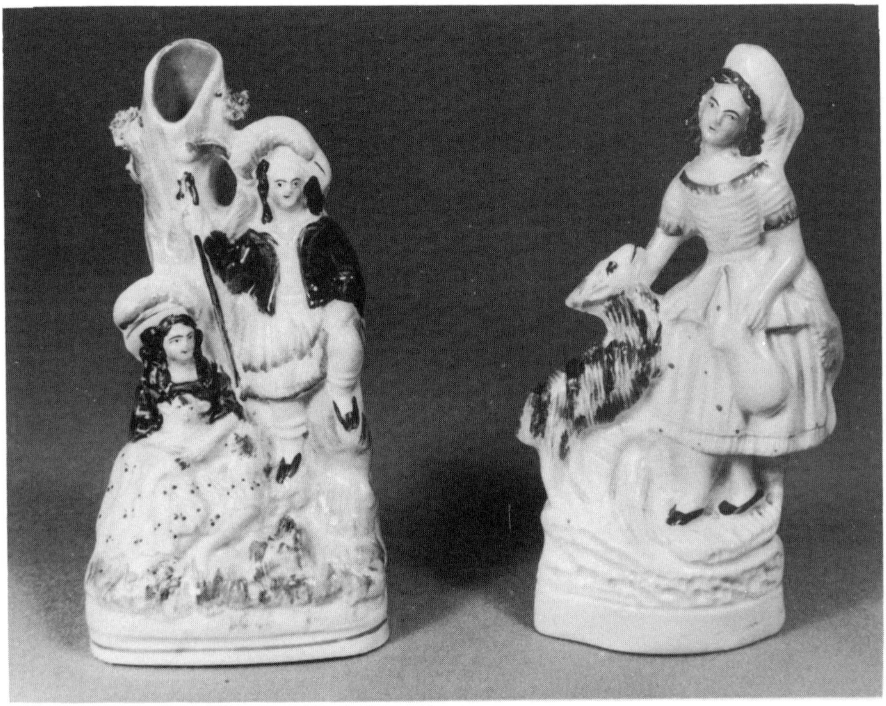

Plate 84. Staffordshire 'flat-back' chimney ornaments by Sampson Smith, *c.*1860. Figures such as these were more or less mass produced in one- or two-piece moulds and sold for a few pennies. Typical children or shepherdesses were not made as portraits and can be bought quite cheaply today.
Stoke-on-Trent City Museum

wares which look too new and those that have had the modern printed marks erased, which leaves a dull patch in the glaze. Principal factory marks are DAWSON, DIXON & SCOTT.

FURTHER READING
The Potteries of Sunderland & District—J. T. Shaw (Sunderland Museum & Art Gallery)

SUSSEX POTTERY

The name given to country wares, often similar to Devon pottery, made at a number of places in Sussex in the eighteenth and nineteenth centuries. The wares often have inlaid and slip decorations.

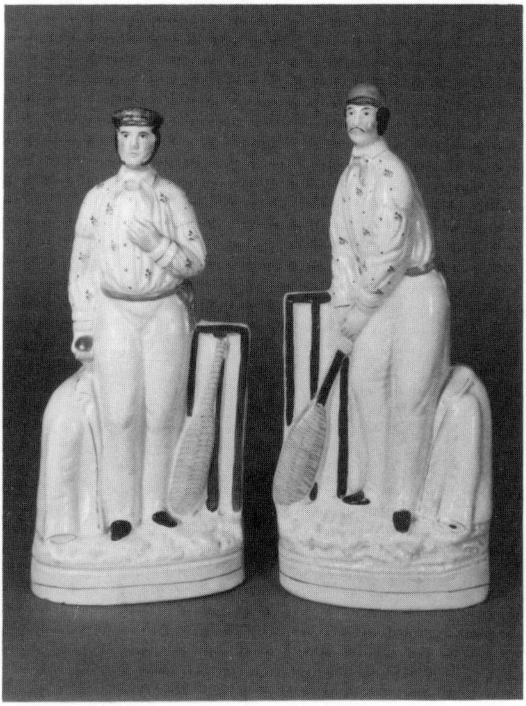

Plate 85. A pair of Staffordshire 'Portrait' figures of cricketers probably representing the batsman Julius Caesar (yes, that was his real name) and bowler George Parr. Sporting figures are among the most sought after Staffordshire figures but the collector should beware of large numbers of reproductions of the cricketers and the prizefighters 'Heenan and Sayers'. The copies are usually very lightweight and smaller than the originals, these figures being 13½ in. and 14 in. high.

Phillips

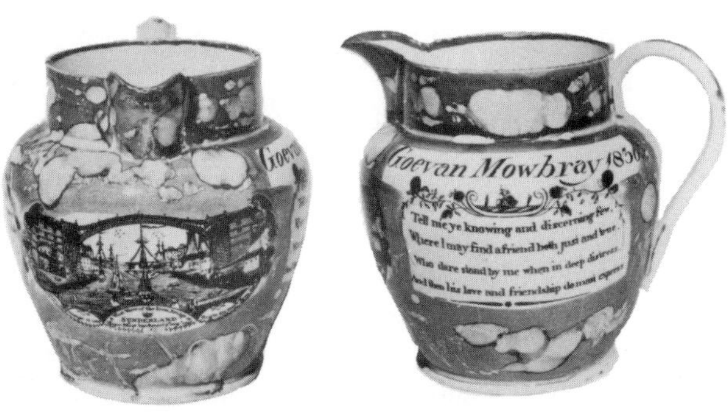

Plate 86. Two views of a Sunderland jug showing the bridge opened in 1797, made for Goevan Mowbray in 1836, decorated with hand-coloured transfer prints and a splashed pink lustre ground with typical irregular patches.

Sunderland Museum and Art Gallery

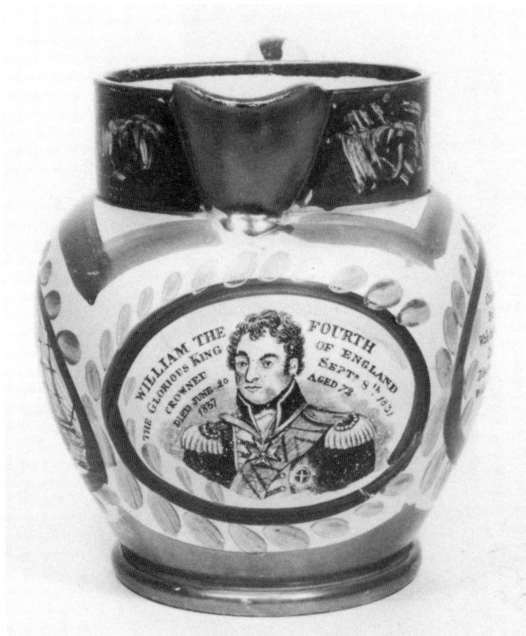

Plate 87. A Sunderland jug bearing a rare print commemorating the death of William IV in 1837, the ground naïvely painted in pink lustre and red and green enamels, probably by young children.
Phillips

SWANSEA to about 1870

Large quantities of pottery have been made in Swansea at the Cambrian Pottery from about 1764, the most interesting being cream-wares with botanical painting, or plates with lustre decoration, sometimes marked 'Dillwyn & Co.' or 'Swansea'. The most sought after wares are fine porcelains produced between 1814 and 1817 by Billingsley and Walker who came to Swansea from Nantgarw at the suggestion of Dillwyn. The translucent warm porcelain was often sent to London for decoration and collectors must beware of fakes. The general mark is the word 'Swansea', the most reliable form being impressed in the body, with or without tridents.

FURTHER READING
Swansea Porcelain by W. D. John
The Pottery and Porcelain of Swansea and Nantgarw by E. M. Nance

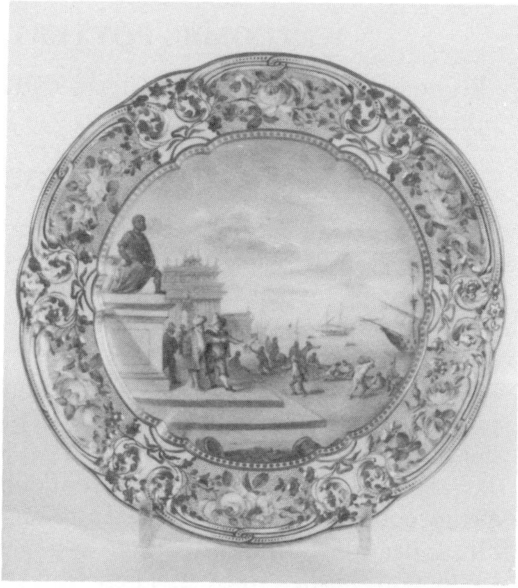

Plate 88. A Swansea plate richly painted by a London decorator with a harbour scene and border of roses and gold dots, 8½ in. diameter. The independent artists painted on wares from several factories but the quality of moulding and superior paste confirm a Swansea attribution.

Bonhams

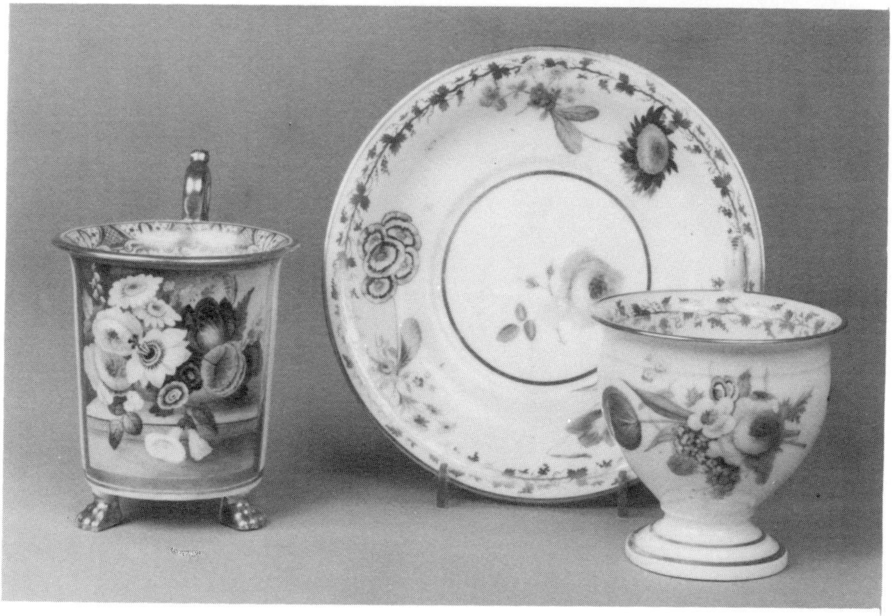

Plate 89. A Swansea cabinet cup, and cup stand, each finely painted with delicate floral designs, the shapes showing the influence of French Empire porcelain.

Christies

WATCOMBE POTTERY CO. 1867–1901

Produced earthenwares and terra cotta, the latter not yet being fully appreciated.

WEDGWOOD

The nineteenth century wares of this great factory are nowhere near as highly priced as the eighteenth century ones and differences in the markings can help to date pieces, these marks being found in *Godden's Encyclopaedia of Marks*, where also is to be found the system of year mark codes.

The earliest interesting wares of the nineteenth century are the all over splashed pink lustres with marbled effects, often called 'Moonlight' lustre (not to be confused with the later 'Fairy' lustre) and made between about 1805–1815. Owing to financial difficulties with earthenware, Josiah Wedgwood the second introduced a china, the glaze of which has a mellow, soft appearance that gives the appearance of being opaque but its production finished in 1822. These wares are relatively rare and generally carry the printed mark 'WEDGWOOD'.

The generally recognised Wedgwood wares of jasper, creamware and basalt continued to be made, although the quality was not as high as in the

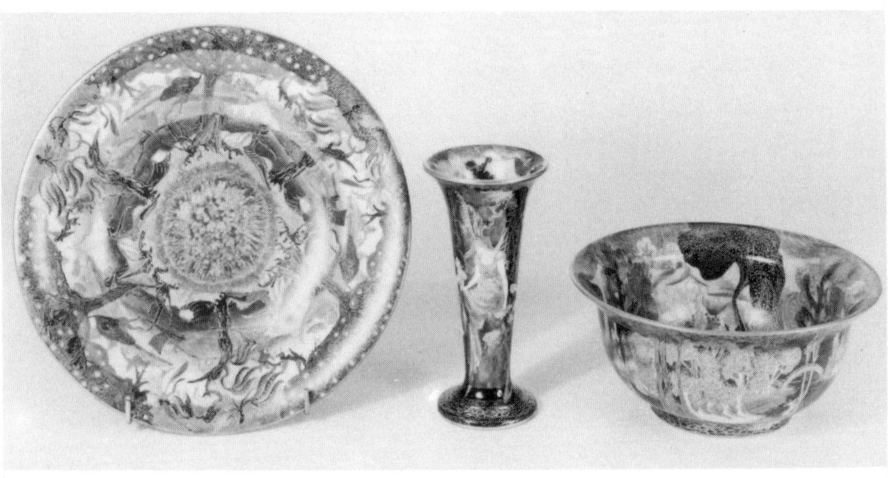

Plate 90. Group of Wedgwood 'Fairyland' lustre wares designed by Daisy Makeig-Jones, the bowl and circular dish with elves and gnomes among trees, the vase with the Queen of the Fairies, each in bright colours and gold. The vase 6 in. high, Portland Vase marks in gold.

Phillips

previous century, apart from some finely painted creamwares painted by the Frenchman Emile Lessore who went to Wedgwood's after a few months at Minton's in 1858. Such was the regard in which he was held that when he returned to France in 1867 to escape from the black smoke of the furnaces, the Company sent blanks over to him for painting, these being returned for subsequent firing and sale. Most of his pieces were signed.

Other interesting wares are majolicas, the parian (called 'Carrara') and three coloured jasper (white and two colours). This century's wares present collectors with an opportunity of buying Wedgwood at considerably lower prices than for those of the previous century and it can also be said that the wares of our present century are very collectable especially the paintings of the Powells. Now highly collectable are the 'fairyland' lustre bowls and vases showing elves, gnomes and fairies in moonlight scenes produced from 1914 by Daisy Makeig-Jones rather under the inspiration of the art nouveau movement, describing her work as 'such stuff as dreams are made of'. She retired in 1935.

FURTHER READING

Early Wedgwood Lustre Wares by W. D. John and J. Sincox
Wedgwood Ware by W. B. Honey
Wedgwood Fairyland Lustre by Una des Fontaine

WEMYSS WARE

Robert Heron and son at the Fife of Gallatown Pottery, Sinclairtown, Kirkcaldy, Scotland, from about 1850–1929 produced earthenwares painted in gaudy colours with bold designs of roses, thistles and other plants and animals—now quite sought after. Especially collectable are models of pigs and cats, which were also painted with typical roses, and commemorative pieces such as those made for Queen Victoria's jubilee.

WORCESTER

As the nineteenth century began there were three fine factories in the City—Flight & Barr, Chamberlain and Grainger.

FLIGHT & BARR

The families of the Flights & Barrs carried on the manufacture of the finest porcelain and later bone china, at Warmstry House, various deaths in the families and the consequent moving up a peg of the members causing changes in the title of the firm which help to date the wares—which are

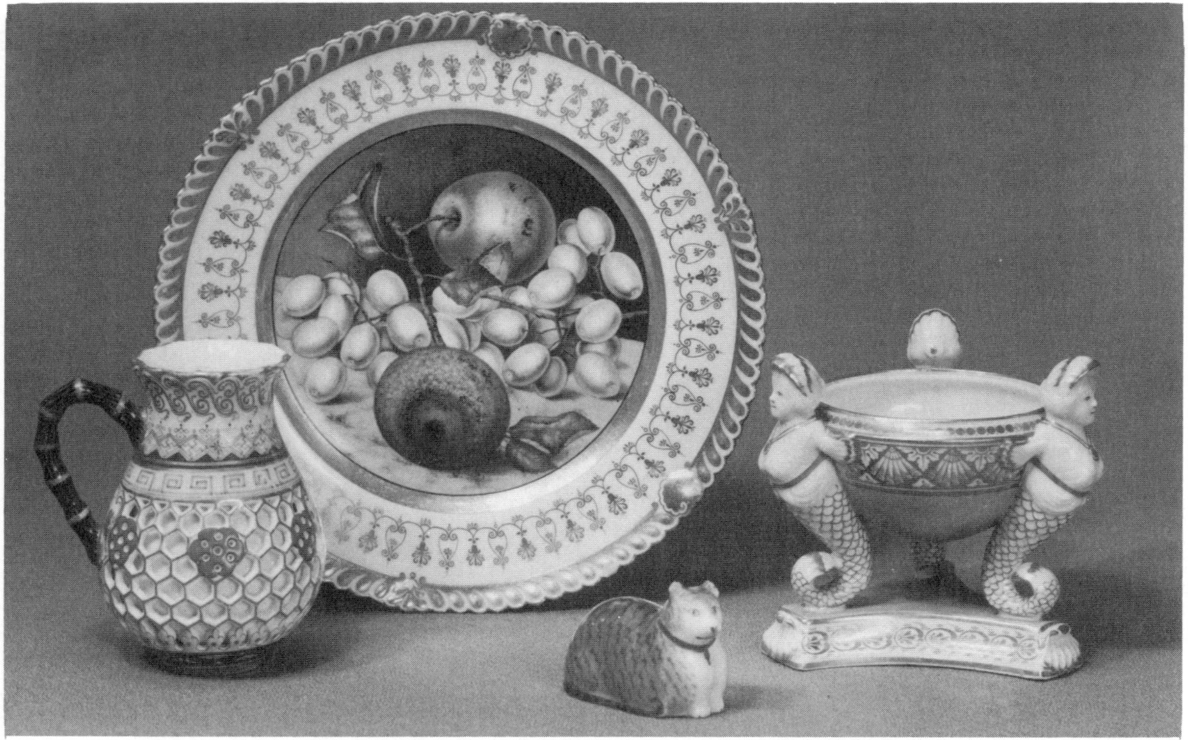

Plate 91. Four pieces from the Worcester factory of Chamberlain, the bowl supported by mermaids *c.* 1820; a hollow model of a cat with painted fur, one of a number of small animal models; a fine 'Regent China' plate with richly painted fruit by Thomas Baxter, *c.* 1820, and a double-walled jug, one vessel luted into another and the outside one pierced, exhibited at the Great Exhibition of 1851.

Dyson Perrins Museum, Worcester

almost invariably marked. Thus Flight & Barr from 1792–1804, Barr Flight & Barr 1804–1813 and Flight Barr & Barr 1813–1840.

In the Flight & Barr period pieces continue to be marked with the curious lop-sided incised 'B' or the words 'Flight & Barr' under a crown. The quality of painting continued the improvement that was seen after Barr joined the factory in 1793 and an interesting introduction was 'bat' printing of a very high standard. Shapes, especially of teapots, are very fine and characteristic and gilding is always of superb quality.

Barr Flight & Barr, from 1804–1813, produced wares of outstanding quality, especially in the field of armorial services, always a great speciality of this factory. The mark is either the full name, with additional details printed or written, or the impressed initials 'B. F. B.'. Sometimes the mark of Flight & Barr is found in addition and this most likely indicates ware made in the earlier and decorated in the later period. Fine decorators were employed in this and the next period, such as Barker and Baxter, shells and feathers and Pennington, figure subjects in monochrome. Billingsley was employed for a short while to carry out experiments on a new translucent porcelain body, but left for Nantgarw, taking the results of his experiments with him, to the annoyance of the firm.

From 1813 the title changed to Flight Barr & Barr, wares being fully marked or having the impressed initials F. B. B. The continuing use of the typical fine blue ground colour is rivalled by a splendid strong green, rather like that of a Granny Smith apple. The quality is always of the highest and contrasts with the other Worcester factories of the period, whose quality could be variable. Flight and Barr really strike one as a dilettante firm of potters, delighting in perfect quality for its own sake and not as if they were in business to make money. An interesting anecdote by R. W. Binns—later Managing Director of Royal Worcester—describes how the partners went round the factory exhorting the workmen to greater and greater artistic effort.

But in 1840 Flight, Barr & Barr amalgamated with Chamberlain and moved to the latter's larger factory site at Diglis, the buildings being enlarged. Mr Binns referred to the amalgamation as a 'marriage of convenience and not of love'. The Warmstry House factory was used by the new firm, Chamberlain & Co. for the production of floor tiles and it was later sold to Messrs Maw, who used it for the same purpose before moving to Shropshire.

FURTHER READING

Flight and Barr Worcester Porcelains by Henry Sandon

CHAMBERLAIN

The Diglis factory of Chamberlain generally produced good quality porcelain in the early years of the century. In 1802 Lord Nelson visited the factory and placed an order for a complete breakfast, dinner and dessert service in one of Chamberlain's favourite Japan patterns with the addition of the Admiral's coat of arms, crests and mottos. So difficult was the service to decorate that only the breakfast service had been completed by the time of Nelson's death at Trafalgar in 1805, the remainder of the order being cancelled; but the capture of such an order quickly led to more including some for royal services and the firm flourished. During the Regency period a fine translucent porcelain called Regent China was produced, but kiln losses were very great and the ware correspondingly expensive. Decoration put on this body was generally of high standard and any Chamberlain ware marked Regent China should be snapped up. Some excellent decorators worked for Chamberlain, such as Humphrey Chamberlain and Thomas Baxter, the most keenly sought type of decoration being shells and feathers.

Most Chamberlain important pieces are marked, although early tea wares can often have the name only on one of the major items of the service, often put under the cover of the teapot or sugar box. The marks are very helpful in dating the piece as the wording of the mark was constantly changing; reference should be made to the *Encyclopaedia of British Pottery & Porcelain Marks* by Geoffrey Godden. In the 1820's and 30's some biscuit porcelain cottages, figures and busts were produced and a number of florally encrusted pieces of fine quality, which, if unmarked may be wrongly called 'Coalbrookdale'. Small animals—dogs and cats—were also made but were very rarely marked and probably masquerade as Rockingham. Favourite scenes used to decorate pieces were, of course, local ones, in particular Worcester and Malvern, but it should not be assumed that every piece decorated with such subjects would have come from the Worcester factories, as books of engravings could be bought and used by any factory.

In 1840 Flight Barr & Barr joined Chamberlain and the factory was called Chamberlain & Co. until 1851. This eleven year period was not a good one, whether through the lack of competition from the other factory or some other cause, the china became crude, thick and often heavily crazed and the factory produced some rather un-Worcester-like items, such as floor tiles, door furniture, false teeth and buttons, the latter, especially, being a financial disaster. The only wares of this period to evoke lukewarm praise at the 1851 Great Exhibition being the interesting double reticulated wares—one pot being luted into another and the outside body

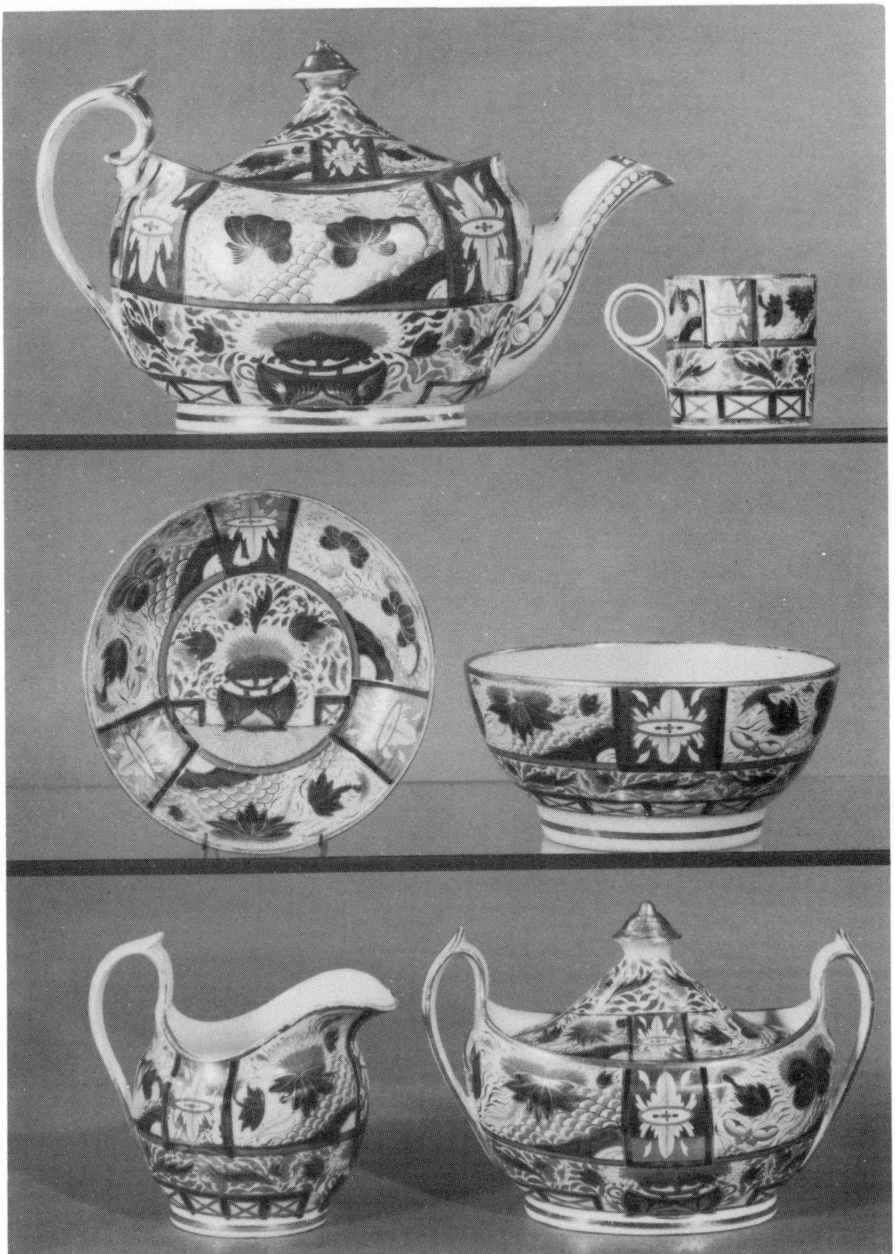

Plate 92. A Grainger Worcester tea service painted with a colourful Japan pattern, the design also used by Chamberlain and at Coalport, but here on typical Grainger shapes *c.*1810, the undersides of the covers marked Grainger & Co. Worcester Warranted, No. 140.

Geoffrey Godden, Chinaman

pierced. These wares are now very keenly sought. In 1852 the factory was taken over by two men W. H. Kerr (a Chamberlain & Co. partner) and R. W. Binns.

KERR and BINNS PERIOD

This period from 1852 to 1862 brought about an incredible revival in the standards of a factory that had almost sunk to rock bottom. Binns was a man of exceptional qualities and seemed to produce an overnight miracle, witness the fantastic 'Shakespeare' service produced for the Dublin Exhibition of 1853, and later bought by the gentlemen of Ireland for presentation to the Lord Lieutenant, the parian modelling added to the large china vessels representing scenes from A Midsummer Night's Dream modelled by W. B. Kirk. An interesting link with Ireland was forged by Kerr, an Irishman, as he helped to discover a suitable source of stone for porcelain manufacture at Belleek, some of the experiments on the ware being done at Worcester, who also used some Irish stone in their body and made some wares which are very similar to the iridescent parian of Belleek. Very fine parian figures and busts were made and also some interesting black coloured wares looking like basalt. A splendid group of decorators were emerging, such as Thomas Bott: white 'Limoges' enamel scenes on dark blue—Joseph Williams: scenes—Josiah Rushton: female figure subjects and copies of classical subjects and the Callowhill brothers; fine gilding was done by Josiah Davis. Three marks were in use in this period, a very rare one using the words W. H. Kerr & Co. Worcester printed in blue, an impressed circle with scrolling W's surrounding a crescent and 51 (standing for 1751, the year of founding of the factory) in the centre, this impressed mark sometimes being very difficult to see unless the piece is held up to a strong light, and a mark of a shield with 'K & B' at the top, the word Worcester in a scroll across the shield the last two numbers of the year of manufacture and sometimes the initials of the decorator. The shield mark was put on pieces of which the proprietors were most proud and can be relied upon to be fine and collectable items. Typical ordinary decorations were of grasses, wild flowers and butterflies.

A fine and most interesting collection could be made of the wares of this ten-year period alone.

ROYAL PORCELAIN COMPANY

When Kerr retired in 1862 Binns took the opportunity of forming a joint stock company under the title it has had ever since. The company was very prosperous but the hopes of building a fine new garden factory in the Arboretum Pleasure Gardens was thwarted by lack of finance so the Diglis

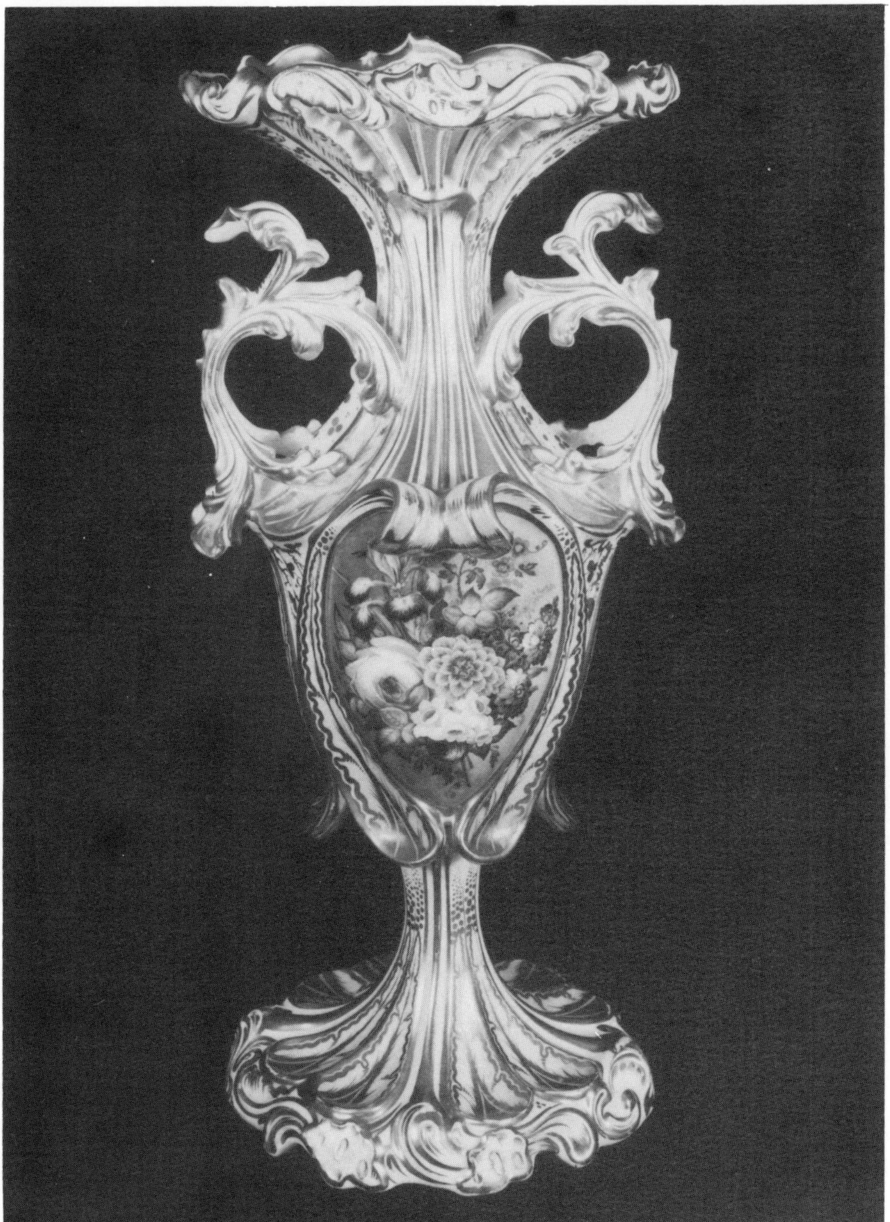

Plate 93. An impressive Grainger Worcester vase of scroll moulded form, the pale green ground with foliate gilding, finely painted with a bouquet of flowers, $16\frac{1}{2}$ in. high, marked G. Grainger, Worcester in red script.

Phillips

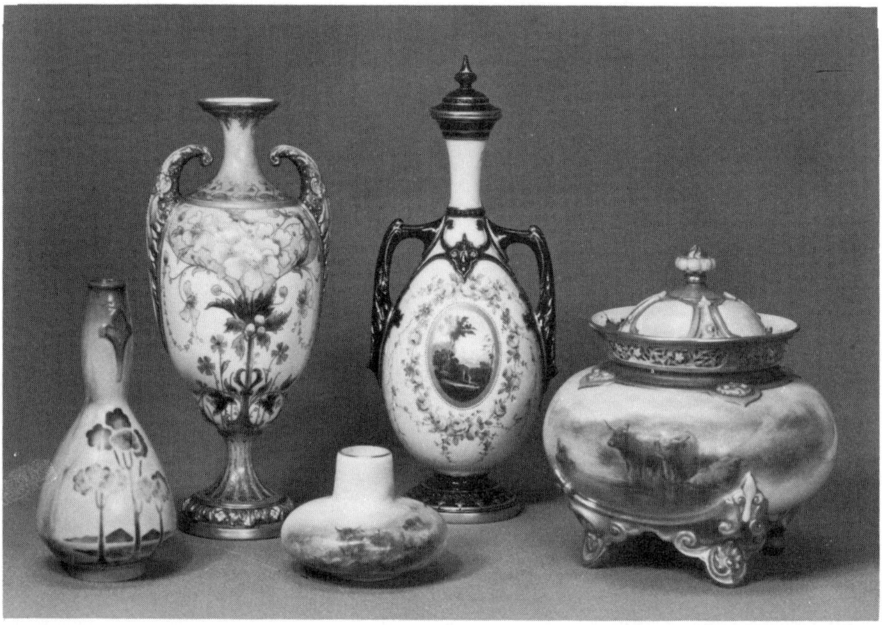

Plate 94. Group of Royal Worcester pieces of the first quarter of this century, from left to right; a Sabrina Ware vase; an Art Nouveau style handled vase; a small pot painted with Highland cattle by Harry Stinton; a vase and cover with dark blue mounts and panel painted in the Claude style by Harry Davis; roses by Hawkins, height 12 in., pot-pourri vase and cover with Highland cattle by John Stinton.
Dyson Perrins Museum, Worcester. Davis Vase in Author's Collection

factory was extended. The Kerr & Binns circle mark was continued with the addition of a crown above the circle. Usually the last two numbers of the year of manufacture are placed under the circle, e.g. 68 for 1868, or a system of code letters or symbols for the various years, which can be found in the mark book previously referred to. As well as fine bone china, parian was continued and also earthenwares were made coloured in the style of majolica or French faience, especially *Henri Deux* type wares. Ivory porcelain decorated with Raphaelesque or Capo di Monte colours were a speciality of the 1860's, sometimes with the addition of beautiful 'jewels' of enamels. Pierced wares continued to be made, the finest of all being by George Owen who had the unique ability to do incredibly intricate geometric piercing without any pattern being impressed or marked on the raw clay, his skill being helped by his being ambidextrous. All Owen's later work has the signature G. Owen scratched into the base and his pieces stand out as pearls among the ordinary reticulated work of other workmen.

Mr. Binns speedily worked through three most interesting art movements—all based on his great love of Eastern ceramics; first Persian shaped vessels, then Japanesque style and finally Stained Ivory. The last two styles are very collectable, especially the curious shapes and decoration based on Japanese art—diamond shaped teaware, bamboo spill vases, pots with elephant head handles and legs and decoration of symmetrical circles, fans and gilded swans. These wares can still be picked up cheaply, not yet being in the public taste again. Stained ivory was an attempt to imitate matured, mellow ivory and was made in different colours which are often inaccurately referred to nowadays as bisque or biscuit wares (a confusing term as biscuit is, of course, the term for unglazed porcelain and china). These wares can look rather sombre and were often encumbered with superfluous ornamentation and seem to be out of favour nowadays, but the qualities of making are so fine that it is necessary sometimes to shut one's eyes to what we think of as eccentricities.

The chief modeller during this period was James Hadley, a modeller of great talent who produced fine models of vases, large figures such as water carriers—male and female making a pair, and small figures for use as ornaments or menu supporters and candle extinguishers which are hollow underneath. Some figures have the name Hadley moulded on them but these figures were not, of course, actually made by Hadley, who only produced the original model. Hadley eventually went freelance, working from his Worcester studio, although his entire production was bought by Royal Worcester. Another modeller who produced two fine models was Thomas (later Sir Thomas) Brock R. A., who created 'The Bather Surprised' and 'The Violinist'. Hadley was later to start his own firm, which Royal Worcester subsequently bought after his death, as they had also bought the factory of Grainger in 1889.

Great painters worked for Royal Worcester, such as the incredible Stinton family, especially John Stinton, who painted highland cattle, signing the work J. Stinton, starting at Grainger's as did his brother James who painted game birds, signing as Jas. Stinton. John's son Harry also painted Highland cattle and signed H. Stinton. The wares of these three are very collectable and always of high quality. John and Harry painted so much Highland Cattle between them that old factory workers said they grew to look like the cattle themselves. John, born in 1854, died in 1956.

Other wares of collectable interest made before the end of the century were art nouveau style vases, Sabrina ware and fruit painting of a naturalistic sort with mossy backgrounds (still done to this day). One of the greatest twentieth century ceramic painters, Harry Davis, joined the factory at the age of 13 in 1898, at first painting landscapes in a style reminiscent of Claude, then specialising in sheep and cattle in Highland settings and English castles. Other great painters, who were allowed to sign pieces about the 1890's, were Hawkins (flowers) Sebright (fruit) and Powell (birds). Hawkins was followed as foreman painter by Harry Davis, who, on retirement as foreman, was in turn followed by Edward Townsend.

GRAINGER'S FACTORY

This factory spans the whole of the nineteenth century—founded in 1801 by Thomas Grainger, who had married Robert Chamberlain's daughter, and production finally finished in 1902, the business having been bought by Royal Worcester in 1889. The period from 1801 to 1812 is called the Grainger Wood period, very few of the wares being marked and most bought in the white from other factories for decoration. In 1812 the factory was rebuilt following a fire and the period to 1837 is called Grainger Lee and Co. Few of the wares of this period are marked and are often ascribed to other better known factories. Sometimes pattern numbers are used, which can be a help in sorting out an ascription, as most of the pattern books are still preserved by Royal Worcester. In 1839 Thomas Grainger died and was succeeded by his son George, the mark becoming G. Grainger & Co. Fine underglaze blue printing was done, good reticulated wares and parian made, and a fine earthenware body called 'semi porcelain' introduced, sometimes marked 'S. P.' From 1870 a shield mark with 'G & Co.' above a 'W' and the City of Worcester crest of three black pears was used, the mark becoming more elaborate in 1889 with the addition of the words 'Royal China Works'.

The best of the factory's wares must be regarded as highly collectable.

JAMES HADLEY & SONS

This short lived factory (1896–1905) produced what must now possibly be the most collectable of Victorian ceramics. Of superb form, as can be assured from the models of James Hadley, often decorated with an interesting method of different coloured clay mounts and additions, produced by putting the different clays into separate parts of the mould. Two main forms of mark were used—the script word 'Hadley' sometimes in a scroll, or a beautiful monogram mark incorporating the letters J. H. & S. Faience of great quality was made, figurines, terrocotta modelled plaques and vases often painted with the unique Hadley flowers typified by very full blown roses. This style of painting and a number of the shapes were continued by Royal Worcester after their purchase of the factory, by Hadley's workmen who moved the few yards back to the main factory.

LOCKE & CO.

This small factory, established under the arches of Shrub Hill railway station, by Edward Locke in 1895, was never bought up by the main

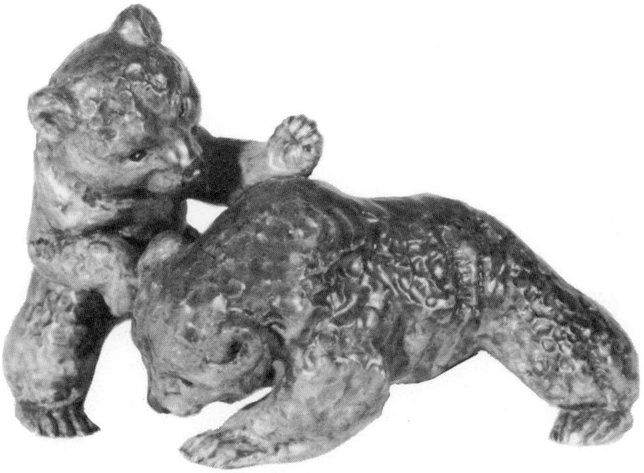

Plate 95. Royal Worcester model of two bear cubs at play, charmingly modelled by Doris Lindner from bears at the London Zoo and produced in 1940 as one of a series of 'Zoo babies'; production was very limited and these animal subjects of the 1930's and 40's are certainly worth looking out for, probably being much rarer than most pieces made in the 18th century, and now starting to show a considerable rise in price.
Author's Collection

factory and their wares do not count as Royal Worcester. Some can be attractively decorated but the material was such a poor one and Locke's mark of a globe with the word Worcester across it was causing confusion in foreign dealers' minds that Royal Worcester finally took the Company to court in 1904, obtaining an injunction forbidding them the use of the word 'Worcester' on their ware, such word being regarded as a Trade Mark, an injunction which still applies and caused Locke to go out of business within a few months. The wares are only of minor interest.

FURTHER READING
Royal Worcester Porcelain from 1862 by Henry Sandon

9 The Twentieth Century

This section brings our story up to the present day.

A few years ago it would not have been thought that ceramics of our own time could seriously be put forward as sensible items to put money into. So many collectors still have the very prejudiced idea that the production of fine ceramics stopped in 1800—nothing of any quality having been made since. But market values, and a great number of people, would not agree with them.

It is a sobering thought that in the great ceramic collection in the Dyson Perrins Museum, devoted only to Worcester ware, it is not the great vases painted by Donaldson or the rare ground coloured vessels of the eighteenth century, nor the fine garnitures of vases or the wine coolers painted by Baxter in the nineteenth century that are insured for the greatest amount, but a pair of limited edition birds from the series modelled by Dorothy Doughty and made just before, during and after the last war for the United States market. One particular pair of Bob White Quails, made in 1940 in an edition of 23 pairs only, fetched an incredible price of 37,000 dollars at public auction in the U.S.A. and the Museum pair from this edition carries the highest insurance in the Collection.

Limited editions are items such as figure groups, vases, mugs, etc. which are made in a strictly controlled number. When this number has been reached the moulds from which they were made are destroyed, so the purchaser knows that there are only so many, say 100 or 500, in existence in the world. Inevitably a number of these end up in Museums, or Board Rooms from whence they will not reach the open market and when one comes up at public auction the interest shown can be very great. As a case in point a Royal Worcester limited edition of 100 models of the Queen on the police horse Tommy, was made in 1947 to commemorate the first time she took the Trooping of the Colour ceremony when Princess Elizabeth. At an original cost of 100 guineas, the last one to come on the open market fetched £6,500 in 1977, an incredible increase in only 30 years.

There is no doubt that limited editions are here to stay and while the last pieces in the edition are still being completed some of the earlier ones can be sold at the major auction houses, sure proof of the seal of approval that is now put upon them. Such figure subjects as Royal Worcester's Arkle modelled by Doris Lindner, who was also responsible for the model of the statuette of the Queen, have become legends in their own time, changing hands at hundreds of pounds above their purchase price even before the edition is completed.

A number of companies have ventured into the field of limited editions, especially to commemorate special events. Not all these pieces can honestly be put forward as the great antiques of the future and many will go down into history with the same regard that we have for a lot of the poor commemorative wares made for the Coronations of King Edward VIII and George VI. One's critical senses should still be keenly applied to pieces, even limited edition ones, but there is no doubt that the best of these make magnificent investments, as well as providing great aesthetic pleasure. A number of illustrations are given in the book which should go a long way to explain the view that is now becoming much more strongly held that the best wares of the present can certainly hold their own against the best of the past, and with the greater technical knowledge that has come in this century, especially the use of modern kilns, has come the ability of making completely free standing figures. One of the most recent firms in the limited edition market is Hereford Fine China whose wares have reached a high standard of realism.

The leading companies of the present day are still producing fine domestic wares, although the increasing use of lithographic printing has taken over from the more traditional, but costly, hand painting and transfer printing. The best of lithos should not be scorned, however, as tremendous work and expertise goes into the production of a finally produced pattern. A considerable quantity of hand work is still done by the best of British factories, and those with great traditions stretching back to the eighteenth century are still among the finest in the world. Some recommended types of wares are shown in the illustrations in this book and the only way in which modern factories can possibly be faulted is their too frequent mere trading on the past, the production of wares that look virtually the same as those that the factory was making a hundred years before.

Forward looking companies are abundant, fortunately, such as Doulton, Minton, Spode, Wedgwood and Worcester, to mention just a few.

The craftsmen potters movement is one of the most interesting of this century and among the best of these wares must lie many potential antiques of the future, although it is unlikely that the rate of increase in values will be as rapid as those previously mentioned. The classical craftsman potter in this country, in general, is very influenced by early Chinese pottery—especially of the Tang and Sung dynasties, and also the wares of the English Medieval period and is typified by the grand old man himself, Bernard Leach, who might also be regarded as the father of the movement.

Most of the finest pieces made in this century are stonewares, with decoration and glaze often based upon that of the early Chinese, the glazes often derived from wood ash and the decoration in resist. There are many fine potters, either still potting or now retired or no longer in this country and a very good selection of most of the country's leading craftsmen can be seen in the Craftsmen Potters' Shop in Marshall Street in London's West End, a non-profit making enterprise which sells the wares of the members, who are only admitted and allowed to show their pots on the approval of their technical qualities by their fellow members.

10 Art Pottery in England

The Art Pottery movement sprang from a reaction against industrially produced artefacts in the 1830's. The idea of National Art Education was formed in the late 1830's and by the 1840's Henry Cole edited the Journal of Design and Manufacture. Cole designed plain elegant shapes for Minton as did A. W. N. Pugin, another exponent of the new ideas in art. Pugin looked back to Gothic art as had John Ruskin, who wrote in *The Nature of Gothic* that imagination and spontaneity characteristic of best Gothic craftsmanship was infinitely finer than engine-turned precision.

Ruskin's work tempted many people to buy crude Doulton rather than elegant Wedgwood and Worcester.

Doulton. In the 1850's Doulton was the leading manufacturer of domestic and industrial stoneware and under the influence of Ruskin and Edward Gresy, a medievalist friend of Henry Doulton, reproductions of Rhenish Stoneware were produced early in the 1860's. John Sparkes, headmaster of the Lambeth School of Art had tried unsuccessfully before this to encourage Doulton to try Art Pottery, but in 1863 he had more successful influence modelling ceramic busts to decorate the façade of Doulton's Lambeth factory. Sparkes also suggested that George Tinworth, a Lambeth School of Art trained sculptor, should join Doulton. In 1867 the Paris Exhibition showed 30 pieces by Tinworth in Gothic style. The Art Pottery Movement had arrived.

Doulton specialised in saltgalzed stoneware with carved Gothic design

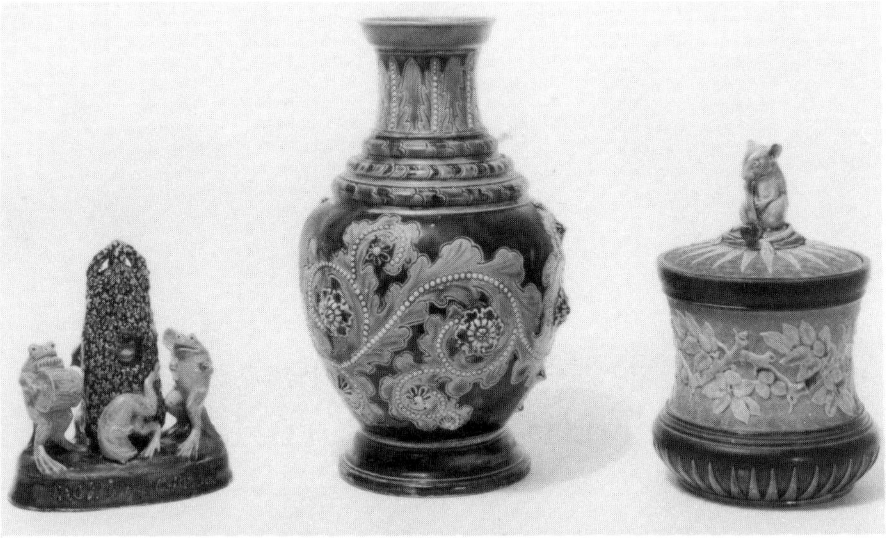

Plate 96. Group of Doulton Wares by George Tinworth. *Left:* an amusing figure group 'Jack in the Green' with playful frogs, one hiding inside a bush, *centre:* an early vase dated 1874, 9½ in.; *right:* a tobacco jar, the finial formed as a mouse smoking a pipe, 7 in., each marked with GT monogram. *Phillips*

in coloured glazes. One of the finest artists was Hannah Barlow, who incised animals into the unfired stoneware, her designs highlighted with coloured staining. John Sparkes wrote 'She possessed a certain Japanese tendency of representing the largest amount of fact in the fewest lines, all correct and all embodying in a high degree the essential character of her subject'. George Tinworth designed some charming animal groups, his subjects having enormous human characteristics. Models of mice and frogs in humorous situations, all signed with his monogram. Arthur Barlow, Hannah's brother, typified Doulton's stoneware. "His ornament is original, a flowering, tumbling wealth of vegetable forms wreath around the jug, now and then fixed by a boss or pinned down by a point of modelled form."

The carved stoneware remained popular until the twentieth century, when other attractive styles were adapted. 'Titanian ware' was painted bone china stained with various colours, rather like the 'Sabrina Ware' of Worcester. 'Sung Ware' with streaks of dark colours on a rich red flambé ground, and the finest of all, 'Chang Ware', devised by Charles Noke, thick dribbling glazes in various colours on a basically red ground. The more standard foliate stoneware can still be bought for reasonable prices, whilst better known artists and Sung and Chang can cost you several hundreds of pounds.

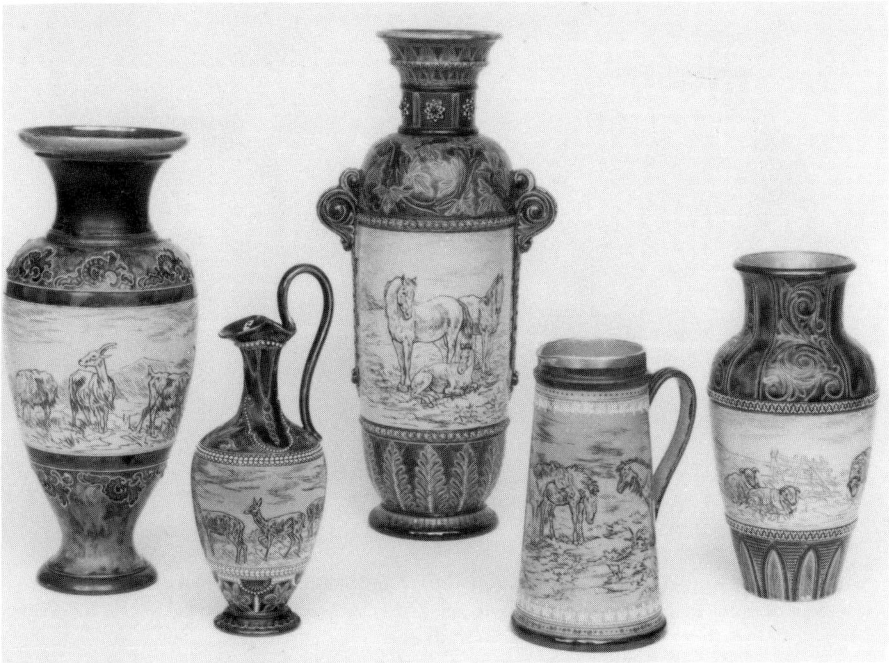

Plate 97. Group of Doulton Wares by Hannah Barlow, each with a typical frieze of sgrafitto scenes of farm animals and deer, dating from the 1870's and 1880's, central vase 16 in. high, each with HBB monogram. *Phillips*

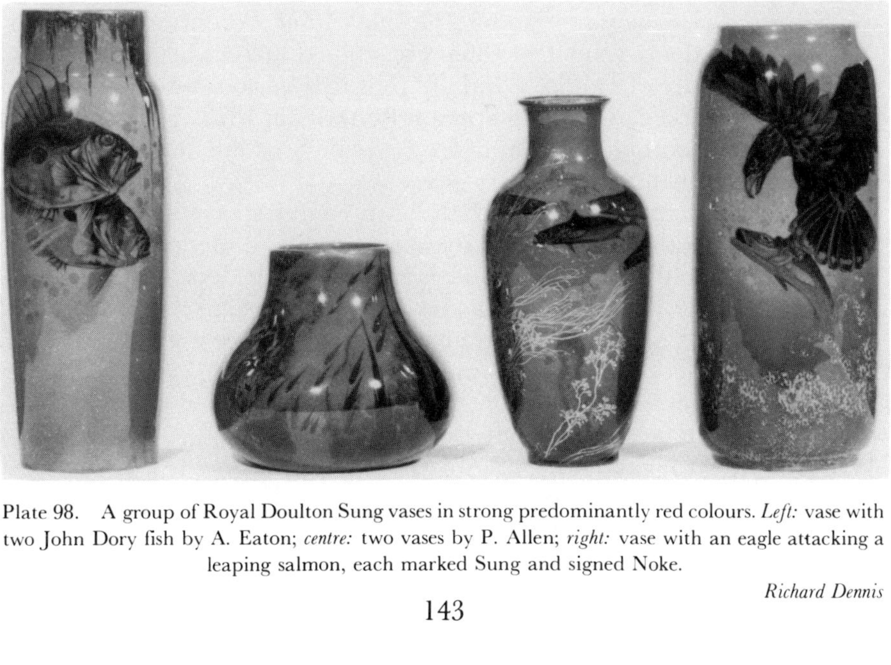

Plate 98. A group of Royal Doulton Sung vases in strong predominantly red colours. *Left:* vase with two John Dory fish by A. Eaton; *centre:* two vases by P. Allen; *right:* vase with an eagle attacking a leaping salmon, each marked Sung and signed Noke. *Richard Dennis*

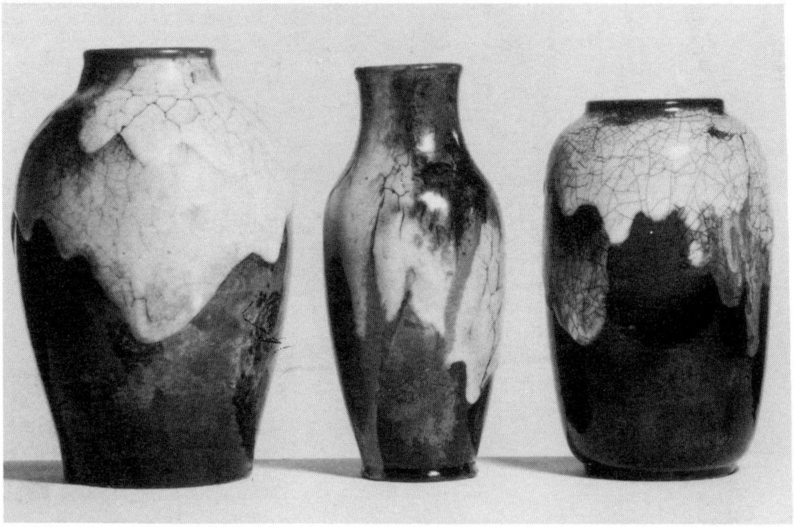

Plate 99. Three Royal Doulton Chang Wares with red and blue Sung-glazed bodies partly obscurred by a thick dripping glaze of strong colours, $9\frac{3}{4}$ in. and 11 in., each signed Noke, with monogram of Harry Nixon.

Richard Dennis

The Martin Brothers. Robert Wallace Martin and his brothers Walter and Charles Edwin formed their own pottery in Lambeth. Robert Wallace was trained as a stonemason under a Gothic carver, becoming a student at the Royal Academy school in 1863. He studied at Lambeth Art School with careful study of Doulton and after visiting various potteries around the country, worked at Bailey's Fulham Potteries in 1872. Two years later he joined his brother Walter and set up in Southall, later joined by Charles and Edwin.

The Martins made saltglazed stoneware and specialised in incised decoration of Gothic scrolls and fabulous beasts with modelled grotesque animals, men and birds. The models of birds with detached heads are perhaps the Martin's most famous projects. The designs are always bold and spontaneous and although limited in colour, possess extremely high degrees of artistic skill. Even the simplest pieces of Martin ware have shown a considerable increase in price recently and other incised pieces or birds are amongst the most sought after studio ceramics.

William de Morgan. This notable novelist experimented in the early 1870's in the production of stained glass and pottery with lustre decoration. His experiments recreated the lustre styles of Hispano Moresque and at 40 Fitzroy Square, London he perfected the techniques, although he

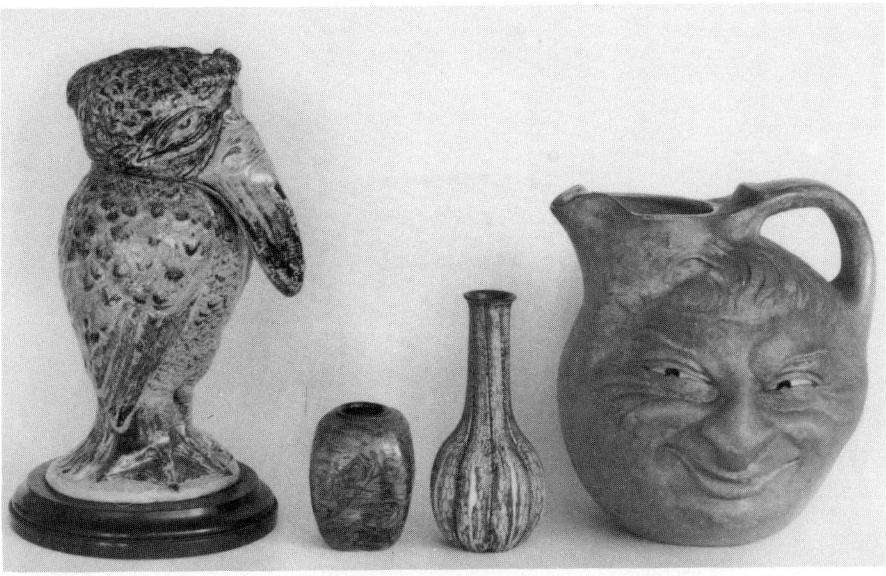

Plate 100. Group of Martinware, the large sad bird has a detachable head, 11 in., dated 10—1886 (i.e. October 1886); square vase $3\frac{1}{2}$ in. high, mottled blue with fish designs, dated 2—1914; vase of gourd shape, 6 in. light grey and cream, dated 8—1894 and a fine face jug, light brown colour, $8\frac{1}{2}$ in. dated 10—1896.

Southall District Public Library, photograph by L. Taylor

succeeded in burning the roof off his house when his kiln, which was linked to the chimney, got out of control. This caused him to move to 30 Cheyne Row, Chelsea. At first he bought various white pottery and decorated it with lustre designs, beginning to make his own tiles in a kiln again connected to the chimney of the house. His decorators were mainly Fred and Charles Passenger, with artistic influence from William Morris. From Chelsea he moved to Merton and then Fulham. His designs were of peacocks and fabulous beasts and lavish foliage, in strong Persian colours or rich ruby and copper lustres, in the style of Italian Majolica from Deruta and Gubbio. Tiles were the bulk of his production right up until the end of the factory in 1907. A typical tile can still be picked up reasonably, but a good dish or vase is again many hundreds of pounds.

Elton Ware. This was started by Sir Edmund Elton, who in about 1880, completely ignorant of ceramics, started a pottery at his house. He first attempted to fire ceramics but failed, he tried again and failed. Many times he tried to perfect his kilns but without proper training failed every time. His diary recalls 'July 15 1880, Built new kiln prepared 248 experiments—kiln gave way, shelves were broken, all experiments spoilt. Pulled down

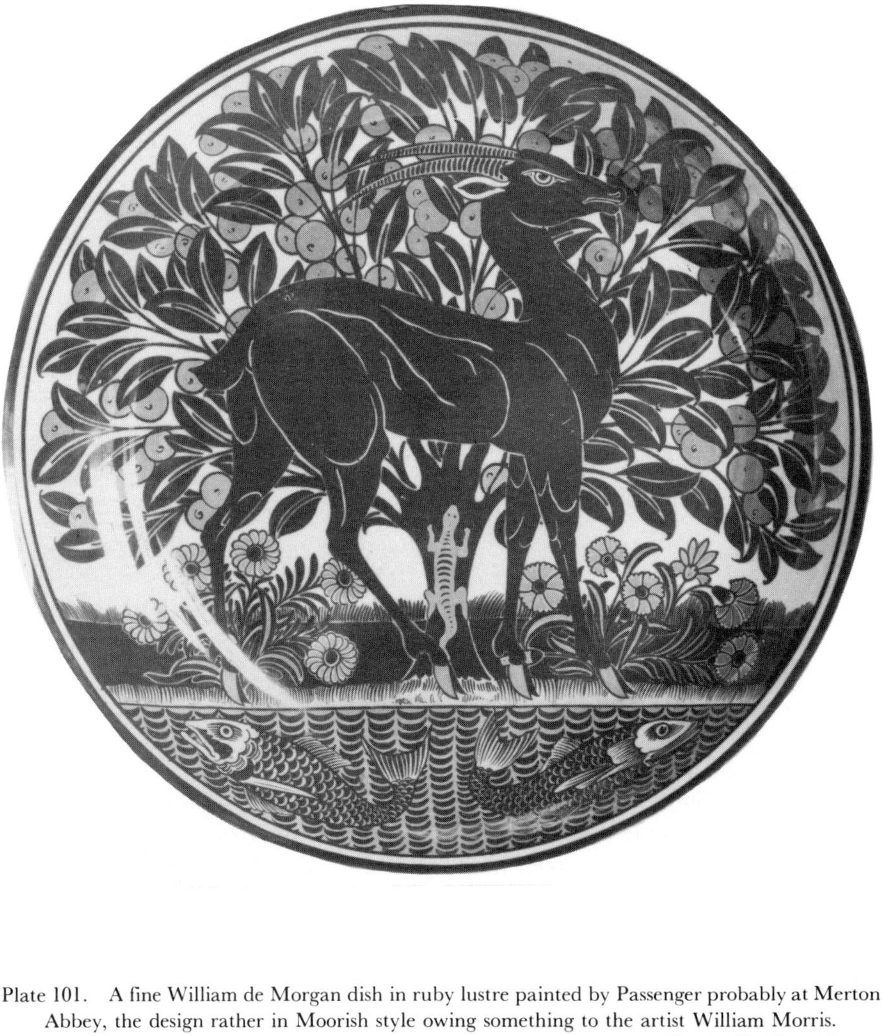

Plate 101. A fine William de Morgan dish in ruby lustre painted by Passenger probably at Merton Abbey, the design rather in Moorish style owing something to the artist William Morris.
Victoria & Albert Museum

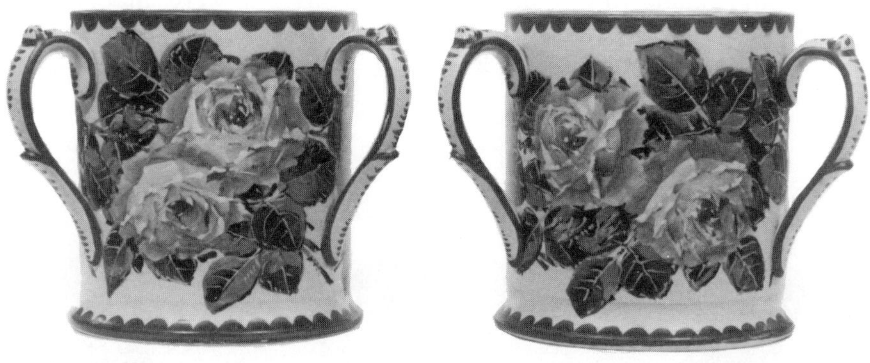

Plate 102. Pair of three-handled loving cups from the Scottish factory of Wemyss (pronounced Weems), painted in typical style with coloured roses.

Sothebys

and rebuilt kilns, fired 58 experiments, sulphur came in and experiments were damaged but results were a trifle better'. But he kept on trying and eventually succeeded in producing slip ware in Barum style. In 1902 he tried to use gold and platinum but unsuccessfully. He found by accident that where they overlapped an attractive result emerged but he was unable to repeat this for a long time. Eventually he perfected a gold and platinum 'crackle' glaze with a crazed foil-like glaze. Elton ware can be very attractive, but although rare is usually very underated, a good example fetching under £50.

Another eccentric potter was Edward Bingham who made slipwares at Castle Hedingham in Essex *c.*1870–1900. Often his wares bore seventeenth century dates and were very crude in workmanship, but with certain primitive charm. They do not command very high prices.

The Della Robbia Pottery was founded in 1894 at Birkenhead, by Harold Rathbone who had connections with Morris and the Pre Raphaelite Movement and designs were Pre-Raphaelite and Aesthetic in influence. Mostly the decoration was in sgraffito—a red body coated with white slip and incised with a design, then colour was added. This technique was used in Italy and influenced by the work of the Della Robbia family. Della Robbia is now being sought and vases are likely to be destined for a steady rise in price.

Charles Brannam rented a pottery from his father in 1879 and his early work was commissioned by Howell and James, well known sponsors of English Art Pottery. Slipware was used to ornament vessels with raised designs and interesting grotesque animal studies were made, some designed by F. Carruthers Gould. Very underated at present, these character pots can be bought for under £20 and surely present great possibilities for investment.

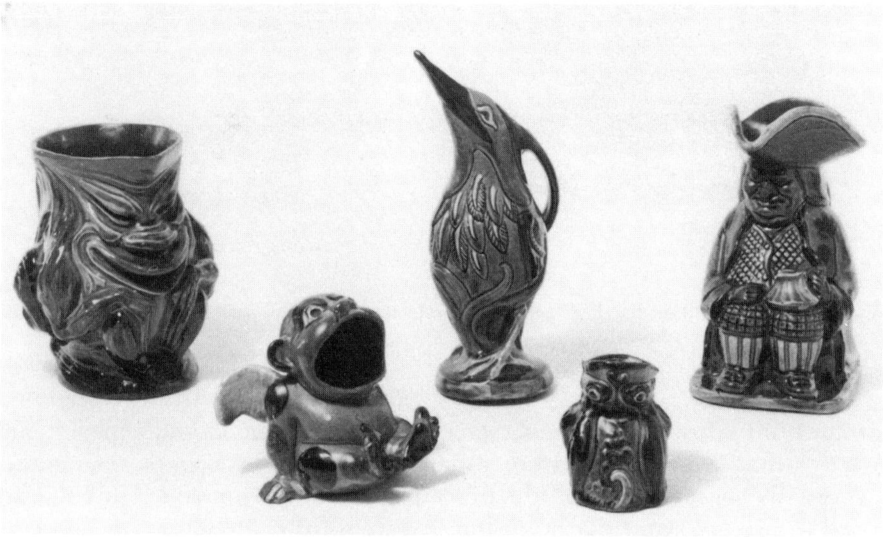

Plate 103. Group of earthenwares by Charles Brannam's pottery in Barnstable, a Toby jug in traditional style and four amusing grotesque animal figures, each glazed mainly in green and deep blue and fully marked in script. Brannam's wares have great charm and as yet are not fully appreciated. *Private Collection, London*

William Moorcroft. The Aesthetic Movement gave way to the Art Nouveau Movement. An early exponent was William Moorcroft who produced Florian ware for James Macintyre & Co. at Burslem. Incised and slip decorations were produced in colours with running glazes. The designs were trees, flowers, fish and fruit, his most usual design of pomegranates and fruit in green and blue grounds, still produced today. Standard small pieces still cost very little, but early Macintyre pieces fetch considerable prices.

Bernard Moore. The twentieth century saw the establishment of many art potteries and studio potters. Bernard Moore produced fine flambé glazes in oriental style from 1905. Two of his pupils—Edwin Wilkes and J. Howson—both produced their own flambé. A relation of J. Howson

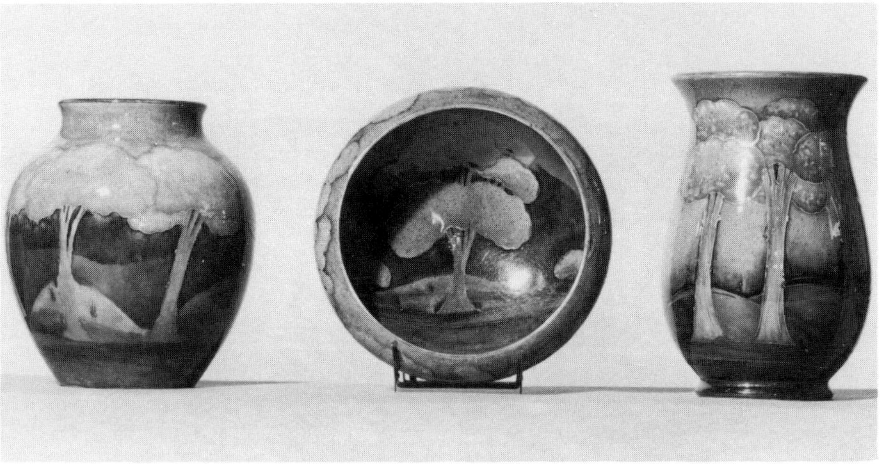

Plate 104. Three pieces of Moorcroft pottery decorated in moonlight blue, with hills and trees in tones of green against a dark blue sky, $8\frac{1}{4}$ in. and $8\frac{1}{2}$ in. each, signed W. Moorcroft, *c.*1924.
Richard Dennis

was William Howson Taylor who built his own pottery at West Smethwick, Birmingham, **Ruskin**, and experimented with high temperature glazes. In 1904 his fine flambé ware won a Grand Prix at the St. Louis Centennial Exhibition. He also produced lustre ware and monochrome glazes known as 'Soufflé'. A plain soufflé pot can be bought for a few pounds while high fired flambés are very much in demand.

Royal Lancastrian. At Clifton Junction near Manchester, William Burton in 1893 established the *Pilkington Tile and Pottery Co.* later known as 'Royal Lancastrian'. Their best known wares were lustres in the de Morgan tradition by talented artists—Richard Joyce who specialised in animals and fish, Gordon Forsyth in heraldic and lettering designs, Walter Crane and William Mycock. Lustre ranges from £70-80 to £400 upwards. Lancastrian is keenly sought and better individual pieces command high prices.

The experimental traditions set up by Elton, Brannam and Bingham have continued into this day with a series of craftsmen potters working in the traditional style.

Bernard Leach studied pottery in Japan, returning to set up a pottery at St. Ives in Cornwall in 1920 with a fine Japanese Potter Shoji Hamada. Leach trained many notable potters and his stonewares influenced by Japanese and Medieval English styles and slipwares are very highly rated. A vase by him sold in 1977 for £1,200, a feat indeed for a then still living potter. David, Janet and Margaret Leach continue the family tradition.

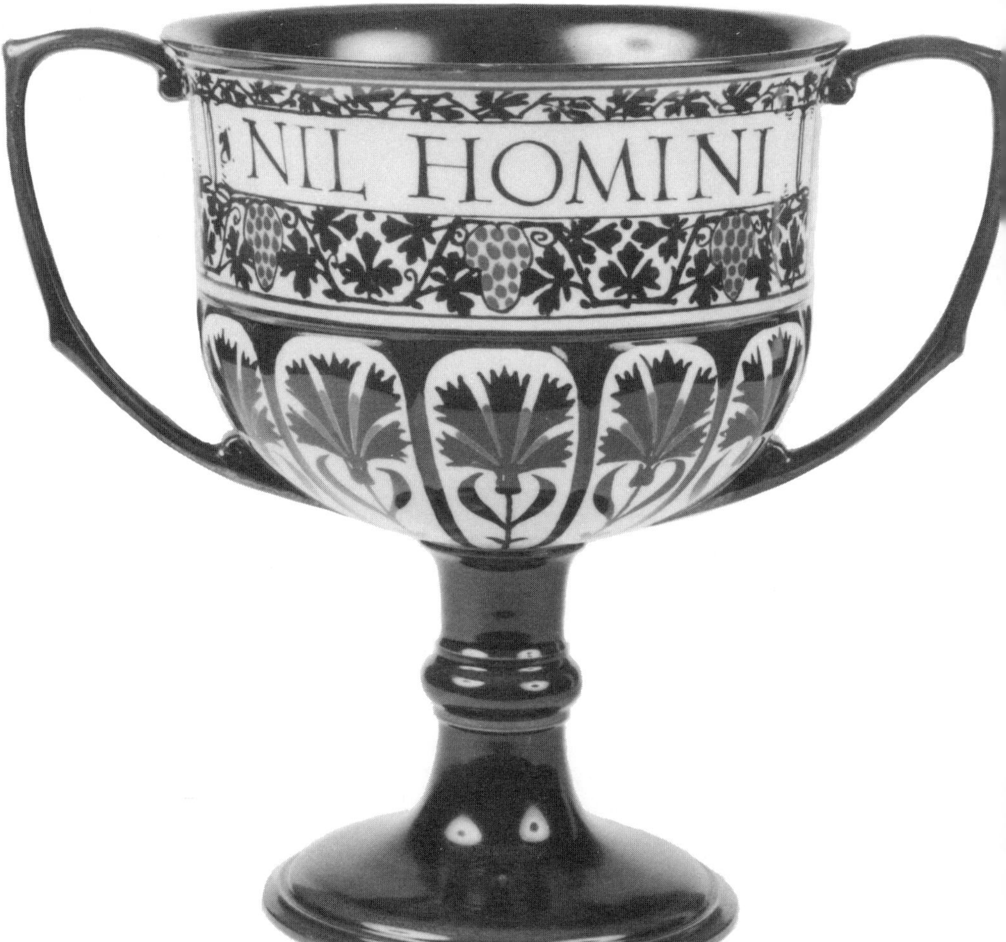

Plate 105. A Pilkington Royal Lancastrian copper lustre twin-handled cup painted by Gordon M. Forsyth with a Medieval design 9 in. high, date code for 1908.

Phillips

William Staite Murray helped establish craft pottery as an art form and not just for use. In 1925 he was made head of the ceramic department of the Royal College of Art, making fine stonewares before going to Rhodesia in 1940.
Michael Cardew learned to pot in Devon. He set up a pottery at Winchcombe in Gloucestershire producing superbly tasteful slipware. He moved to Wentford Bridge and then to Africa before retiring to England. His early work is now well sought after.
Raymond Finch continued the Winchcombe pottery making slipwares, again in traditional style.
Charles Vyse in the 1930's made attractive stonewares with celadon and tenmoko glazes in the Chinese style, as well as modelling character figures. He made especially fine models of cats with rock glazes.
Geoffrey Whiting worked with Indian potters, then started the Avoncroft Pottery—makes fine stoneware and Tenmoko glazes.

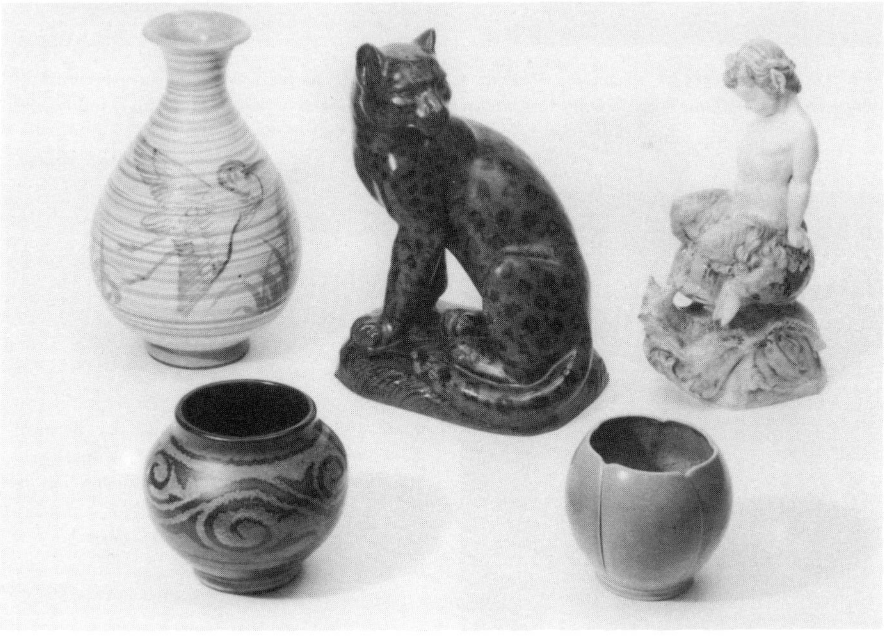

Plate 106. A group of contrasting pottery by Charles Vyse; the three vases showing how heavily the potter was influenced by Oriental ceramics, while the figure on a snail is much more European in style. The leopard is strikingly modelled with a rich almost metallic glaze. Vyse made a number of cat studies and these must rank very highly in the league of modern ceramic masterpieces, the leopard 11 in. high.

Phillips

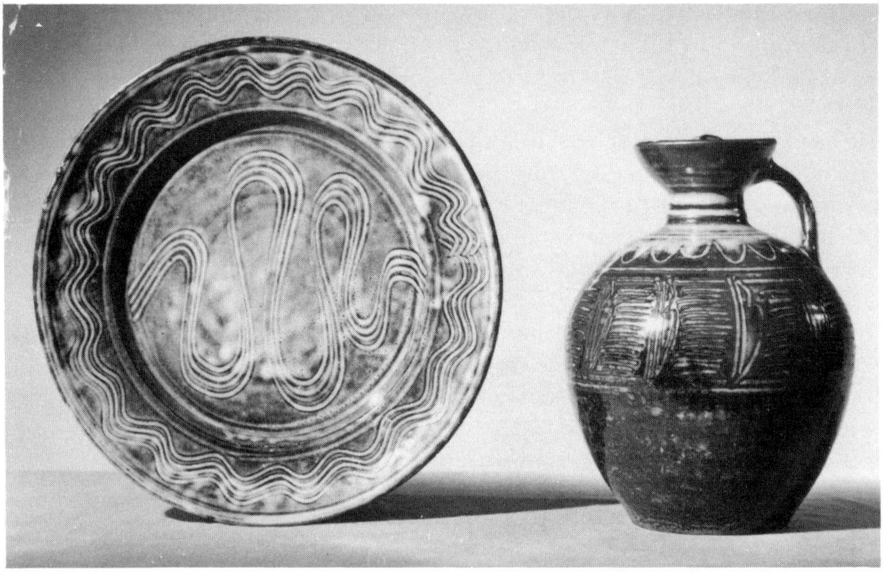

Plate 107. Two Slipware pieces by Michael Cardew, made at his pottery at Winchcombe in Gloucestershire. Although Cardew had worked with Bernard Leach he was more strongly influenced by Traditional English Pottery than by Oriental.

Victoria & Albert Museum

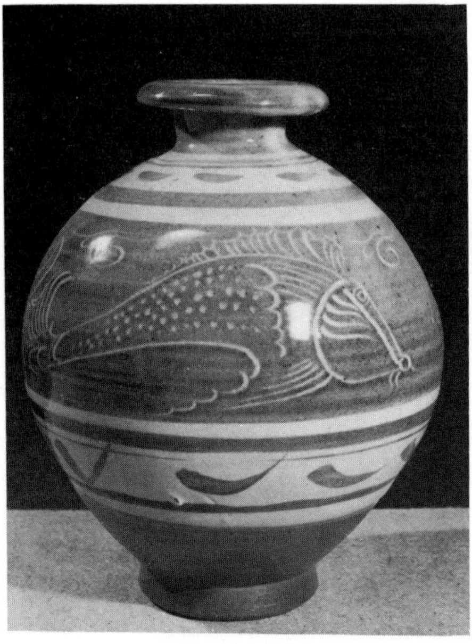

Plate 108. A Stoneware Vase by Bernard Leach made at St. Ives in 1931, showing clearly the great effect the Oriental influence had on Leach.

Victoria & Albert Museum

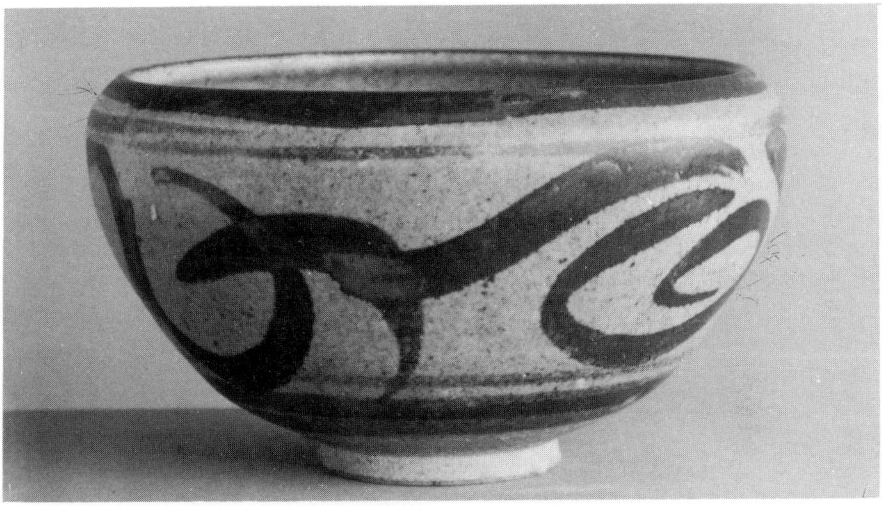

Plate 109. A Stoneware Bowl by William Staite Murray, another English potter who was heavily influenced by the tasteful simplicity of Oriental pottery; here bold brush strokes enhance an iron flecked grey stoneware.

Victoria & Albert Museum

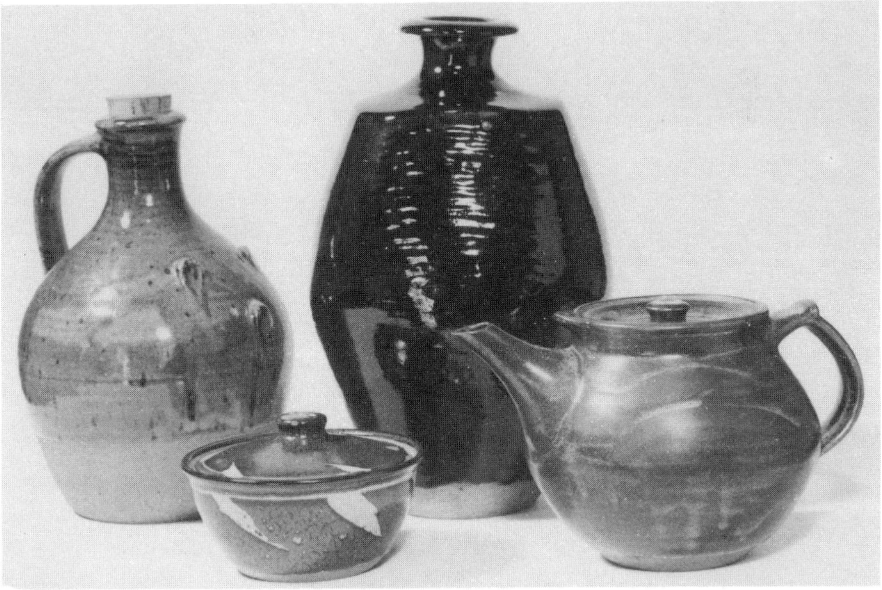

Plate 110. A group of modern Stonewares by Geoffrey Whiting; the cider jar is decorated with an oatmeal glaze, the covered bowl has wax resist decoration and the fine large jar is covered with a black Tenmoko glaze.

Large jar in Author's Collection

Alan Caiger-Smith produces fine modern stonewares and lustres and tin glaze effects, specialising in bold brush strokes.
Adrian Lewis-Evans makes stonewares in traditional Dorset style, with fine porcelain wares in peachbloom glazes.

These last are typical of the skilful contemporary craft potters who follow on from the Martins and the de Morgans, all with their own individual styles, yet typically English. Do not expect to make a fortune overnight by buying modern craftsmen potters' work but the purchase of really fine pieces can bring great joy, whether bought for practical use or as objects of delight or investment. It is often worth buying a good piece by a modern potter, rather than a more common piece by an established firm for the same price.

FURTHER READING
English Art Pottery 1865–1951 by Malcolm Haslam.

Appendix I
Public Museums

The following list of museums which have important or interesting collections of ceramics is not an exhaustive one, but will be of help if a collector is planning a holiday trip and wishes to visit as many collections as possible. It can be assumed that the local museums contain much that is pertinent to any local manufactories, but most museums contain wider collections. The three greatest general collections in this country are in the British Museum and Victoria & Albert Museum in London and the Stoke-on-Trent City Museum and a visit to these would make the finest possible introduction to an interest in ceramics.

ABERYSTWYTH
BARNARD CASTLE
Bowes Museum
BASINGSTOKE
BATH
Holburne Museum
Victoria Art Gallery
BEDFORD
Cecil Higgins Museum
BELFAST
BERWICK-ON-TWEED
BIDEFORD
BIRKENHEAD
DURHAM
EDINBURGH
EXETER
GLASGOW
GATESHEAD
HASTINGS
HEREFORD
HOVE
KING'S LYNN
LANCASTER
LEAMINGTON SPA
LEEDS
City Art Gallery

BIRMINGHAM
BLACKBURN
BOURNEMOUTH
BRIGHTON
BRISTOL
BURNLEY
CAMBRIDGE
Fitzwilliam Museum
CANTERBURY
CARDIFF
National Museum of Wales
CASTLEFORD
CHELTENHAM
DERBY
DEVIZES
DONCASTER
DOVER
DUDLEY
Temple Newsam
LINCOLN
Usher Art Gallery
LLANDUDNO
LONDON
Bethnal Green
British Museum
Kew Palace
Kingston-upon-Thames
Southhall Library
Syon House
Victoria & Albert Museum
Wallace Collection
MAIDENHEAD
MAIDSTONE
MANCHESTER
City Art Gallery
Heaton Hall
Wythenshaw Hall
METHYR TYDFIL
NEWCASTLE-UNDER-LYME
NEWCASTLE UPON TYNE
NORTHAMPTON
NOTTINGHAM
OLDHAM
OXFORD
Ashmolean Museum
PAISLEY
PLYMOUTH
PORT SUNLIGHT
PRESTON
READING
ROTHERHAM
RYE
SAFFRON WALDRON
SALISBURY
SHEFFIELD
SHREWSBURY
SPALDING
STOCKPORT
STOKE-ON-TRENT
City Museum
Minton
Spoke/Copeland
Wedgwood
SUNDERLAND
SWANSEA
TAUNTON
TRURO
WADDESDON
WAKEFIELD
WARRINGTON
WOLVERHAMPTON
Municipal Art Gallery
Bantock House
WORCESTER
City Museum
Dyson Perrins Museum
WORTHING
Art Gallery
YORK
Art Gallery
Yorkshire Museum

Appendix II
Bibliography

As well as the specialised books given after the respective sections there are a great number of others that would be found of general interest. A short list of the most useful of these follows:

BALL, A.	*Price Guide to Pot Lids*, Antique Collectors' Club, 1970
BATTIE, D.	*Price Guide to Nineteenth and Twentieth Century Porcelain*, Antique Collectors' Club, 1975
BEMROSE, G.	*Nineteenth Century English Pottery and Porcelain*
COYSH, A. W.	*Blue and White Transfer Ware 1780–1840*, David & Charles, 1974
CUSHION, John	*Pottery and Porcelain Tablewares*, Studio Vista, 1976
GODDEN, Geoffrey	*British Pottery and Porcelain 1780–1850*
	British Porcelain: an illustrated guide, Barrie & Jenkins, 1974
	British Pottery: an illustrated guide, Barrie & Jenkins, 1974
	Illustrated Encyclopaedia of British Pottery and Porcelain
	Encyclopaedia of British Pottery and Porcelain Marks, Barrie & Jenkins, 1968
	Handbook of British Pottery and Porcelain Marks, Barrie & Jenkins, 1975

	Victorian Porcelain
	Godden's Guide to English Porcelain
HALL, John	*Staffordshire Portrait Figures*
HASLAM, Malcolm	*English Art Pottery 1865–1915*, Antique Collectors' Club, 1975
HENDERSON, Ian	*Pictorial Souvenirs of Britain*, David & Charles, 1974
HUGHES, G. B. & THERLE, T.	*English Porcelain and Bone China, 1743–1850*
LAWRENCE, Heather	*Yorkshire Pots and Potteries*, David & Charles, 1974
LEWIS, Griselda	*A Collector's History of English Pottery*, Barrie & Jenkins, 1978
MAY, John & Jennifer	*Commemorative Pottery 1780–1900*, Heinemann, 1972
MOUNT, Sally	*Price Guide to Eighteenth Century English Pottery*, Antique Collectors' Club, 1972
PUGH, P. D. G.	*Staffordshire Portrait Figures of the Victorian Era*, Barrie & Jenkins, 1971
RACKHAM, B.	*Medieval English Pottery*, Faber 1972
SANDON, Henry	*Coffeepots and Teapots*, Bartholomew, 1972
SEKERS, David	*Popular Staffordshire Pottery*, Joseph, 1977
SOLON, L. M.	*The Art of the Old English Potter*, E.P., 1973
SPERO, S.	*Price Guide to Eighteenth Century English Porcelain*, Antique Collectors' Club, 1970
STRATTON, Deborah	*Mugs and Tankards*, Souvenir Press, 1975
THOMAS, E. Lloyd	*Victorian Art Pottery*, Guildart, 1974
WATNEY, B.	*English Blue and White Porcelain of the Eighteenth Century*, Faber, 1973

Appendix III
Marks

As mentioned in the book, marks, especially on supposed eighteenth century wares, should be used with discretion in identification. The ones given below are some of the most frequently met with or ones that cause most confusion. The most helpful encyclopaedia are those by Geoffrey Godden: the large Encyclopaedia of British Pottery & Porcelain Marks and the smaller Handbook of British Pottery & Porcelain Marks.

Mark 1 is Bow, 2 and 3 Caughley, 4 and 5 Coalport, 6 to 9 Chelsea, 10 Chelsea/Derby, 11 to 12 early Derby, 13 to 15 later Derby, 16 Stevenson & Hancock, Derby, 17 Derby Crown Poreclain Co., 18 Davenport 19 Doulton, 20 Longton Hall, 21 to 24 Minton, 25 Plymouth, 26 Bristol, 27 Swansea, 28 Wileman, 29 to 33 Dr Wall Worcester, 34 to 35 Davis/Flight Worcester, 36 Flight & Barr, Worcester, 37 to 38 Kerr & Binns, Worcester, 39 Worcester Royal Porcelain Company, 40 Grainger, Worcester, 41 James Hadley, Worcester.

1-6

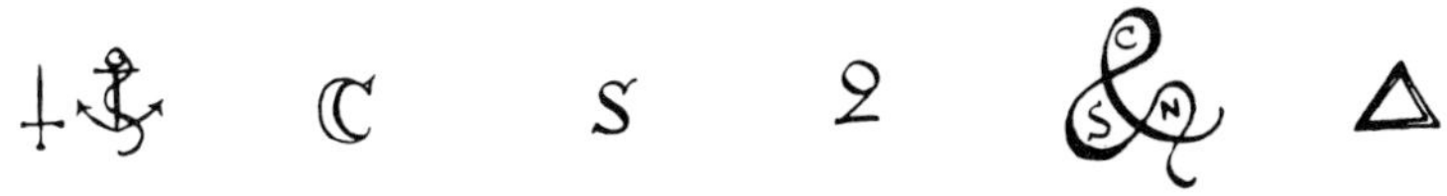

7-12

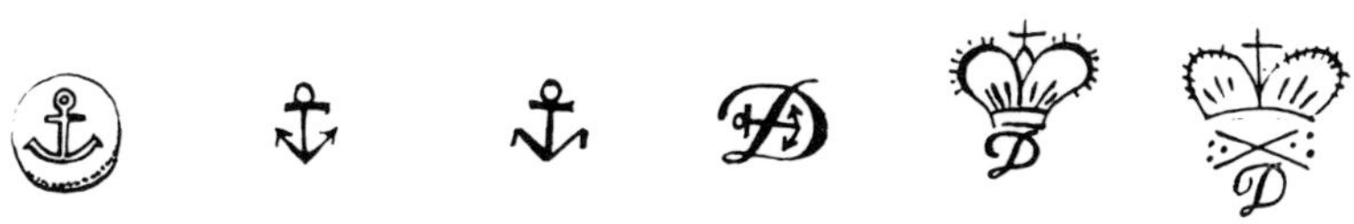

13-18

19-24

25-30

31-36

37-41

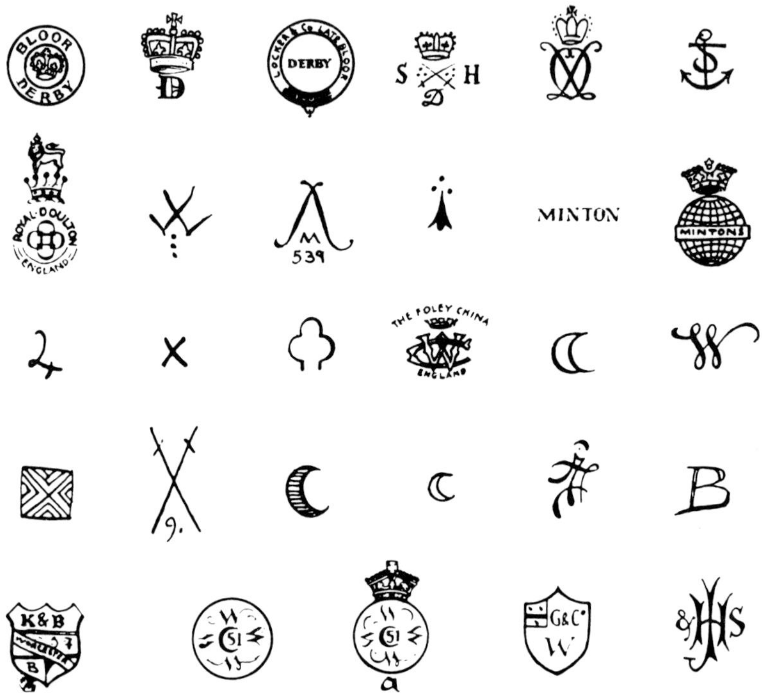

Glossary

Acid gilding: A process of eating away by acid a part of a design left matt, the finished gilding being raised and burnished in contrast to the matt etched area.
Applied flowers: flowers that are modelled or moulded separately and then affixed onto the vessel or figure.
Art Pottery Studio: An idea of Mintons, who established a studio in London for Art School students to decorate ceramics in a new free way. Examples can be marked 'Mintons Art-Pottery Studio Kensington Gore'.
Ball clay: a very plastic clay from the West of England.
Basalt: a black body appearing like Egyptian basalt stone and sometimes referred to as 'Egyptain Black'. It has a matt surface and was a popular body from the 1760's into the 19th century; Wedgwood's still produce it to this day, plate 22.
Bat printing: in this process the pattern is transferred from copper plates by means of a thin glue bat, a very soft and delicate effect was obtained, as opposed to the hard lines of paper transfer printing plate.
Biscuit: unglazed ceramics, a name given because of the rather biscuit like appearance of ware before glaze. Unglazed porcelain and china is vitreous but earthenware porous.
Bisque: unglazed porcelain or china, more generally called biscuit. The term should not be applied to the stained ivory forms of decoration.
Bocage: Foliage added to the back of 18th and 19th century figure groups, often necessary to support the figure.

Body: The material that comprises the basic ingredients of the ware.
Bone Ash: The ash produced by calcining and then grinding animal bone. Though used in the eighteenth century in some porcelains, it was perfected in the fine bone china of the nineteenth and twentieth centuries.
Bone china: the standard fine English porcelain since about 1800. Spode is credited with its first making and the finest bone china can have up to 50% of bone in the body, a very expensive material, but cheaper bone china may have little bone.
Botanical services: these were often inspired by magazines of botanical drawings.
Burnishing: The brightening up of gold after firing. This is done by hard rubbing with soft silver sand or with an agate or bloodstone.
Cabaret: a group of pieces, generally on a tray, which make up a dejeuner service.
Cadogan: a teapot filled from a hole in its base, said to be named after Lord Cadogan who brought a Chinese original to England.
Calcine: to reduce by heat to a powder.
Camaieu: a painting *en camaieu* is generally in different shades of a single colour.
Campana vase: a neo-classic shape of the early 19th century in form of an inverted bell.
Can: a cup of cylindrical shape.
Caneware: a tan coloured stoneware, generally left unglazed.
China clay: The purest, whitest form of clay, in England coming from Cornwall and Devon.
China stone: Felspathic rocks that fuse at great heat; the 'petuntse' of the Chinese.
Chinoiserie: a Europeanised version of an Oriental scene.
Clobbering: colours added onto a blue and white pattern which is complete in itself in an attempt to make it richer, usually badly done.
Cobalt Oxide: the principal material for blue on ceramics.
Colour printing: multi-coloured prints, often referred to as Pratt prints were introduced in the Victorian period, and by means of the super-imposition of different colour prints a fully coloured picture could be obtained.
Combed ware: two or more different coloured slips blended together by combing to produce marbling and feathering patterns.
Cottages: many cottages and houses were made, generally in Staffordshire, some being used as pastille-burners and night lights.
Cow creamers: a vessel in the shape of a cow, the milk or cream being put into the hole in its back and poured out through its mouth.
Cracked ice: decoration representing cracked ice.

Cradles: earthenware cradles, often decorated in slip, were probably given to newly-married couples as fertility symbols.
Crazing: the breaking of the glaze into minute spider webs of lines; although crackle was deliberately included by the Chinese, it was an unwished for fault in some English ware.
Creamware: cream-coloured earthenware introduced in about 1740. Wedgwood refined the body and called it 'Queen's Ware'.
Delft: pale coloured clay covered with an opaque white glaze (oxide of tin).
Doctor Syntax: "the Tours of Doctor Syntax in search of the Picturesque," illustrated by Rowlandson from 1809 led to a number of copies on ceramics.
Dry blue: an onglaze blue enamel which looks rather dry, used principally at Worcester.
Egyptian Black: see basalt
Enamel colours: colours which combine with a flux and melt into the glaze at different temperatures. These are painted or printed on the ware after the glaze has been fused.
Encaustic: frequently applied to medieval tiles with inlaid patterns and to 19th century reproductions of them; also to a Wedgwood style of decorating.
Engine-turning: decoration produced by turning the leather-hard unfired pot on a lathe having an eccentric motion to obtain geometrical, fluted, diced and other patterns.
Excise marks: royal cyphers and crowns applied on pads onto mugs and other vessels as a check on capacity.
Faience: originally coming from the names of Faenza or of Fayence it is now used to refer to French and some other European tin-glazed wares or majolicas.
Fairings: literally pieces sold or given as prizes at fairs, particularly applied to the amusing little chimney ornaments, such as 'Last in bed put out the light', great quantities of which were made on the Continent.
Fazackerley colours: a distinctive palette of colours on Liverpool delft ware, green, dark blue, brick red and bright yellow.
Flambé glaze: A Chinese technical achievement of producing glazes with clouded or mottled effects. In England the great exponents were Bernard Moore and Doulton.
Flow blue: 19th century method of blue printing in which the blue flows considerably, causing a halo-like effect of pattern.
Flux: A fusible glass which combines with enamel colours to fuse them in the glaze.
Footrims: the turned foot upon which cups, bowls and plates sit.
Frit: a glassy, vitreous compound of silica and alkali, some early English porcelain was made from frit.

Galena: lead sulphide - *lead ore*.
Gilding: Gold applied to a piece and refired at a low temperature. Gold can vary in quality; in the eighteenth century it was mixed with honey to make it flow (this produces a soft brown colour) later an amalgam of mercury and gold was used; producing a brighter colour. Raised gold is applied over built up enamels. After firing gold has to be burnished.
Girl in a swing figures: figures of a primitive form whose factory of origin is not certain, possibly inspired by Chelsea.
Glaze: the fusible glass-like skin that is put over most ceramics either to allow earthenwares to hold liquids or to enable the piece to be kept clean. Lead glazes were early, marvellously useful ones but being dangerous to the workmen are not now allowed. Later forms of glaze were salt and those using materials such as feldspar, quartz, flint, borax, potash and soda; a vessel can be dipped in the glaze, or glaze can be sprayed or painted on.
Glaze free margin: the raw biscuit line around the inside of porcelain footrims, a feature often found on Worcester and Caughley 18th century porcelain - often inaccurately termed glaze shrinkage or retreating glaze.
Glost: the name given to glazed wares, also the name of the kiln in which glazed wares are fired.
Grog: crushed fired ceramics added to a new body to reduce shrinkage during firing.
Groundlaying: a method of obtaining an even band of colour by dusting powdered colour upon the prepared oiled surface and dabbing it with a silk boss.
Hard Paste: Term used to describe porcelain of a very hard surface, impervious to the scratching of a knife or file. The feel is much harder and glassier than that of soft paste.
Imari: name given to a range of Japanese porcelain from Arita; English copies and versions were made at such factories as Derby, Spode and Worcester, which were generally called 'Japans'.
Incised decoration: Decoration cut into the body.
Ironstone china: not a china in the sense of bone china, but really a highly vitrified stoneware. Typified by the firm of Mason.
Jackfield: a generic name given to earthenware covered with a glossy black glaze.
Jasper: a fine-grained hard earthenware which was stained various colours; the body normally decorated with added white relief decorations.
Jewelling: droplets of enamel applied to the surface of a piece to simulate jewels, such as pearls.
Kakiemon: a symmetrical Japanese decoration, extensively copied by Bow, Chelsea and Worcester.
Lace work: could be made by dipping real lace in slip, allowing it to dry and

then firing it; a speciality of Meissen and Dresden, but done in England at a number of factories.

Leadless Glaze: it was long realised that lead was a noxious substance, dangerous to the potters, but an effective substitute was difficult to find. Nowadays no lead is used.

Limoges enamels: white enamels built up on a dark blue ground, the speciality of Thomas Bott at Worcester.

Lithographic printing: colour printing by photo litho or off-set process, the majority of printing today is done by this method, which at its best is very effective, but at its worst can be poor.

Lithophanes: Sometimes called Berlin Transparencies, these are thin porcelain plaques moulded with a pattern that only comes to life when a light is placed behind it, rather like a photographic negative. These were popular in Victorian times and could be mounted in sets to form lamp shades. Originally made in Berlin—these examples generally being marked with the K.P.M. impressed mark, the first British patent was taken out by R.G. Jones in 1828. They were produced in great quantities by Grainger, Minton's, Copelands and Adderley & Lawson, but are very difficult to find nowadays, especially marked ones. They can be very charming and should be sought.

Long Eliza: paintings of elongated Chinese women, a term corrupted from the Dutch LANGE LYZEN.

Lustre: lustres are colours on a body such as gold (produced from copper) and silver, either covering the whole surface or used as decorative motifs.

Maiolica: term used to describe Italian and Spanish tin-glazed earthenware.

Majolica: Victorian period earthenware covered with coloured glazes.

Martha Gunn: a female Toby jug made in the likeness of the Brighton bathing superintendant.

Matt glaze: glaze with a dull, non-glassy appearance.

Moons: small patches in the body of porcelains seen by transmitted light; they are noticed particularly in Chelsea.

Moulds: Plaster of paris cases into which slip is poured, allowed to form, the surplus poured away, the remainder of the liquid being absorbed by the plaster, allowing the cast object to be turned out when formed. Other forms of Moulding involve pressing solid clay into plaster moulds.

Moustache cup: a cup having protective ledge which stopped the large moustaches popular at the turn of the 19th/20th centuries from dropping into the tea.

Muffle kiln: a small kiln for firing enamel colours and gilding, the ware being protected by flues.

Nankin: chief exporting town from whence came the huge quantities of Chinese blue and white wares.
Oeil-de-perdrix: decoration of small circles, often upon a coloured ground; literally partridge eye.
Ogee shape: cups and bowls of a double curved shape, like the curved parts of a letter B; popular each side of 1800.
Painters' Marks: symbols and initials that are put on the base of pieces to identify the painter (or gilder or other workman).
Parian: a porcelain body made of felspar and china clay which was easily moulded and translucent. Many figures and much useful ware was made in it of the appearance of marble and the name actually derives from the Island of Paros, where Greek marble for sculpture was mined.
Pastille-burners: cottages and other buildings or containers with perforated lids in which a fragrant pastille was burnt.
Pate-sur-pate: a very difficult process of painting in slip on the biscuit body under the glaze gradually building up the decoration and tooling it. The finest pate-sur-pate of the nineteenth century, such as the work of Solon, at Mintons, are among the most sought after wares of the century.
Pearl ware: a body similar to cream ware but having more flint and white clay.
Pitcher mould: a mould made of fired clay.
Porcelain: a translucent body (as opposed to opaque earthenware or pottery) but its translucence depends on its thickness and firing temperature. Most English 18th century porcelain was soft paste; present day porcelain is of the hard paste variety.
Porringer: a basin or bowl for broth or porridge, generally covered.
Posset pot: vessel with multiple loop handles and spouts with an elaborate cover with a crown as a knob, used for posset, a beverage containing such things as hot ale, milk, sugar and spices.
Pot-lids: lids that were put on ointment and other pots, often decorated with coloured prints by such firms as F. & R. Pratt, hence called Pratt pot-lids.
Punch-bowls: from which a beverage comprising spirits blended with hot milk or water sweetened with pure loaf sugar was ladled.
Redware: red coloured high fired earthenwares, or stonewares, generally left unglazed.
Resist: negative decoration produced by painting on the surface with something which will resist the other coverings put on.
Rococo style: vigorous use of scrolls, rockwork, seaweed, etc. used in the mid-18th century and revived in the early 19th century.
Saggar: a container made of high fired clay in which delicate wares are put to protect them during their firings in the kiln.
Saltglaze: stonewares either white or coloured, glazed by throwing salt into

the kiln at the highest point of firing; the resultant glaze is hard and usually pitted rather like orange peel.
Sgraffiato: incising through the slip to reveal the natural coloured body underneath.
Slip: Clay mixed with water so that it can be poured into moulds, or painted on the surface of vessels, as on slip-ware, or pate-sur-pate.
Soft paste: Term used to describe porcelain of very soft appearance, the surface of which can be scratched.
Sponged wares: decoration produced by dabbing with a sponge.
Sprigging: application of relief ornament, made in moulds, onto the surface of vessels.
Spur marks: marks under the base caused by the spurs or stilts upon which the piece rested during firing.
Stoneware: a hard body made from stoneware clays, which although earthenware, can sometimes show an orange translucence in their thinnest parts.
Terra Cotta: reddish unglazed earthenware, made in this country from the 1840's.
Throwing: The process of forming pots on the wheel, a ball of clay is thrown upon a wheel, which is turned either by foot or electrically, is centred and with water as a lubricant is worked up and down once or twice by the two hands working together, then a hole is opened up in the centre of the clay and with the right hand working outside and the left inside pressure is exerted which squeezes the clay upwards into a cylinder—this is the 'throwing'; more throws can be made to thin out the clay and gain greater height and the vessel can be shaped by the hands. When fnished the pot is cut off the wheel by a wire and placed aside to dry.
Toby jugs: jugs in the form of a man holding a mug of beer and a pipe, made from the 18th century to the present day, great quantities being made in the 19th century especially. The clothing and attitude can vary enormously.
Transfer printing: introduced in 1757, probably at Worcester and then Bow, at first onglaze (black, violet and lavender colour) then, by 1760, underglaze in blue. The process involves pressing colour into the incised lines of an etched or engraved copper plate, priming a tissue paper with soapy water, pressing the paper onto the copper through a press and fixing the resultant print onto the varnished surface of the vessel and rubbing it hard in. The colour is then fused onto the vessel by a further firing.
Transparencies: see Lithopanes.

Index